My Century

Günter Grass

My Century

Translated by Michael Henry Heim

A Helen and Kurt Wolff Book • Harcourt, Inc.
New York   San Diego   London

This is a translation of *Mein Jahrhundert*

Library of Congress Cataloging-in-Publication Data
Grass, Günter, 1927–
[Mein Jahrhundert. English]
My century/Günter Grass; translated by Michael Henry Heim.
p.   cm.
"A Helen and Kurt Wolff book."
ISBN 0-15-100496-X
I. Heim, Michael Henry.   II. Title.
PT2613.R338M4513   1999
833'.914—dc21   99-38690

Designed by Lori McThomas Buley
Text set in Granjon
Printed in the United States of America
First edition
A C E D B

In memory of Jakob Suhl

My Century

1900

I, TRADING PLACES WITH MYSELF, was in the thick of things, year in and year out. Not always in the front lines, because there were wars going on all the time and a soldier's better off in the rear, but in the beginning, when we were up against the Chinese and our battalion reported to Bremerhaven, I was in the front of the middle unit. We were volunteers, nearly all of us, but I was the only one from Straubing, even though I'd just been engaged to Resi, my dear Therese.

We were waiting to board ship, the North German Lloyd building at our backs and the sun in our eyes. The Kaiser stood on a platform high above us and gave a spirited speech out over our heads. We had these new broad-brimmed hats to keep the sun out. Sou'westers, they were called. We looked real dapper. The Kaiser, though, he wore this special helmet with the eagle shining against a blue background. He talked about solemn duties and the cruel foe. We were all carried away. He said, "Keep in mind the moment you land: No mercy shall be shown, no prisoners taken...." Then he told the story of King Attila and the Huns. He praised them to the skies even though they wreaked all kinds of havoc. Which is why the Social Democrats later published those shameless Hun letters and made nasty remarks about the Kaiser's Hun speech. He ended with our orders for China: "Open the way to culture now and forever!" We gave three cheers.

For someone like me from Lower Bavaria the long sea voyage was hell. When we finally landed in Tientsin they were all there: the British, the Americans, the Russians, even real live Japanese and small troops from minor countries. The British turned out to be Indians. There weren't many of us to start with, but luckily we had the new five-centimeter rapid-fire cannons, the Krupp ones, and the Americans were trying out their Maxim machine gun, which was one hell of a weapon. So Peking fell in no time. In fact, by the time our company marched in, everything seemed over and done with, which was a pity. Though some of the Boxers were still making trouble. They were called Boxers because they had this secret society they called I Ho Ch'uan or "righteous fists" in our language. That's why the English—and then everybody else—talked about the Boxer Rebellion. The Boxers hated foreigners because they sold the Chinese all kinds of stuff. The British particularly liked selling opium. That's why things went the way the Kaiser ordered: There were no prisoners taken.

For the sake of order the Boxers were rounded up in the square at Tienanmen Gate, right in front of the wall dividing the Manchu city from the ordinary part. Their pigtails were tied one to the other. It looked funny. Then they were either executed in groups or had their heads chopped off one by one. But I didn't write my fiancée a blessed word about the horrors; I stuck to hundred-year-old eggs and steamed dumplings Chinese style. The British and us Germans we liked using our guns, we wanted to get things over with, while the Japanese followed their time-honored tradition of head chopping. The Boxers liked being shot better because they were afraid of having to run around hell with their heads under their arms. Otherwise they were fearless. I saw somebody licking his chops over a rice cake dipped in syrup just before he was shot.

There was a wind blowing through Tienanmen Square; it came from the desert, stirring up clouds of yellow dust. Everything was yellow including us. I wrote that to my fiancée and enclosed a little desert sand in the letter. And because the Japanese executioners got a clean cut by chopping the pigtails off the Boxers, who were just young fellows like ourselves, there were lots of little piles of them lying around in the dust, and I picked one up and sent it home as a souvenir. Back in Germany I wore it at Fasching and everybody was in stitches until my fiancée threw it in the fire. "It could've haunted the house," Resi said two days before we were married.

But that's another story.

1901

SEEK AND YE SHALL FIND. I have always enjoyed rummaging in junk, and late in the fifties there was a Chamissoplatz dealer whose black-and-white shop sign promised antiques, though the valuable pieces lay buried deep in junk. Since my interest was piqued by curios as well, I discovered three picture postcards bound with a string and depicting mosque, sepulchre church, and wailing wall through a dull sheen. Postmarked January '45 in Jerusalem, they were addressed to a certain Doctor Benn in Berlin, but the post office had been unable to locate the addressee amid the city's debris and had marked them undeliverable. I was lucky that Kurt Mühlenhaupt's treasure trove in the Kreuzberg district had offered them shelter.

The message—interspersed with curlicues and stick figures and continuous over the three cards—was difficult to decipher, but ran as follows: "Truly the times are out of joint! Today, the first of March, with the burgeoning new century resplendent in its stiff-legged "one" and you, my barbarian and tiger, stalking the far-off jungles for prey, my father, Herr Schüler, took me by his Eulenspiegel hand and he, I, and my glass heart boarded the suspension railway on its maiden journey from Barmen to Elberfeld. Up over the black Wupper! It is a hard-steel dragon winding and wending its thousand-footed way over a river blackened by Bible-pious dyers with the effluents of their inks for little recompense. On, on the ship cruises, roaring through the skies, while the dragon advances on heavy ringèd feet. If only you, dear Giselher, at whose sweet mouth I have shuddered with bliss, could float across the Styx, the other Wupper, with me, your Sulamith— or shall I be Jussuf the Prince?—until falling rejuvenated reunited we were consumed. But no, I have been saved here on holy ground and live only for the Messiah, while you are lost, apostate, my hard-faced betrayer, barbarian that you are. O lamentation! Can you see the black swan on the black Wupper? Can you hear my song playing plaintively on a blue piano?... But now we must disembark, Father Schüler says to his Else. On earth I was in the main his good little girl...."

It is a known fact that on the day the opening of the first, four-and-a-half-kilometer, stretch of the Wuppertal Suspension Railway was celebrated Else Schüler was no child but a woman of thirty or more, wife to Berthold Lasker and mother of a two-year-old son, but age in her scheme of things was always flexible, which only makes the three signs of life from Jerusalem addressed to Doctor Benn and posted only weeks before her death that much more informative.

I did not haggle long; I paid a collector's price. And Kurt Mühlenhaupt, whose junk was always special, gave me a wink.

1902

It was a minor event in Lübeck when the student in me bought his first straw hat to wear while strolling to the Mühlentor or along the banks of the Trave. Not a soft felt or a bowler; no, a flat-topped, buttercup-yellow, vainglorious straw hat, which, having just become the rage, was called either the elegant *canotier* or more folksy *boater*. Women too wore straw hats, theirs trimmed with ribbons, but for a long time they also laced themselves into fishbone corsets: few were brave enough to parade in front of, say, the Katharineum in the health movement's new, free-flowing dresses that aroused and mocked us students.

There was much new at the time. The Imperial Post Office, for instance, had just issued uniform stamps for the entire Reich featuring a metal-bosomed Germania in profile. And since progress was the keynote of the day, many straw hatters were curious about the times to come.

My hat had all kinds of adventures. I shoved it back on my neck while admiring the first Zeppelin. I laid it next to the newly published scourge of bourgeois sensibility, *Buddenbrooks,* while sipping coffee at the Café Niederegger. Then, during my first year at the university, I wore it through Hagenbeck's Zoological Garden, which had just begun operation, and, thus protected, I observed apes and camels in the open while they covetously observed me and my hat.

Mistaken for another's on the dueling floor, forgotten altogether in the Alster Pavilion—time after time a new straw hat was wanted, to doff with verve (or dispassion) to the ladies. After a while I started tilting it to the right the way Buster Keaton did on the screen, only nothing could make me sad like him; everything made me laugh, which meant that in Göttingen, where, now wearing glasses, I earned my degree, the gangling, comic, photogenic Harold Lloyd of the later years, fumbling with his straw hat while hanging from a clock hand, was more my look.

Back in Hamburg, I was in the throng at the opening of the Elbe Tunnel. From the Chamber of Commerce to the Warehouse District, from court to chambers we ran waving our straw hats when the world's largest ship, the high-speed North Atlantic steamer *Imperator,* sailed out of the harbor on her maiden voyage. There were plenty of occasions for hat waving. And once when I was taking the air along the banks of the Elbe near Blankensee with a minister's daughter on my arm— she later married a veterinary surgeon, that spring or autumn, I can't remember which—a gust of wind made off with my flimsy headdress. It rolled, it sailed. I chased it in vain. Disconsolate—not even Elisabeth, the object of my love at the time, could give me solace—I watched it drift downstream.

Only after completing my apprenticeship and entering the civil service could I afford straw hats of better quality. They remained in fashion until many thousands of straw hatters in small towns and large metropolises—including me at the

Supreme Court in Schwerin—crowded around gendarmes in the street reading off proclamations of war in the name of His Majesty. Many tossed their boaters in the air, relieved at being released from civilian life and willingly exchanging—quite a few for good—their shiny, buttercup-yellow straw hats for the field-gray headgear known as spiked helmets.

1903

THE FINALS BEGAN just after half past four on Whitsunday. We'd taken the night train from Leipzig—the team, three substitutes, the coach, and two gentlemen from management. Sleeping cars? Not a chance! No, the whole Leipzig club—me included—went third class. (The fare wasn't peanuts, you know. It took a lot to scrape it together.) But our fellows stretched out on the hard seats, and till just before Uelzen the train was a symphony of snores.

Anyway, we pulled into Altona bushed, but in high spirits. As usual, they took us to an ordinary parade ground; it even had a gravel strip running through it. We protested, but a lot of good it did us. Herr Behr, the referee from Altona Soccer Club 93, had roped off the sandy but otherwise perfectly even playing field and marked the center line and penalty area with wood shavings.

The only reason our opponents, the Prague team, got to play was that those birdbrains in the Karlsruhe Club management fell for a dirty trick: they believed a misleading telegram and failed to show for the preliminary round in Saxony and the German Soccer League decided on the spot to put the Prague Club in the finals. It was the first match and the weather was perfect, so Herr Behr had a nice crowd of roughly two thousand spectators, though the five hundred marks they tossed into his tin bowl didn't nearly cover expenses.

Things got off to a bad start: just before the whistle the ball was nowhere to be found. The Prague team protested, but the spectators laughed more than they hooted, and everybody was in high spirits when the ball finally lay there on the center line and our opponents, the wind and sun at their backs, kicked off. Before we knew it they were down at our goal making a cross from the left wing, and it was all that Raydt, our bean-pole of a goalie, could do to save us from falling behind so early in the game. But then Friedrich of Prague scored a goal. We held our own for a while, though the passes came fast and furious from the right. We finally squeezed a goal out of the flurry and pressure in front of Prague's penalty area, but Prague, who had a strong goalkeeper in Pick, tied the score just after halftime. From then on they couldn't hold us back. In the space of a few minutes Stany and Riso managed to score five goals between them. All hell broke loose and the crowd kept going wild. There was barely time for the cheers to die down. Not even their star center halfback, Robitsek— who, by the way, fouled Stany really hard—could stop us. Herr Behr gave bad-boy Robi a warning, and Riso scored a seventh goal for us just before the whistle blew.

Prague had been praised to the skies, but turned out to be quite disappointing, especially the forward line. Too many re-turn passes, lax in the penalty area. Later, people said Stany and Riso were the big heroes, but that's wrong: it was the teamwork. Even so, Bruno Stanischewski—whom everybody called Stany—was a perfect example of what players of Polish extraction had been for German soccer over the years. Because I've been in management for quite some time now—I'm treasurer—and I go to lots of away matches, I had the privilege of watching Fritz Szepan and his brother-in-law Ernst Kuzorra, the Schalke stars, play, I saw their great victories, and I can state without fear of contradiction that if after the Altona championship German soccer started looking up, it was due in great measure to the spirit and skill of Germanized Poles.

But to get back to Altona: it was a decent match, if nothing spectacular. Still, even in those days, when Leipzig was the undisputed champion of Germany, reporters liked to spice up their stories with the stuff of legend. In any case, word got round that the reason Prague had been so slow on the uptake, especially during the second half, was that the night before, they'd had a grand old time with the ladies of the Reeperbahn. Well, I have it from Herr Behr, the referee, in his own hand: "The best team won!"

1904

"At our mine in Herne it started up right before Christmas...."

"Hugo Stinnes's mine, you mean...."

"But there's cart problems all over the place. At the Harpener Mines, when they don't fill 'em full up or there's too many chunks that ain't pure coal..."

"And then there's a penalty...."

"Right, inspector. But us miners we're peace-loving folk, and there's other reasons for the strike. The worm sickness, for one. It's all over the district. Every fifth miner's got it. And the bosses they play it down...."

"The horses got it too, you want my opinion...."

"No, it was them Poles brought it with them...."

"But everybody's striking, Poles included, though they're a cinch to keep in their place...."

"With schnapps, you mean!"

"Bullshit! We're all of us blotto half the time...."

"In any case, the strike committee is quoting the Berlin Peace Treaty of May '89, where it calls for an eight-hour shift...."

"Eight-hour shift, ha! The cart trips are getting longer and longer...."

"At our mine in Herne we're up to ten hours a day...."

"And there's more and more cart trouble these days, you want my opinion...."

"Over sixty shafts are being picketed...."

"There's blacklists again too...."

"And in Wesel the Fifty-seventh Infantry Division is standing ready...."

"Come off it! All we've ever had are gendarmes...."

"But at our mine in Herne the inspectors like you they're going around with armbands. And clubs..."

"Pinkertons is what they call them, after that American, the one who came up with the dirty trick...."

"Hugo Stinnes is closing down his mines, 'cause there's a general strike...."

"Well, all over Russia they're having what you might call a revolution...."

"And Comrade Liebknecht in Berlin..."

"But the army marched right in and shot up a storm...."

"The way our boys down there in Africa take care of them Hottentots…"

"Still, more than two hundred mines in the district are out on strike.…"

"Eighty-five percent all told…"

"Though it's been pretty quiet so far, inspector.…"

"Not like in Russia, where the revolution's on the upswing…"

"Which is why they're starting to take action against the Herne strikebreakers, comrades.…"

"Stinnes is dead set against a settlement.…"

"Russia's in a state of war.…"

"Our boys really gave it to the Herero and them other Hottentots.…"

"The Russians will have a harder time of it with the Japanese.…"

"At our mine in Herne there's even been some shots fired.…"

"Yeah, but in the air only…"

"Still, you should've seen us run.…"

"From the mine gate clear across the forecourt…"

"No, inspector. Not soldiers. Just police…"

"But that didn't stop us from running.…"

"Time to make tracks, I said to Anton.…"

1905

MY FATHER BEFORE ME worked for a Bremen shipping company in Tangier, Casablanca, and Marrakesh, and that long prior to the first Moroccan crisis. He was a man plagued by worries, a man for whom politics, especially in the far-off person of Chancellor Bülow, muddied the balance sheet. As his son, who managed to keep our concern above water in the face of powerful French and Spanish competition but made the rounds of the saffron, fig, date, and coconut dealers with no true passion and therefore spent less time in the office than in the teahouse and prowled the souks for entertainment, I found the constant crisis banter at table and club absolutely ludicrous. I consequently viewed the Kaiser's spur-of-the-moment call on the Sultan from a distance and through an ironic monocle, especially as Abd al-Aziz himself proved capable of reacting to the unannounced state visit with remarkable pomp, shielding his eminent guest with a picturesque bodyguard and English agents while secretly securing the favor and patronage of France.

Despite the much mocked mishaps at the port—where the launch, sovereign and all, nearly capsized—the Kaiser made an impressive entrance, riding into Tangier on a borrowed, clearly nervous white horse, but firm in the saddle. The people even cheered. However, it was his helmet and the light signals it beamed to the sun that elicited spontaneous admiration.

Later, the teahouses and even the club were flooded with cartoons showing the eagle-bedizened helmet engaged in lively dialogue with His Majesty's mustache—and no face in between. Moreover, the cartoonist—no, I was not the perpetrator; he was an artist I'd known in Bremen, one of the Worpswede art colony crowd—succeeded in drawing the helmet and handlebar mustache in such a manner that the rounded, richly decorated headpiece and its sharp spike harmonized perfectly with the domes of the mosques and their minarets.

The grandiose entrance gave rise to nothing more than worried telegrams. While His Majesty made spirited speeches, France and England formed ententes to deal with Egypt and Morocco. I found the whole thing laughable. As laughable as the sudden appearance of our gunboat the *Panther* in the waters outside Agadir six years later. It made a sensation, of course, but all that remained was the impression of the Kaiser's helmet flashing in the sun. Industrious local coppersmiths soon had imitations for sale in every marketplace. For many years—more years than our trade with the country held up—one could buy Prussian spiked helmets *en miniature* and larger-than-life as souvenirs or utilitarian spittoons.

My father, though, who always feared the worst in more than matters of trade, and who, not entirely without reason, would call his son "Flighty Golightly," found nothing in all this to make him laugh; instead, he took it as further grounds for uttering beyond the dinner table his painful pronouncement: "We are being surrounded, the British and French are surrounding us in league with the Russians." And on occasion he disturbed us with its corollary: "The Kaiser may be good at sword-rattling, but his politics are made by others."

1906

CALL ME CAPTAIN SIRIUS. My creator's name is Sir Arthur Conan Doyle, better known as the author of the world-famous Sherlock Holmes novels, which offer a strictly scientific account of criminology. But almost as a sideline he attempted to warn his insular England of a danger in the offing when, eight years after our first seaworthy submarine was launched, he published a brief book which he called *Danger! and Other Stories,* which came out in German translation during the war, in 1916, under the title *The Submarine War, or How Captain Sirius Did England In,* and was reprinted here seventeen times before the war was over, but now unfortunately seems to have fallen into oblivion.

Thanks to this prophetic little book I, in the person of Captain Sirius, succeeded in convincing the King of Norland, the Reich's ally, of the daring yet perfectly rational possibility of using a mere eight submarines—which was all we had—to cut England off from her supplies and literally starve her to death. Our submarines were called the *Alpha,* the *Beta,* the *Gamma,* the *Theta,* the *Delta,* the *Epsilon,* the *Iota,* and the *Kappa.* Unfortunately, the last was lost in the Irish Sea during our otherwise successful mission. I was the captain of the *Iota* and commanded the entire flotilla. We scored our first successes at the mouth of the Thames near Sheerness: aiming my torpedoes amidships, I sank in quick succession the *Adela,* laden with mutton from New Zealand, the Oriental Company's *Moldavia,* and the *Cusco,* the latter two laden with grain. After further successes along the Channel coast and all the way to the Irish Sea, involving the whole flotilla either in squadrons or one by one, prices—first in London, then throughout the island—began to rise: a fivepenny loaf of bread soon cost a shilling and a half. By systematically blocking all major ports of entry we drove already exorbitant prices higher and unleashed a countrywide famine. The starving populace protested against the government with acts of violence. It stormed the Empire's sanctuary, the Stock Exchange. Anyone belonging to the upper classes and able to afford it fled to Ireland, where there were still at least potatoes to be

had. In the end proud Albion was forced to conclude a humil-
iating peace with Norland.

The second part of the book consists of statements by naval
officers and other experts, all of whom confirmed Sir Arthur's
warning of the submarine menace. One of them, a retired vice
admiral, advised England to build storehouses for grain, like
Joseph in Egypt, and to protect homegrown agricultural prod-
ucts by means of tariffs. There were urgent pleas to abandon
England's dogmatic insular mentality and finally get down to
building the tunnel to France. Another vice admiral suggested
that trading vessels be allowed to ply the seas only in convoys
and that swiftly moving dirigibles be specially equipped to
hunt out submarines. Intelligent propsals all, their worth
alas, having been corroborated during the course of the war. I
could wax particularly eloquent on the subject of the depth- or
water-bombs.

My creator, Sir Arthur, unfortunately forgot to report that
while a young lieutenant in Kiel I was present as the crane
lowered the first seaworthy submarine into the water—all
hush-hush, top secret—at the Germania Shipworks on 4 August 1906. Before that I had been second officer on a torpedo
ship, but I volunteered to test our new underwater weapon
in its early stages. As a member of the crew I was in the *U-1*
when it was lowered thirty meters under water and made it to
the open sea on its own steam. I should point out, however,
that Krupp, using the design of a Spanish engineer, had
even earlier built a thirteen-meter craft that went five-and-a-
half knots under water. This *Forelle* aroused even the Kaiser's
interest. Prince Heinrich himself went down in it once. Regret-
tably, the Reich's Naval Office obstructed the *Forelle*'s expedi-
tious development. There were, moreover, difficulties with the
gasoline engine. But when the *U-1* was put into commission in

Eckernförde a year behind schedule, nothing could stop it, even though the *Forelle* and our thirty-nine-meter ship, the *Kambala,* which came equipped with three torpedoes, were later sold to Russia. I was unfortunately detailed to attend the ceremony at which they were handed over. Orthodox priests, dispatched specially from Petersburg, anointed the vessels with holy water fore and aft. Following a lengthy overland journey they were launched in Vladivostok—too late to use them against Japan.

Still, my dream came true. Much as he shows an instinct for sleuthing in his books, Sir Arthur could never have suspected how many German youths—like me—had dreamed of the speedy descent, the wandering eye of the periscope, the bobbing tanker just waiting to be torpedoed, the command of "Fire!," the many and much acclaimed hits, the intimate camaraderie, and the pennants waving on the triumphant return home. And not even I, who have been involved from the start and have entered literature along the way, not even I could have suspected that tens of thousands of our lads would never emerge from their underwater dream.

Thanks to Sir Arthur's warning, our repeated attempts to bring England to her knees unfortunately came to naught. All those deaths. But only Captain Sirius was condemned to survive every descent.

1907

AT THE END OF NOVEMBER our Celler Chaussee plant burned down. Down to the ground. And we were going great guns, let me tell you. Turning out thirty-six thousand discs a day. Why, people would tear the things out of our hands. We were making twelve million marks' worth of sales a year by then. One reason business was so good was that the Hannover plant manufactured double-sided discs. Only other place that made them was America. Lots of um-pah-pah. Not much in the way of art. And then yours truly—Rappaport's the name—signed up Nellie Melba, "the Great." At first she made the same kind of fuss as Chaliapin, who was scared stiff that the devilish contraption—which was what he called our up-to-the-minute equipment—would gobble up his smooth bass voice. Joseph Berliner—who, with his brother Emil, had had the nerve to start up Deutsche Grammophon in Berlin just before the turn of the century with a measly twenty thousand marks—said to me one fine morning, "Pack your bags, Rappaport. You're off to Moscow, and don't ask me how, but you're bringing Chaliapin back alive."

Well, let me tell you, I was on the next train with next to no clothes but with our first shellac pressings of Melba as a bread-and-butter gift, you might call it. And what a time I had! You know the Yar Restaurant? First class! Well, we spent a whole night there in a private dining room. We started out with straight vodka in water glasses, and before long Fyodor was crossing himself and singing. No, not the big Boris aria; just that pious stuff the monks mumble in their booming basses. Then we switched to champagne. It was sunup before he signed, all teary-eyed and crossing himself still. I've limped since I was a child, and I bet he thought I was the devil pushing him to sign. The only reason he did was that we'd struck a deal with Sobinov, the tenor, so I could show him the contract as a kind of sample. Anyway, Chaliapin was our first real star.

That paved the way for the rest: Leo Slezak, Alessandro Moreschi, whom we billed as the last castrato on disc. And then—in the Hotel di Milano, believe it or not, one floor above the room where Verdi died—I managed to get the very first recordings of Enrico Caruso: ten whole arias! And an exclusive contract—you can be sure of that. Soon we had Adelina Patti on board and others too. With worldwide distribution. The royal houses of England and Spain were regular customers. And with a little trick or two Rappaport took care of the American competition for the house of Rothschild in Paris. But I'd been in the record business long enough to know you can't stay put, quantity is everything, you've got to decentralize, so we set up plants in Barcelona, Vienna, and—get this—Calcutta to hold our own in the world market. That's why the fire in Hannover wasn't a total catastrophe. Though it did get us down. After all, we started out real small there, the Berliner brothers and me, in that little Celler Chaussee plant. Sure the two of them were geniuses and I'm just a businessman, but Rappaport always knew that the record and the record player meant the dawn of a new era. Though Chaliapin kept crossing himself madly before each recording.

1908

IT'S STANDARD PRACTICE in our family for the father to take the son along. My grandfather, a railwayman active in the union, would take his son and heir to hear Wilhelm Liebknecht whenever he spoke in the Hasenheide in Berlin, and my father, another railwayman and comrade, drummed into me the more or less prophetic statement he'd heard at the mass rallies (which were banned as long as Bismarck was in power), namely, "Annexing Alsace-Lorraine will bring us war, not peace!"

Then he took me, when I was only a nine- or ten-year-old whippersnapper, to hear Wilhelm's son, Comrade Karl Liebknecht, in smoky taverns or, once they banned him there, in the open. He took me to Spandau when Liebknecht was campaigning there. And in 1905 he let me ride the train with him—we got free tickets because Father was an engine driver—all the way to Leipzig, where, in the Felsenkeller in Plagwitz, Liebknecht gave a speech about the big strike in the Ruhr district that made headlines all over the country. But he didn't just talk about the miners, he didn't just rail against the Prussian tycoon- and squirearchy; his main topic was the general strike as a potential weapon of the proletarian masses, and in that he was downright prophetic. He spoke off the cuff, building his argument as he went and alluding directly to the revolution in Russia and the bloodstained tsarist regime. He was constantly interrupted by applause. When he was through, the entire audience—my father claimed there were over two thousand present—voted unanimously to support the heroic militants in the Ruhr district and in Russia.

There may have been as many as three thousand crushed together in the Felsenkeller. I had a better view than my father because he put me up on his shoulders, as his father had done when Wilhelm Liebknecht or Comrade Bebel spoke on the situation of the working class. It was standard practice in our family. Anyway, I always both saw and heard him from my elevated whippersnapper vantage point. He knew how to reach the masses. He could go on forever. He was especially good at inciting the young to action. I once heard him shout out over a field of umpteen thousand heads, "Get the young and you've got the army!" Which—that too—was prophetic. And I was scared out of my wits up there on Father's shoulders when I heard him roar at us, "Militarism is capitalism's bloody butcher and buttress!"

I remember as if it were yesterday the day he spoke of the inner enemy we must all repel, because he scared me so that I suddenly needed to pee and started fidgeting on Father's shoulders. But Father was so involved he didn't notice, and there came a point when I just couldn't hold it in. And so it happened that in the year 1907 I pissed not only my pants but also my father's neck. Comrade Liebknecht was arrested the following year and sentenced by the Supreme Court to one and a half years' imprisonment in the Glatz Fortress for his antimilitarist pamphlet. But I was immediately removed from my father's sopping back, the result of my time of need, and right in the middle of the rally, before Comrade Liebknecht had even finished inciting the young to action, was given such a spanking that I felt the hand long after.

And that is the reason why—the only reason why—the minute things came to a head I made a beeline for the local recruiting office and enlisted. I was even decorated twice for bravery and, after being wounded at Arras and outside Verdun, made it to N.C.O. But never, not even at the head of a raiding party in Flanders, did I doubt that Comrade Liebknecht, who—later, much later and with Comrade Rosa—was beaten to death and tossed into the Landwehrkanal by some fellow soldiers from the Freikorps, was perfectly justified in inciting the young.

1909

BECAUSE I USED TO SWEAT my way daily to the Urban Hospital on my bicycle and had the reputation of being a cycling enthusiast, I was appointed Dr. Willner's assistant for the six-day race that was held in the winter velodrome at the zoo, a first not only for Berlin and the Reich but also for Europe as a whole. Only in America had the agony been going on for several years, because over there everything bigger than life attracts a crowd. So it made sense that the victors of the previous New York season, Floyd MacFarland and Jimmy Moran, were favored to win. It was a pity that the German racer Rütt, who had won the American competition the year before with his Dutch partner, Stol, was unable to take part. A deserter, he could not enter the Reich with impunity. But that handsome devil Stol was on hand and soon became everybody's darling. Naturally I hoped that Robl, Stellbrink, and our ace Willy Arend would do the German colors proud.

Dr. Willner manned the infirmary nonstop, that is, round the clock. Like the cyclists we were allotted chicken-coop-sized bunks that were set up on the long side of the grandstand just next to the small workshop for the mechanics and our poorly concealed first-aid station. We had plenty to do. On the very first day Poulain took a tumble and brought down our Willy Arend with him. Georget and Rosenlöcher took their places, when, for several rounds, they had to sit on the sidelines, and Rosenlöcher had to drop out later from exhaustion.

According to our plan, Dr. Willner had all participants weighed before the race and after. He also gave them all, not only those of German blood, the option of oxygen inhalations, an offer nearly everyone took him up on. The six to seven bottles they consumed a day testifies to the enormous strain placed on them by the race.

After being remodeled in the spring, the hundred-and-fifty-meter track looked completely different. The fresh cement was painted green. The standing room in the back was packed with young people; the boxes and front rows were occupied by gentlemen from Berlin-W. in tails and white cummerbunds, their top hats blocking the ladies' view. The royal box was visited by Prince Oskar and his retinue as early as the second day, when our Willy Arend was behind by two laps, but on the fourth day, which was characterized by twenty-five rounds of fierce attempts on the part of the favorites MacFarland-Moran and Stol-Berthet to outstrip each other and a blow delivered by the French cyclist Jacquelin to our Stellbrink with the result that the gallery all but rioted and was on the point of lynching Jacquelin until the race was called to a halt for a brief interval and the Frenchman disqualified, His Imperial and Royal Majesty the Crown Prince appeared with his royal household in exquisite array and stayed on well past midnight in the best of moods. There was much jubilation at his appearance—that and some brisk military marches, though popular tunes as well for the cheering back rows. Even when things were quiet, when the cyclists circled the track almost serenely, there was vigorous music in the background. Stellbrink, a tough customer who played a mandolin as he rode, was no match for it.

And even in the early morning, when absolutely nothing exciting was going on, we had a lot to do. Thanks to Sanitas, the electricity company, we were equipped with the latest Rotar X-ray machine, and Dr. Willner, supervised by Dr. Schjerning, head of the hospital, took sixty X rays of all participating cyclists, whether they made it through to the end or not, and showed them to Dr. Schjerning. Dr. Schjerning advised Dr. Willner to publish that and related material in a major professional journal, which he subsequently did, though without mentioning my part in the project.

But our most esteemed Dr. Schjerning was also curious about the race itself and watched the top-rated Stol-Berthet team yield to the American favorites on the fifth day. Later, after Brocco got in Berthet's way during his final spurt, Berthet claimed that his partner, Stol, had been bribed by the MacFarland-Moran team, though he could not prove it to the officials. Despite lingering suspicions, therefore, Stol retained his darling status with the public.

Dr. Willner recommended high-in-nutrition Biolecithin, Biomalt, raw eggs and roast beef, rice, noodles, and custard to our racers. Robl, a rather sullen loner, downed huge portions of caviar on the advice of his private physician. Nearly all the participants smoked and drank champagne. Jacquelin even drank port until he was eliminated. We had reason to believe that some of the foreign participants were using stimulants made of more or less dangerous poisonous compounds. Dr. Willner suspected strychnine and caffeine preparations. I noticed Berthet, a millionaire's son with black locks, chewing away on a ginger root in his bunk.

Be that as it may, the Stol-Berthet team eventually fell behind, and at ten o'clock P.M., on the seventh day, Floyd MacFarland and Jimmy Moran emerged victorious, pocketing a prize of fifteen thousand marks. Our Willy Arend came in seventeen laps behind them, thereby disappointing even his most devoted followers. Yet the velodrome was packed, sold out, despite the fact that it cost twice as much to get in at the end. Of the sixteen teams that started, only three were left. The applause at the final bell was thunderous. Even though the handsome devil Stol got a special burst of his own, the Americans had their fair share when they made a final victory round. It goes without saying that the royal box was occupied by the Crown Prince and Princess, the Princes of Thurn and Taxis, and other such notables. A bicycle-mad patron gave our Arend and Robl hefty consolation prizes. Stol presented me with a souvenir, an air pump made in Holland. And Dr. Willner found it noteworthy that throughout the race participants excreted considerable amounts of protein.

1910

ANYWAYS, NOW I WANT to tell you about the nickname the boys here pinned on me just 'cause my name's Bertha and I'm pretty big. It all goes back to the time we was living in the workers' colony, they called it. It was right next to the factory, so we got all the smoke, but whenever I squawked about the wash being all gray and the kids coughing all the time and all, my old man he'd say, "Forget it, Bertha. When you do piecework for Krupp, you keep your mouth shut and you work fast."

Which we did all those years, even when things got cramped 'cause we had to give up the back room, the one near the rabbit warren, to two of the men, bachelors, boarders, and there was no room for my knitting machine that I saved up for with my own money. But my Köbes said to me, he said, "Forget it, Bertha. All that counts is it don't rain in on us."

He worked in the foundry. Where they made cannon barrels and the rest of that stuff. It was a couple years before the
war. We had our hands full. And they came up with this thing
they were so proud of; they said there'd never been anything
like it so big before. Well, our colony was full of foundry
men—both our boarders worked there—and people kept
going on about it even though it was supposed to be this big
secret. Thing was, they couldn't finish it. It was supposed to be
like a mortar. That's the one with the stump of a barrel. But
this one was forty-two centimeters in diameter, forty-two on
the dot. A couple times the mold broke or something, but my
old man he'd say, "You ask me, we'll finish it before all hell
breaks loose. Or else, Krupp being Krupp, he'll sell it to the
tsar in Russia if he can."

But when all hell did break loose a couple years later, they
didn't sell it; they used it to shoot at Paris from far away. And
they called it Big Bertha everywhere. Even where nobody
knew me. At first it was only the foundry boys, the ones in the
colony, who called the thingummy that. Named it after me
'cause I was so big. Can't say as I liked being talked about like
that all over the place, though my Köbes said to me, he said,
"They don't mean no harm." I can't say as I particularly liked
them cannons, even though we lived off of 'em. And not so
bad either, you ask me. We had chickens and geese, and most
everybody kept a pig in their shed. And then all them rabbits
in spring...

Didn't use 'em all that much during the war, their Big
Berthas. I bet the Frogs they laughed themselves silly when
the thingummy missed its target. And my Köbes—who Ludendorff called up out of the reserves at the very end of the
war and now he's a cripple so we can't live in the colony no

more and gotta rent this shack and get by on my savings—my Köbes says to me, he says, "All that counts is you've got your health...."

1911

My dear Eulenburg,

If I may still call you same after that canaille of a Harden has vilified us in his press campaign and I have been obliged, much against my will, to bend to *raison d'état* and dismiss my loyal majordomo. And yet, dear Count, may I ask you to celebrate with me. For I have capital news: Today I promoted Tirpitz, my Minister of the Navy, who has done such an admirable job of making things uncomfortable for the left liberals in the Reichstag, to Admiral of the Fleet. You remonstrate mildly with me on occasion over my punctiliously detailed sketches of the fleet and because all through our colossally boring meetings I indulge my modest talent, adorning, as a warning to us all, not only folders but also their dry-as-dust contents with France's *Charles Martel* and her first-class cruisers, the *Jeanne d'Arc* above all, and Russia's latest, armored vessels like the *Petropavlovsk,* the *Poltava,* and the *Sebastopol* with their myriad gun turrets. With what could we have countered England's Dreadnoughts before the naval bill gradually gave us a free hand? The four Brandenburg cruisers, nothing more. But now—as you will see, dearest friend, from the materials enclosed—we have a response to my sketches of the potential enemy; nor is it merely a sketch, for it is at this very moment plowing the North and Baltic Seas or on the stocks at Kiel, Wilhelmshaven, and Danzig.

I realize we have wasted years, our people being, alas, un-conscionably ignorant *in rebus navalibus*. We had to find a way to make them understand and, even more, champion the navy. It took the Naval Association and the naval bill to do so, though we were aided by the English—or should I say, my es-teemed English cousins?—against their will, when during the Boer War—as you will recall, my dear Eulenburg—they seized two of our steamships in a perfectly illegal action off the east coast of Africa. Everyone in the Reich was outraged, which helped us in the Reichstag. Though my quip—"We Germans must counter the English armored Dreadnoughts with German armored Frightnoughts"—also raised a com-motion. (I know, I know, my dear Count: I have a shameful weakness for Wolff's News Agency.)

But now the first fruits of my dreams are on the waters. What is to come? That is for Tirpitz to decide. I still find it an inviolable pleasure to sketch both commercial- and war-ships, though now I do it in earnest at my writing desk, where I sit, as you know, in the saddle, primed for the attack. After my constitutional morning ride I make it my obligation to commit to paper a daring draft of our still so callow fleet in the face of the foe's superiority, aware as I am that Tirpitz, like myself, is putting his money on capital ships. We must be speedier, more mobile, better shots. I am bombarded by new ideas on the subject. The ships fairly tumble out of my head in the act of creation. I had a few heavy cruisers in my mind's eye yester-day—the *Seydlitz,* the *Blücher*—and out they came through my hand. I see whole squadrons lining up. We still lack the necessary capital ships. If only for that reason the submarines must wait, Tirpitz feels.

Dearest friend and kindred spirit, if only you were here at hand as you once were. The lively, clearheaded talks we would have. I would do everything to calm your fears. Yes, dear Count, I wish to be a prince of peace—but well armed.

1912

THOUGH GAINFULLY EMPLOYED by the Potsdam Department of Hydraulic Engineering as a riverbank inspector, I also wrote poetry in which the end of the world was at hand and death reigned supreme; in other words, I was ready for any and all horrors.

It happened in mid-January. I had heard him read for the first time two years earlier at the Kleiststrasse Nollendorf Casino, where the New Club met on Wednesday evenings. From then on I attended the readings as often as I could, given the distance. My sonnets went all but unnoticed, whereas his work could not be ignored. I came across it again at the Neopathetic Cabaret. Blass and Wolfenstein were there too. His verse filed past in thundering columns, the march of a monotonous monologue leading straight to the slaughter. But then the childlike giant exploded. It was like the eruption of Krakatoa the year before. He had been writing for Pfemfer's *Aktion*; it was just after the latest Moroccan crisis, when things were touch and go and we were eager for the fray. Then, suddenly, his poem "War." I can hear it now: "Countless corpses hidden midst the reeds / Covered over white by death's strong birds…" He was very much taken with black and white, white especially. No wonder a black hole seemingly awaiting him turned up in the endless white of the long since frozen and walkable Havel.

What a loss! And why, we wondered, hadn't the *Vossische Zeitung* published an obituary? Only a brief statement: "On Tuesday afternoon, while skating on the Havel at Kladow, Dr. Georg Heym, doctor of jurisprudence, and Ernst Balcke, law student, fell into a hole in the ice made for waterfowl."

Precious little, though accurate as far as it went. We had noticed something wrong at Schwanenwerder. My assistant and I made our way to the spot with several skaters, but all we found was what later proved to be Heym's elegantly knobbed walking stick and gloves. Perhaps he had tried to help his friend out of the water and fallen in himself. Or Balcke had pulled him in when he fell. Or both of them had willingly sought out death.

The *Vossische* article also mentioned, as if it had any bearing on the matter, that he was the son of a retired counsel for the military who lived in Charlottenburg, Königsweg 31. The law student's father was a banker. But nothing, not a word about what possessed two young men to leave a safe path marked with sticks and bundles of straw, to leave it willingly. Nothing about the inner needs of our even then lost generation. Nothing about Heym's poetry. Yet a young publisher by the name of Rowohlt had brought out some of that poetry, and a volume of stories was to follow. Only the *Berliner Tagblatt* mentioned—as an afterthought to the accident report—the drowned man's literary activities, pointing out that he had recently published a volume of verse, *Life Eternal,* which showed signs of talent. Signs! Ridiculous.

The Department of Hydraulic Engineering was very much involved in retrieving the corpses. True, my colleagues mocked me when I called Heym's poetry "terribly important" and quoted one of his most recent poems—"The people standing forward in the streets / Look up to see the wondrous signs of heaven"—yet they hacked away tirelessly at the ice and probed the riverbed with "death anchors." Back in Potsdam, I wrote a poem dedicated to Heym entitled "Death Anchors." Pfemfer expressed interest in publishing it, but then sent it back with apologies.

The one-year-younger Balcke, as the *Kreuzzeitung* was quick to report, was sighted by a fisherman, who made a hole in the ice and hauled the corpse out of the water with a hook he had on board. Balcke looked peaceful, while Heym had his legs tucked under him like an embryo. Tense, his face distorted, his hands bruised. Lying on the crusty ice with both his skates still on. Outwardly—but only outwardly—robust. Torn by conflicting desires. Repelled as he was by the military, he had volunteered for the Alsatian infantry in Metz only weeks before. He had other plans as well, however. I know he was thinking of writing for the theater.

1913

CAN I REALLY HAVE BUILT this ominous mass, this fossilized colossus, this expression of a granite-shitting architect's mania, no, not planned and designed it but—for the good fourteen years I was in charge of construction—dug the foundation and laid layer upon layer as it towered up to heaven?

What I said to Court Counselor Thieme, who heads the Society of Patriots and cadged nearly six million marks across the length and breadth of the Reich, what I said today one year after the keystone was laid with great pomp and just after one of my men had filled in the last cracks, "Pretty colossal, the whole affair."

"Which is as it should be, Krause. Which is as it should be. Our ninety-one meters outdoes the Kyffhäuser Monument by—would you believe it?—twenty-six...."

To which I responded, "And the Kaiser's Temple at the Porta Westfalica by nearly thirty."

"And the Berlin Victory Column by exactly thirty."

"To say nothing of the Hermann Monument. Or the Bavarie in Munich, which comes to a piddling twenty-seven."

My irony must have registered. "In any case," he continued, "our patriotic commemoration of the Battle of the Nations will be duly opened to the public on its hundredth anniversary."

After adding a pinch of doubt to his patriotic broth—"A few sizes smaller would have done the trick just as well"—I started talking shop. I opened by redigging the foundation: "A hundred percent debris from Leipzig and environs. Year after year. Layer after layer." But all my warnings—"You can't build on that stuff, you'll have cracks before you know it; with slipshod work like that you can expect repair bills galore"—had fallen on deaf ears.

Thieme looked at me sheepishly, as if all the exorbitant bills had just landed on his shoulders.

"But if we hadn't built on a refuse heap," I went on, "if we'd sunk the foundation into the solid base of the battlefield, we'd have uncovered a vast number of skulls, sabers and lances, uniforms in tatters, whole and cracked helmets, officers' braid and foot soldiers' buttons—Prussian, Swedish, Habsburg, even Polish, and French of course. There were plenty of deaths to go around. A hundred and twenty thousand if you put all the nations together."

I went on with my figures, citing the hundred and twenty thousand cubic meters of cement and fifteen thousand cubic meters of granite. But Court Counselor Thieme, who had been joined in the meantime by the architect of the complex, Professor Schmitz, looked quite proud and called the moment "worthy of the dead." Then he congratulated Schmitz, who for his part thanked Thieme for funds sponged and confidence shown.

I asked the gentlemen whether they had confidence in the granite inscription at the exact center of the pediment: GOD WITH US. Both gave me a quizzical look, then shook their heads and walked off in the direction of the fossilized colossus perched on a refuse heap. The two of them should have been sculpted in granite and placed among the musclemen decorating its upper reaches shoulder to shoulder.

The opening was scheduled for the next day. Not only Wilhelm would be there but the King of Saxony as well. The clear October sky promised glorious weather. One of my masons, a Social Democrat if there ever was one, had the following to say: "Now *there's* something us Germans are good at. Monuments. At any price."

1914

FINALLY, IN THE MID-SIXTIES, after two of my colleagues at the institute tried and failed several times, I managed to bring the two elderly gentlemen together. Perhaps I had better luck because I was a young woman, and Swiss to boot, that is, I had the bonus of neutrality. My letters, despite the

dispassionate tone I used to describe the object of my research, were meant as a sensitive if not timid knock at the
door. The acceptances arrived within a few days and almost
simultaneously.

I characterized them to my colleagues as an impressive, if
slightly fossilized pair. I had booked them quiet rooms in the
Zum Storchen. We spent much of our time in the Rôtisserie
there, with its view of the Limmat, the Town Hall directly opposite, and the Zum Rüden house. Herr Remarque, who was
sixty-seven at the time, had come from Locarno. Clearly a bon
vivant, he seemed more fragile to me than Herr Jünger, who
had just turned seventy and made a sprightly, pointedly athletic impression. He lives in Württemberg, but had come to
Zurich via Basel after making a foot tour through the Vosges
to the Hartmannsweiler Kopf, the scene of severe fighting
in 1915.

Our first session was anything but promising. The conversation of my "witnesses of an era" centered on Swiss wines,
Remarque preferring Ticino vintages, Jünger those of La Dôle
in the canton of Vaud. Both made a show of plying me with
their well-conserved charm. I found their attempts to use
Schwyzerdütsch amusing but tiresome. It wasn't until I quoted
the opening of "The Flemish Dance of Death," an anony-
mous song popular during the First World War—"Death
rides on a raven-black steed, / Wearing a stocking cap over his
head"—that things changed. First Remarque, then Jünger
hummed the haunting, melancholy melody, and both knew
the lines that brought the refrain to a close: "Flanders is in
danger. / Death is there no stranger." They looked off in the
direction of the Cathedral, its spires towering over the houses
along the embankment.

Following this meditative interlude, broken only by some clearing of throats, Remarque said that in the autumn of 1914—he was still on a school bench in Osnabrück while volunteers at Bikschote and Ieper were lying in their own blood—the Langemark legend, that is, that German soldiers had responded to English machine-gun fire by singing "Deutschland über alles," had made a great impression on him. That, together with their teachers' exhortations, had moved many a class to enlist in the war effort. Every second soldier did not return. And those who did—like Remarque, who was not allowed to continue his education—were tainted to this day. He still thought of himself as one of the living dead.

Herr Jünger, who had followed his fellow writer's account of his school experiences with a delicate smile, qualified the Langemark legend as "patriotic balderdash," though he admitted that long before the war began he had been obsessed with a craving for danger, a yen for the unusual—"be it only a stint in the French Foreign Legion." "When it broke out at last, we felt we'd been fused with an enormous body. Yet even after the war showed its claws, I was fascinated, during the raiding parties I led, by the idea of battle as inner experience. Fess up, my friend. Even in *All Quiet on the Western Front,* your excellent debut, you described the camaraderie unto death among soldiers in highly moving terms."

The novel did not record what he himself had experienced, Remarque replied. It brought together the front-line experiences of a generation sent to the slaughter. "My service in the ambulance corps provided me with all the material I needed."

I wouldn't go so far as to say the gentlemen began to argue, but they made a point of showing how they differed on matters military, how opposed their very styles were, and that in other respects as well they came from opposing camps. While one of them still considered himself "an incorrigible pacifist," the other wished to be seen as an "anarch."

"Don't be silly," Remarque said at one point. "Why, in *The Storm of Steel* you were like a holy terror bent on adventure. Until Ludendorff's final offensive. You would throw together a raiding party for the bloodthirsty pleasure of taking a quick prisoner or two—and possibly a bottle of cognac..." But then he admitted that his colleague's diary gave a partially valid description of trench and positional warfare and of the character of the matériel battle.

Toward the end of our first round—by which time the gentlemen had emptied two bottles of red wine—Jünger returned to the issue of Flanders. "Digging trenches along the Langemark front two and a half years later, we came across belts, weapons, and cartridge cases from 1914. We even found spiked helmets, the kind worn by whole volunteer regiments marching off to war...."

1915

OUR NEXT ROUND took place at the Odeon, a café so venerable that, until the German Reich granted him safe-conduct to Russia, Lenin sat there reading the *Neue Zürcher Zeitung* and the like, secretly planning his revolution. We concentrated on the past rather than the future, though the gentlemen insisted on opening the meeting with a champagne breakfast. I was served orange juice.

They laid their evidence, their once hotly debated novels, on the marble table between the croissants and the cheese platter.

All Quiet on the Western Front had had much larger editions than *The Storm of Steel*. "Once my book was burned publicly in '33," Remarque said, "it was out of print for a good twelve years—and not only in Germany—while your hymn to war has obviously been available everywhere and at all times."

Jünger made no response. But when I brought the conversation round to the trench war in Flanders and the chalky soil of the Champagne region and placed pictures of the areas under siege on the table, which had since been cleared, he immediately started in on the Somme offensive and counteroffensive and made a point that set the tone for the rest of the conversation: "That miserable leather spiked helmet—which you, my most worthy colleague, were spared—was replaced as early as June 1915 in our section of the front by a steel helmet. It was developed by an artillery captain named Schwerd after a number of false starts in a race with the French, who were also introducing steel helmets. Since Krupp was not in a position to manufacture a suitable chrome alloy, contracts went to other companies, including the Thale Iron Works. By February 1916 steel helmets were in use on all fronts. Troops at Verdun and on the Somme received them first; the eastern front had to wait the longest. You have no idea, my dear Remarque, how many lives were lost to that useless leather cap, which, leather being in short supply, was actually made of felt. The losses were particularly great in positional warfare, where every well-aimed shot meant one man fewer, every bomb fragment blasted its way home."

Then he turned to me and said, "The helmet used by your Swiss police today—true, in modified form—is modeled after our steel helmet down to the pins that provide ventilation."

My response—"Fortunately our helmet has not had to stand up to the bombardments of matériel you so powerfully celebrate"—he passed over in silence, inundating instead the pointedly tight-lipped Remarque with further details, from the battle-gray finishing process used for rust protection to the neck protector in the back and the horsehair or quilted-felt lining. Then he lamented the poor visibility in trench warfare as a result of the front rim's having to protrude enough to provide protection down to the tip of the nose. "You can be sure I found the heavy steel helmet a terrible burden while leading raids. It was admittedly frivolous of me, but I preferred my good old lieutenant's cap, which, I should add, was lined with silk." Then something else occurred to him, something he qualified as amusing. "By the way, I keep a Tommy helmet on my desk as a souvenir. It's completely different, flat as it can be. With a bullet hole in it, naturally."

After a lengthy pause—the gentlemen were having plum brandy with their coffee—Remarque said, "The M-16 steel helmets, later M-17, were much too large for the green replacement recruits; they kept slipping. All you could see of the childlike faces was a frightened mouth and quivering chin. Comical and pitiful at once. Nor need I tell you that infantry bullets and shrapnel could pierce even steel...."

He called for another brandy. Jünger joined him. The nice Swiss *Meidschi* was served another glass of freshly squeezed orange juice.

1916

AFTER AN EXTENDED STROLL on the Limmat Embankment past the Helmhaus and along Lake of Zürich's promenade, followed by a quiet period imposed by me and respected, I believe, by both gentlemen, we were invited to dinner by Herr Remarque—who, thanks to the screen versions of his novels, clearly belongs to the category of well-to-do authors—in the Kronenhalle, a solid, upscale restaurant with an artistic ambiance and authentic Impressionists as well as Matisse, Braque, and even Picasso hanging on the walls. We had whitefish, then *Rösti* and strips of stewed veal in the Swiss manner, and finally espresso and armagnac for the gentlemen and a *mousse au chocolat* for me.

Once the waiter had cleared the table, I concentrated on positional warfare along the western front. Without consulting their works, both gentlemen were able to recount instances of reciprocal drumfire lasting for days and putting their own trenches in jeopardy; they described the staggered trench system, the breastworks, the saps, the dugouts, the tunnels burrowed deep in the earth, the underground passageways, the galleries for explosives and espionage, the tangle of barbed-wire barricades, but also foxholes and whole trenches under water. Their experiences sounded extraordinarily fresh, and if Remarque qualified his by saying he had only built trenches, never fought in them, he also said, "I did see what became of them, though."

Whether they spoke of building trenches, going for food, or laying barbed wire at night, every detail was vivid. Their memories were precise, and only occasionally did they sink into anecdotes, like the talks Jünger had at the far ends of the saps—that is, at a distance of no more than thirty paces—with the Tommies and Frogs in his school English and French. After a few descriptions of offensives and counteroffensives I had the feeling I'd been there.

Then they turned to English mines and their effectiveness,

the "rattler," the bottle mine, and shrapnel; they spoke of duds and heavy grenades with percussion fuses and time fuses, of the noises made by approaching guns of various calibers. Both men were able to imitate the voices that went to make up the disturbing concerts known as "cordons of fire." It must have been hell.

"And yet," Herr Jünger said, "there was one element alive in us all, an element that spiritualized the desolation of war: the objective pleasure we took in danger, the chivalrous impulse to persevere in battle. Yes, I can state without compunction: As the years went by, the flame of the prolonged battle produced an increasingly pure and valiant warrior caste...."

Herr Remarque laughed in Herr Jünger's face. "Oh, come off it, Jünger! You sound like a country squire. Cannon fodder quaking in oversized boots — that's what they were. Animals. All right, maybe they were beyond fear, but death never left their minds. So what could they do? Play cards, curse, fantasize about spread-eagled women, and wage war—murder on command, that is. Which took some expertise. They discussed the advantages of the shovel over the bayonet: the shovel not only let you thrust below the chin; it gave you a good solid blow, on the diagonal, say, between neck and shoulder, which then cut right down to the chest, while the bayonet tended to get caught between the ribs and you had to go all the way to the stomach to pull it loose...."

As none of the Kronenhalle's reticent waiters dared approach our boisterous table, Jünger, who had chosen for what he called our "working dinner" a light red, poured himself another glass and, after a pointed pause, took a swig. "True, true, my dear Remarque, but I still maintain that when I saw my men lying motionless, stonelike, in the trenches, rifles pointed, bayonets fixed, when I saw steel helmet after steel helmet, blade after blade shining by the light of a flare, I was suffused with a feeling of invincibility. Crushed we could be, yes, but not conquered."

During the ensuing silence, which no one seemed able to break—Herr Remarque was on the point of saying something, then dismissed it with a wave of the hand—both men raised their glasses, but looked past each other as they simultaneously downed what was left in them. Remarque kept tugging on the handkerchief in his breast pocket, Jünger shot me glances that made me feel like a rare insect he needed for his collection, while I focused on my formidable portion of *mousse au chocolat.*

Eventually they loosened up and started in on the "cannon fodder's" slang. Latrine rumors, to be precise. Apologies were duly proffered when the language got too rude for the "little Swiss Miss," as Remarque called me in jest. In the end, each praised the other for the graphic quality of his coverage of the front. "Who else is there but us?" Jünger asked. "The French have got only that madman Céline."

1917

RIGHT AFTER BREAKFAST — nothing opulent this time, no champagne; in fact, the gentlemen decided to accept my recommendation of Birchermüsli—we resumed our conversation. As if talking to a schoolgirl they were afraid to shock, they gave me a cautious account of chemical warfare, that is, the deliberate use of chlorine and mustard gas as ammunition, referring partly to their own experience but also to secondary sources.

We had come to chemical weapons without beating around the bush, when Remarque brought up the Vietnam War, which was going on at the time of our conversation, and called the use of napalm and Agent Orange "criminal." "Once you drop an atom bomb," he said, "you lose all inhibitions." Jünger condemned the systematic defoliation of the jungle by surface poisons as a logical continuation of the use of poison gas in World War I and agreed with Remarque that the Americans would lose this "dirty war," which had no use for true "soldierly behavior."

"Though we must admit," he added, "that we were the first to use chlorine gas. In April 1915, at Ieper, against the English."

Whereupon Remarque cried out—so loud that a waitress came to a halt not far from our table and then rushed off— "Gas attack! Gas! Gaaas!" and Jünger imitated the ring of the alarm with a teaspoon. Then, suddenly, as if obeying some inner command, he was serious and to the point: "We immediately started oiling our rifle barrels and anything made of metal. Those were our orders. Then we buckled on the gas masks. Later, in Monchy, just before the Battle of the Somme, we saw a group of gas victims writhing and moaning, water streaming from their eyes. But the main thing chlorine does is to eat away at your lungs, burn them up. I saw what it could do in enemy trenches as well. Not long thereafter the English began using phosgene on us. It had a sickly-sweet smell."

Then it was Remarque's turn: "They would retch for days, spewing out their burned-up lungs. The worst thing was when they were caught in a shell hole or funk hole during a barrage of fire, because clouds of gas would settle in any depression like jellyfish, and woe unto those who took their masks off too soon.... The replacements, inexperienced, were always the first to go.... Poor young, helpless boys bumbling about... Baggy uniforms... Turnip-white faces... Still alive but with the deadpan gaze of dead children... I once saw a dugout filled with the poor beasts.... All blue heads and black lips... Taken their masks off too soon... Hemorrhaging to death."

They both apologized; it was too much so early in the morning. I could tell they found it odd and unpleasant for a young lady to be interested in the bestialities war naturally entailed. I assured Remarque—who, more than Jünger, saw himself as a gentleman of the old school—that he needn't worry about me: the report that Bührli has commissioned from us had to be comprehensive, after all. "I'm sure you're aware of the quality of the weapons Bührli turns out for export," I said, and asked them for more detail.

Since Herr Remarque gazed off in the direction of the Town Hall bridge and the Limmat Embankment and did not respond, Herr Jünger, more in control of himself, filled me in on the development of the gas mask and then of mustard gas, which was first used—and by the Germans—in June of 1917 during the third battle at Ieper. It formed an all but odorless, barely perceptible cloud, a kind of mist that stuck to the ground and didn't start taking effect—eating away at your cells—until three or four hours after you breathed it. Dichloroethyl sulfide, an oily compound sprayed in tiny drops. No gas mask could keep it out.

Herr Jünger went on to explain that entire trench systems would be infected with the gas, whereupon they would be evacuated without a fight. "But late in the autumn of '17," he said, "the English captured a major cache of mustard-gas grenades and immediately used them against us. Many soldiers lost their sight.... Tell me, Remarque, wasn't that what landed the greatest corporal of all time in sick bay at Pasewalk? Where he spent the rest of the war in safety. And where he decided to go into politics."

1918

AFTER A SHORT SHOPPING SPREE—Jünger stocked up on cigars, including the Brisago variety, while Remarque followed my advice and bought his Frau Paulette a silk fichu at Grieder's—I took them to the station in a cab. Since we had time to kill, we went to the bar. I proposed a light white wine for our farewell drink. Although everything had in principle been covered, I did keep a record of the hour-long conversation. When I asked whether they had had direct experience of the tanks the English deployed in large numbers during the last year of the war, they jested that they had never been run over by them, but both had come across "burned-out colossi" during counteroffensives and said the only defenses were flamethrowers and tied-together hand grenades. "The tank," Jünger pointed out, "was still in its infancy. The time of rapid encirclement was still to come."

They both proved keen observers of the war in the air. Remarque recalled bets made in the trenches and behind the lines: "A portion of liverwurst or five cigarettes against whether a Fokker or an English single-seater would be the first to sprout a tail of smoke and go into a spin. Though we were outnumbered in any case: by the end there were five English or American planes to every one of ours."

"Their superiority in matériel was overwhelming across the board," said Jünger by way of confirmation, "but it was especially noticeable in the air. Still, I was always a little jealous of our boys in their triplanes. Air battles were such chivalrous undertakings. How daring it was for a single plane to sail out of the sun and pick its opponent out of the enemy pack. What was the motto of the Richthofen squadron again? Oh, I remember: 'Steadfast yet wild!' And they were a credit to it. Cold-blooded yet fair. *The Red Baron* is still worth reading, my friend, despite the fact that toward the end of his extremely animated memoirs even the Herr Baron had to admit that by 1917 at the latest the idea of a bright and cheerful war was a thing of the past. Down below, the landscape was all muck and shell holes. Everything dogged and determined. Yet he remained brave to the very end, to the moment he was called down from the sky. It was the same on the ground. Only their matériel was strong. 'Undefeated in the field!' was the way we put it. Even with the revolt on the home front. But when I count up my wounds—at least fourteen hits, of which five were from guns, two from shell splinters, one from shrapnel, four from hand grenades, and two from miscellaneous flying metal, which comes to a good twenty scars, because some of them both went in and came out—I can only conclude it was worth it." He delivered the bottom line of his balance sheet with a peal of ringing, or, rather, venerable yet youthful laughter.

Remarque listened, withdrawn. "Can't say I agree," he finally ventured. "I was hit only once, digging trenches, and that was enough for me. I can't match your exploits: I was in the ambulance corps later, nothing more; I can't compete with your *Pour le mérite* chain. But we were defeated in the end. In every respect. And you and your kind lacked the courage to admit defeat. Clearly you lack it even now."

Was that all that needed saying? No. Because Jünger brought up the influenza epidemic that made the rounds of both camps as the war drew to a close: "Over twenty million deaths from influenza, approximately the same as the number of deaths on the battlefield. But when you fell in battle, at least you knew what for."

"What for, in heaven's name?" Remarque muttered under his breath.

Slightly embarrassed, I chose this point to put my copies of their two most famous books on the table and asked for their signatures. Jünger immediately wrote, "For our brave Vreneli" above his, while Remarque signed beneath a clear-cut message: "How soldiers turn to murderers."

Now everything had been said. The gentlemen emptied their glasses, stood at almost the same time—Remarque first—and made a quick bow, thereby managing not to shake each other's hand and making a symbolic attempt at kissing mine. They both assured me I did not need to accompany them to the platform: they had nothing but hand luggage.

Herr Remarque died four years later; Herr Jünger clearly intends to live out the century.

1919

A BUNCH OF WAR PROFITEERS, the lot of them. Know the one who made a pile with his Bratolin? Chops, he called them, and they were all corn and peas and turnips. The wurst too. And now these wursterfeiters are yelling and screaming about how the "home front"—that's us—didn't make enough grenades and the German housewife stabbed our soldiers in the back... In the back!... Well, they stuck my husband in the Home Guard at the very end and he came home a cripple. And the two girls were so sickly they got the grippe and died. And then Erich, my only brother, Erich, who was in the Navy and with a little bit of luck came out of Dogger Bank, Skagerrak, and all those shooting galleries in one piece, well, here he marches into Berlin from Kiel with his battalion on the side of the Republic and gets his brains blown out on the barricades. Peace? Don't make me laugh. There's shooting everywhere. And turnips everywhere too. In bread, in meatballs. I even made a turnip *cake* the other day. With a pinch of beechnut. For Sunday company. And then you get these swindlers that charge an arm and a leg for some pasty goo with "flavoring" and call it gravy, you get them talking in the papers about stabs in the back. Well, string 'em up on the lampposts is what I say. Maybe that'd stop all this ersatz business. What makes us traitors? All we want is no more Kaiser and no more turnips. We don't want revolutions going on all the time, and we don't want stabbings, in the back or the front. We want real bread and enough of it; we want marmalade and not "Frux"; we want chicken eggs and not your "Eirol" starch balls; we want a slice of pork and not your latest fake. That's all. Nothing more. Because peace *has* come. Which is why I'm for a Council Republic here in Prenzlau. I'm even on the Women's Food Council, and we've made this appeal and had it printed and pasted up all over the place. "Housewives of Germany!" I shouted from the steps of the Town Hall. "It's time to call the bluff of all the war profiteers! What do they mean with their 'knife in the back'? Didn't we fight year in and year out on the home front? Way back in November 1915 they started feeding us their margarine-and-turnip diet. And it was downhill from then on. No milk! No! Doctor Caro's Milk Tablets. And then came the grippe with its heavy toll and a bad winter with no potatoes. No. Turnips, turnips, and more turnips. "It's like eating barbed wire," my husband said when he came home on leave. And now that Wilhelm has made off with all his riches to that castle in Holland, they tell us that us German housewives took our knives and stabbed our soldiers in the back....

1920

YOUR HEALTH, GENTLEMEN! After a few hard weeks we can celebrate at last. But before we drain our glasses, let me ask you straightaway: What would the Reich be without its trains? And now we have them back! There it was, plain as day, in the otherwise questionable constitution: "It is the responsibility of the Reich..." And believe it or not, it was the "comrades," who in other respects don't give a tinker's damn about the Fatherland, it was the "comrades" who insisted upon it. What Chancellor Bismarck was unable to achieve, what not even His Majesty was vouchsafed, and what we paid for dearly in the War—because for want of standardization, we had two hundred and ten varieties of locomotives, spare parts were often unavailable, and replacement troops or urgent supplies like ammunition for Verdun stood waiting on the tracks—this deplorable state of affairs, which may well have

cost us our victory, has now been rectified by the Social Democrats. Let me repeat: The very Social Democrats who accepted
the November betrayal have, if not turned the proposal into
long overdue reality, then at least made that reality possible.
For I ask you: Of what use was the most elaborate system of
railway networks as long as Bavaria and Saxony balked—
balked, let us be frank, out of sheer hatred for Prussia—at
uniting with the rest of the Reich, that is, at uniting what belongs together on the basis of both human reason and God's
will? That is why I have said over and over: The train to true
unity will ride the tracks of a truly unified rail system. Or, as
the venerable Goethe put it in his infinite wisdom, "What the
princes' intransigence hampers, the railway will accomplish
and unite the Germans." But it took the forced armistice,
which, to compound our misfortune, required us to deliver up
eight thousand locomotives and many thousands of passenger
and freight cars to the shamelessly voracious enemy, to make
us willing to do the dubious Republic's bidding and conclude
a treaty with Prussia and Saxony, Bavaria and Hessen, and
Mecklenburg-Schwerin and Oldenburg stipulating that the
Reich shall take over all the local railways, which, I should
point out, were so deeply in debt that the amount paid could
have equaled the debt outstanding had not inflation made a
mockery of any such calculation. Yet looking back on the year
1920 with glass in hand, I can state without compunction: Yes,
gentlemen, now that the new railway legislation has provided
the Reich with ample funds in stable *Rentenmark* currency, we
have moved out of the red; indeed, thanks to your commend-
able assistance we are in a position to set funds aside for the
reparation payments brazenly imposed on us even as we un-
dergo top-to-bottom modernization. I have been called—first

in secret, then for all to hear—I have been called the "father of
the standard German locomotive," and I have known from the
outset that standardization can succeed only on the basis of
united efforts. Hanomag with its axle linings or Krauss & Co.
with its steering apparatus, Maffei, which produced the cylin-
der covers, or Borsig, which did the assembly work—all these
firms, whose executives are gathered here today in all their
glory, have understood that the standard German locomotive
represents not just the Reich's know-how; it represents the
Reich's unity! Yet no sooner have we begun making profitable
exports—most recently even to Bolshevik Russia, where Professor Lomonosov has spoken highly of our hot-steam freight-
train engines—than we hear the first calls for privatization.
People want speedy gains; they want to cut personnel, shut
down "unprofitable" routes. All I can say is: The time to stop
is now! Placing the Reich's railways in private hands—which
can only mean foreign hands—will do nothing but harm our
poor, humiliated Fatherland. For as Goethe, to whose perspi-
cacity I now call upon you to drain your glasses, once said to
his faithful Eckermann...

1921

Dear Peter Panter,
This is the first time I've ever sent a letter to a newspaper, but
when my fiancé, who reads just about everything he can get
his hands on, shoved some of those hilarious things you write
under my eggcup at breakfast the other day they really gave
me the giggles. I don't get all the political stuff—you've got a

sharp tongue, you have—but you're always funny too. I like that. The only thing is, you don't know beans about dancing. When you talk about doing the shimmy "with your hands in your pockets," you really miss the boat. That may work with the one-step or the foxtrot, but I got to know Horst-Eberhard—as you point out in your little article, he works for the post office, but behind the counter, nothing high up—anyway, I got to know him last year at Little Walter's Shimmy Palace, and he uses both hands when we shimmy together up close. For all to see. And last Friday, even though my wages for the week would barely buy me a pair of socks, the two of us threw on our glad rags—maybe I'm the "little Miss Rattle-head" you make snide remarks about—and went to the Admiral's Palace, where they have dancing contests, and you should have seen our Charleston—that's the latest rage in America. We were the bee's knees—him in a rented monkey suit, me in an above-the-knee gold lamé creation.

Now don't go thinking we were dancing around some golden calf or something. No sirree bob. We dance for the pure joy of it. In the kitchen to the record player. Because we've got it in us. All over. From the solar plexus on up. To the ears, which—as your little article makes a point of saying—in the case of my Horst-Eberhard do stick out. Because shimmy or Charleston, it's not just the legs. It comes from inside and runs all through you. In waves. From down below to up above. All the way to the scalp. There's a shiver goes with it too. You feel happy. And if you don't know what feeling happy is—happy-go-lucky happy, I mean—why not come and take some lessons with me. Every Tuesday and Saturday. At Little Walter's. Free.

Honest! Don't worry, we'll take it in stages. We'll warm up

with a one-step across the floor. I'll lead. You can follow for a change. Trust me. Besides, it's easier than it looks. Then we'll try "Yes, We Have No Bananas." You can sing along. It's fun. And if you've got the stamina for it and my Horst-Eberhard has no objection, we'll go from there to a real Charleston. You feel it down in your calves right away, and soon you're all warmed up. And if I'm in the mood, I'll open up my pouch just for you. Don't worry. One sniff only. You won't get hooked. Just to keep your spirits up. Honest!

My Horst-Eberhard says you usually use a pen name or something: Panther or Tiger or sometimes Herr Wrobel. And he read somewhere you're a short, fat, Polish Jew. Well, I don't care. My name ends in -ski too. And most fat people are good dancers. So if you happen to be feeling generous next Saturday, in a good mood, we'll start off with a bottle or two of bubbly and I'll tell you all about the shoe business. I'm in the men's department at Leiser's. Just promise me one thing: no politics! OK?

Yours affectionately,
Ilse Lepinski

1922

WHAT MORE DO YOU WANT from me? You reporters always know everything anyway. The truth? I've told you everything there is to tell, but nobody believes me. "Unemployed and unreliable" is what went into the court records. "Theodor Brüdigam? An informer, that's what he is. In the pay of the left—and the right too." True enough. But only the Ehrhardt

Brigade paid up, or, rather, the people who kept going after the Kapp Putsch came to grief and the Brigade was forced to disband. What else could they do? And what does "illegal" mean when just about everything going on makes a mockery of the law, and the enemy is the left and not, as Chancellor Wirth would have it, the right. No, it was Captain Hoffmann, not Lieutenant Commander Ehrhardt, who was in charge of the money. And he definitely belongs to the Consul Organization. No one can be certain about the others: they themselves don't know who belongs and who doesn't. A few small contributions came from Tillessen. He's the brother of the Tillessen who shot Erzberger, the Center Party bigwig, though he's as Catholic as Erzberger ever was. Tillessen's in hiding in Hungary or some place like that. But Hoffmann's the one who hired me, hired me to get the lowdown on a number of left-wing groups, not only the Communists, and he just happened to mention who was next on the list after the "November traitor" Erzberger. Scheidemann the Social Democrat, of course, and Rathenau the "Versailles appeaser," though there were plans afoot for Reich Chancellor Wirth as well. Right, I was the one who warned Scheidemann in Kassel. Why? Well, because the way I see it you don't overthrow a system by killing people; you do it semilegally. And the best place to start is Bavaria. You set up a tightly run national state, as your Mussolini has done in Italy. You can even use that Corporal Hitler, batty as he is, because he's a born crowd pleaser and has a big following in Munich. But Scheidemann refused to listen. Nobody believes a word I say. Luckily it fell through; I mean, the acid they splashed in his face in the Habichtswald. Right, it was the mustache that saved him. Sounds like a joke, but that's how it was. Which is why we've stopped using acid. Right, I found it revolting. That's why I wanted to work for Scheidemann only. But the Social Democrats refused to believe me when I said, Scratch the C.O. and you get the Reichswehr Counter Intelligence. And Helfferich, of course, whose bank provides the funds. And von Stinnes. The plutocrats see the money as a kind of tip. Anyway, Rathenau—who is nothing if not a capitalist and whom I personally warned—must have suspected what was going to happen. Because Helfferich and his "Down with Erzberger!" campaign clearly brought about the Erzberger assassination—"Only a traitor to the fatherland could think of negotiating a shameful armistice with that Frenchman Foch"—and just before Rathenau was shot down Helfferich branded him an "appeasement politician." But Rathenau refused to take it to heart. And his idea of calling a last-minute meeting of capitalists—that is, with Hugo Stinnes—couldn't save him, if only because he was a Jew. When I told him, "You are particularly exposed during your morning drive to the Ministry," he responded with the arrogance typical of the Jewish moneyed aristocracy: "Why should I believe a man like you, sir, when my sources tell me you have a bad reputation?" No wonder the public prosecutor prevented me from being sworn in as a witness at the trial: he suspected me "of having taken part in the crime under investigation." Clearly the court wished to keep the C.O. out of it: the men behind the scenes had to be kept behind the scenes. At most there were some rumors about the involvement of possibly illegal organizations. The only one who blabbed at the investigation was von Salomon, a pipsqueak who liked to think of himself as a writer and just wanted to show off. All he gave them was the name of the Hamburg driver and he got five years. Anyway, my warnings fell on deaf ears. Things went the way they had with the Erzberger affair. Even then the boys in the Brigade were trained in absolute discipline, which is why the C.O. could choose the perpetrators, Schulz and Tillessen, by lot. From that point on, the outcome was clear. As you must know from your own newspapers, gentlemen, they gunned him down in the Black Forest, where he was on holiday with his wife and daughter. They lay in wait for him while he was taking a walk with another Center Party man. Of the twelve shots they fired, the one that got him in the head did the job. His walking partner, a Dr. Diez, was merely wounded. The perpetrators then wended their tranquil way to the nearest village, Oppenau, where they had coffee. What you don't realize, gentlemen, is that the perpetrators of the Rathenau assassination were also chosen by lot. One of them spilled the beans in confession, and his priest reported it to Chancellor Wirth, though keeping his vow of secrecy by refusing to reveal the culprit's identity. But Rathenau didn't believe the priest any more than he believed me. He even refused to listen to the pleas for caution made by the Frankfurt Committee of German Jews, which I had informed of the situation as well; he refused to accept police protection. And on the 24th of June he insisted on being driven from his Königsallee house in Grunewald—in an open motorcar, as usual—to Wilhelmstrasse and refused to listen to his chauffeur. So it was a textbook case. Everyone knows by now that even before they'd left Königsallee the chauffeur had to brake at the corner of Erdener Strasse and Lynarstrasse because a horse and cart—whose driver, by the way, has never been interrogated—blocked their way. There were nine shots fired from the Mercedes-Benz saloon car following them. Five hit home. A hand grenade was hurled at Rathenau's car as the Mercedes

passed it. The perpetrators were instilled with a martial spirit
and a hatred for all things non-German. Technow was at the
wheel, Kern manned the machine gun, and Fischer, who
killed himself during the getaway, tossed the hand grenade.
But the only reason it worked was that nobody would believe
Brüdigam the informer, the man with the bad reputation.
Soon the C.O. stopped making payments, and a year later
Corporal Hitler's march on Munich's Feldherrnhalle ended in
failure after much bloodshed. My attempt to warn Ludendorff
was to no avail. And this time I asked for no money; I was interested in other things. Besides, it was losing its value daily.
Only my concern for Germany made me... I felt it my patri-
otic duty to... But nobody will listen to me. You won't.

1923

THEY LOOK PRETTY NOW, the old banknotes, and my great-
grandchildren like to play at buying and selling houses with
them. When the Wall came down, I put away a few of our
East German ones, with the compasses and ears of corn on
them, but the children think them less valuable because
they've got fewer zeros, and use them only as change.

I found the inflation banknotes after Mother died, in the
book where she kept her household records. Now I often leaf
through the price lists and recipes for both the cheery and the
sad memories they bring back. Dear me, Mother had a hard
time of it. We four girls made a lot of work for her, not that
we meant to. I was the eldest. In other words, the apron here,
which cost three and a half thousand marks at the end of

1922, was meant for me, because every evening I helped to wait on the boarders she cooked for so inventively. And that dirndl there, my sister Hilde wore forever, even though she won't remember its green-and-red pattern. Hilde, who went over to the West in the fifties and was headstrong even as a child, broke with her past long ago.

Dear me, those exorbitant prices. We grew up with them. And in Chemnitz—though elsewhere too, I daresay—we used to chant a rhyme my great-grandchildren still find what they call "neat":

> One, two, four, five, eight, nine million.
> Mother cooks beans by the trillion.
> Each pound costs ten million marks.
> Without ham?
> You're out, ma'am!

And we had beans three times a week. Beans or lentils. Because legumes, which are easy to store, increased in value if Mama happened to find them at the right time. The same held for corned beef, which she would buy in tins, several dozen at a go, and squirrel away in the kitchen cupboard. So what Mama would make for our three boarders, who were forced by the galloping prices to pay daily, were cabbage rolls and corned-beef patties. Fortunately, one of the boarders, whom we children called Uncle Eddy and who had been a steward on big luxury liners before World War I, had a supply of silver dollars, and because Uncle Eddy and Mama became close after Father's untimely death I see in Mama's book that the American dollar went first for seven and a half thousand marks, later for twenty and more million. And by the end, when only a very few silver pieces were left jingling in his sack—hard as it is to believe—for trillions! Be that as it may,

Uncle Eddy kept us supplied with fresh milk and cod-liver oil and Mama with her heart medicine. And sometimes, when we were good, he rewarded us with chocolate bars.

But the petty clerks and civil servants, to say nothing of everyone on the dole, were in a pretty bad way. As a widow, Mama would hardly have been able to make ends meet on her own, that is, with Father's pension. And all the beggars and disabled soldiers! Herr Heinze, who lived on the ground floor and had inherited a tidy sum just after the war, clearly did well by investing in some forty hectares of land suitable for farming and grazing and collecting the rent from the peasants in kind. He was said to have sides of bacon stashed away, and when the currency was still all zeros and the government issued emergency money or, here in Saxony, even coal, he would exchange them for bolts of cloth, for worsted and gabardine, so when stabilization finally came he was in business, he had it made.

Still, I wouldn't call Herr Heinze a war profiteer, the way others did. There were plenty of those without him. And Uncle Eddy—who was a Communist even back then, and later, in Karl-Marx-Stadt, as Chemnitz came to be called in the workers-and-peasants state, made quite a career for himself—Uncle Eddy could name them all. "Sharks in top hats," he called them. It's a good thing neither he nor Mama lived to see the introduction of West German currency and they'll be spared the trouble that comes with the Euro.

1924

THE DATE COLUMBUS weighed anchor was the date we chose. Columbus set sail from Genoa in 1492, heading for

India, though in fact he landed in America; our venture, our more accurate instruments notwithstanding, was every bit as risky. The dirigible was actually ready on the morning of the eleventh: it lay in its open hangar with precisely calculated quantities of fuel for the five Maybach engines and water for ballast on board; the ground crew had ropes in hand. But the LZ-126 refused to float: it was heavy and remained so because a layer of fog and warm air masses had suddenly rolled in and settled over the entire Lake Constance region. Since we could not spare either water or fuel, we had to postpone the takeoff until the following morning. The jeering crowd was hard to bear. We did take off on the twelfth, however.

Twenty-two men strong. For a long time it was touch and go whether I would be allowed to serve as mechanic: I was one of the ones who by way of national protest had destroyed the last four military airships waiting in Friedrichshafen to be delivered up to the enemy, just as more than seventy ships from our fleet—including a dozen battleships and regular-service ships due to be handed over to the English—were scuttled by our own people in July 1919 at Scapa Flow. The Allies promptly demanded compensation; the Americans alone wanted us to cough up three million gold marks. But then the Zeppelin people proposed that the debt be paid off by our delivering an airship built to the latest standards. And since the American military had shown more than lively interest in our most recent model, which had a capacity of seventy thousand cubic meters of helium, the horse trading worked. LZ-126 was to be flown to Lakehurst, New Jersey, and presented to the Americans upon landing.

Many of us looked upon that as a disgrace. I did. Hadn't we

been humiliated enough at Versailles? Hadn't the enforced peace placed a heavy enough burden on the Fatherland? We—that is, several of us—toyed with the thought of undermining the sordid deal. Only after long inner turmoil was I able to discern anything positive in the undertaking, and not until I had expressly promised Dr. Eckener, whom we all respected as our captain and an honest man, that I had given up any idea of sabotage was I allowed to take part.

LZ-126 was so stunning I can picture her even today. Yet at first, while we were still above the European continent, only fifty meters above the saddles of the Côte-d'Or, I was still obsessed with the idea of destroying her. Though designed to provide luxurious accommodation for two dozen, she had no passengers aboard, only a few American military personnel who kept a sharp eye on us round the clock. But when we hit some strong downdrafts over the Spanish coast at Cape Ortegal and the ship started swaying so violently that all hands were occupied keeping her on course and the Americans had to turn to matters of navigation, a takeover would have been possible. All we would have had to do was force an early landing by pitching a few fuel containers overboard. I was tempted again when the Azores lay beneath us. Indeed, day and night I sought opportunities, suffering doubt and temptation. Even when we climbed two thousand meters over the Newfoundland fog or shortly thereafter, when a stay snapped during a storm, I harbored thoughts of averting the imminent ignominy. But thoughts they remained.

What held me back? Certainly not fear. During the war I had been exposed to mortal danger over London whenever the searchlights reached our airship. No, I knew no fear. The only thing that kept me from acting was Dr. Eckener's will.

Although I could not share his conviction—namely, that in the face of the victors' despotism it was our duty to give proof of German productivity in the form of our shiny, silver, celestial cigar—in the end I bowed totally to his will, for a piddling, merely symbolic, as it were, breakdown would have made little or no impression, especially as the Americans had sent two cruisers to meet us and we were in constant radio contact with them: they would have come to our aid had we had an emergency, whether a strong headwind or the slightest hint of sabotage.

Only now can I see how right I was to renounce all attempts at an "act of liberation," but even then, when the LZ-126 drew close to New York, when the Statue of Liberty greeted us through the mist of the morning of 15 October, when we headed up the bay and the metropolis with its mountain chain of skyscrapers lay beneath us and the boats in the harbor welcomed us with their sirens, when we flew the entire length of Broadway, back and forth, twice, at middle altitude, then rose up to three thousand meters to give all the inhabitants of New York a chance to admire German productivity sparkling in the morning sun, and when we finally headed for Lakehurst and made ourselves presentable, washing and shaving with the last of our water supply, I felt proud, unrestrainedly proud.

Later, when the sad delivery ceremony was over and our pride and joy was rechristened the *Los Angeles,* Dr. Eckener thanked me and told me that he had experienced the same turmoil as I. "But one's inner swinish tendencies are easier to resist," he said, "than the inborn commandment to maintain one's dignity and achieve results." I wonder what he felt when thirteen years later the finest expression of the Reich restored, the *Hindenburg,* powered unfortunately by flammable hydrogen rather than helium, went up in flames upon landing at Lakehurst. Was he as certain as I that it was sabotage? It was the Reds! They didn't hold back. Their dignity hinged on another commandment.

1925

MANY PEOPLE THOUGHT I was just a brat. None of the conventional methods could stop my whining. Even the Punch-and-Judy theater my father lovingly built for me, with its colorful panel and half a dozen hand puppets, failed to hold my attention. I went on whining. Nothing anyone could do would turn off the now swelling, now fading, but never-ending drone. Neither Grandma's fairy tales nor Grandpa's "Here! Catch!" kept me from whimpering, bawling, getting on the nerves of both family and friends, destroying their pointed attempts at witty conversation. True, I could be bribed for five minutes with chocolate "cats' tongues," but there was nothing that could shut me up for the time, say, my mother's breast once did. I wouldn't even let my parents quarrel undisturbed. Then, finally, with the help of a crystal radio receiver and a headset, that is, even before we signed up for the Reich Broadcasting Company, my family turned me into a placid introvert.

We lived in the Breslau area, where Radio Silesia provided a wide range of morning and afternoon programs, and I was soon able to manipulate the few knobs in such a way as to ensure clear, static-free reception. I listened to everything: Karl Loewes's ballad "The Clock," the glorious tenor voice of

Jan Kipura, the divine Erna Sack. Whether Waldemar Bonsels read from *Maja the Bee* or an exciting regatta was broadcast live, I was all ears. Lectures on oral hygiene or entitled
"All You Need to Know About the Stars" provided me with a
well-rounded education. Because I listened to the stockmarket reports twice a day, I learned of heavy industry's economic recovery. (My father exported agricultural machinery.) I
learned of Ebert's death before my parents, who, relieved of
the burden I'd been on them, could get on with their quarrels
full time. Shortly thereafter I learned of Field Marshal Hindenburg's election—in the second round—as Ebert's successor to the presidency. But I was also grateful for children's
programs in which Rübezahl, the spirit of the Sudeten Mountains, roamed his domain frightening poor wood gatherers. I
was less enchanted with the "Good Night" program's elves,
those bustling little forerunners of "The Sandman," who
made such a hit later on TV in both East and West. My personal favorites were the early radio plays, in which the wind
blew, rain pattered on the roof, thunder rumbled, doors
creaked, or a child whined as I had been wont to do.

In spring and summer I was often sent outside to the spacious garden surrounding our house and thus grew up in the
lap of nature, but I reveled in my crystal set there as well. So
birdcalls came to me less from the sky or the branches of our
fruit trees than through the headset, when Dr. Hubertus, a
brilliant imitator of animal voices, did his siskin and titmouse,
his blackbird and chaffinch, his oriole and yellowhammer, his
lark. No wonder I was so far removed from the strife threatening my parents' marriage. And if their divorce seemed not
all that terrible, it was because Mother and I kept our suburban house and garden including all the furniture and the radio
receiver and headset.

The crystal set came equipped with an amplifier for low frequencies, and Mother bought cloth covers to lessen the pressure of the earphones. Later the much-loved crystal set was superseded by vacuum-tube sets with loudspeakers. We had a five-tube Blaupunkt. That meant we could bring in Königswusterhausen and even listen to Hamburg harbor concerts and the Vienna Boys' Choir, but I missed the exclusivity that came with the headset.

By the way, Radio Silesia was the first station to use a pleasant triad to identify itself between programs. The practice soon spread all over Germany. No wonder I remained faithful to the radio. I even made it my profession. During the war I was responsible for a series of much-loved broadcasts from the Arctic Ocean to the Black Sea, from the Atlantic Wall to the Libyan desert. Remember the Christmas vignettes from every front? And when we had to start from scratch, I decided to specialize in radio plays for Northwest German Radio. I've watched the genre die out since then, but seen headsets make a comeback as headphones. When they're plugged in, the young people are silent and introverted, out of it, yet with it.

1926

I KEPT COUNT. When His Imperial Highness was forced into exile, it fell to me to keep the record: four vertical lines, one diagonal across the four. HIH took to felling trees with his own hands at his first Dutch residence, continuing subsequently in the Doorn Palace, which was located deep in the woods. Keeping count was not part of my duties: I was engaged to look after the coaches in the carriage house. And

there—in fair weather and foul, together with myself and
occasionally his aide-de-camp, Herr von Ilsemann—HIH
would saw the trunks into logs for the fireplaces in the main
house and the orangery, which served as a guest house. And
he alone would chop kindling—with his sound hand, of
course. First thing in the morning after prayers, which he said
with the servants, he would go off into the wood, even when it
rained. Day in and day out. Felling trees had helped HIH to
relax at Headquarters in Spa back in late October, when Ludendorff was given his marching orders, so to speak, and
General Groener took over. I can still hear HIH sawing away
in the shed and cursing Ludendorff—"It's all that Ludendorff's fault!"—and all the others to blame for the armistice
and everything that went with it: the Reds of course, but also
Prince Max von Baden, the ministers, the diplomatic corps,
even the Crown Prince. He tried to strip Grand Admiral Tirpitz of the Order of the Great Black Eagle, but his advisers—
the privy councillor first and foremost—persuaded him to
settle for a warning. HIH continued to grant medals—rather
too freely, if I may say so—especially to those who chanced to
put in an appearance just after his sawing-and-chopping ses-
sions, among them a number of lickspittles who later left him
in the lurch. And so it went for weeks and months.

As I was the one who kept count, I can state categorically
that, after a year in the Dutch haven of Amerongen, HIH had
felled eleven thousand trees. When, in Doorn, he felled the
twelve thousandth, it was sawed into chunks, each of which
was initialed with a large W and presented to a guest. No, I
was never granted the favor of such a treasure.

But picture it! Twelve thousand trees. More than twelve. I
preserved the record. Yes, for later, when Germany awakes at

last and the Empire is reborn. And things appear to be stirring in the Reich. All hope is not lost. That and only that keeps HIH going. And now that the people have roundly rejected the ballot calling for the dispossession of the royal family—we received the news in a brief but gratifying telegram during a chopping session—there are even more grounds for hope. In any case, His Imperial Highness's spontaneous reaction was: "I stand ready the moment the German people call."

In March we had a visit from the famous explorer Sven Hedin, who cheered the Emperor greatly at his morning felling session when he pointed out, "Anyone who can fell tree after tree with his right hand alone can also bring order to Germany." Later he spoke about his journeys though East Turkestan, Tibet, and the Gobi Desert. The next morning, between trees, HIH made a point of telling the Swede how much he hated war and had wanted to avoid it. I can attest to that, because he was prone to talk through the issue with himself while chopping. "I was on a summer jaunt in Norway," he would say, "and the French and Russians were at the ready .... I was a staunch opponent of war.... I always wanted to be a prince of peace.... But if it had to be... Besides, our fleet was in ruins.... And the English at Spithead... Yes, full steam ahead... I had to act...."

The thing that came up most often after that was the Battle of the Marne. He cursed the generals, Falkenhayn in particular. He enjoyed letting off steam as he chopped. Every blow—with his right hand only, his sound hand—every stroke hit home. Especially when he had November 1918 on the brain. The first to get their comeuppance were the Austrians and their rebel of a kaiser, Karl, then the cowards behind the front, the first hints of subordination, red flags in furlough trains.

He also condemned the government, blow after blow, from Prince Max—"A chancellor of revolution!"—down the line. As the pile grew, he would turn to his abdication. "No!" he would shout. "Forced into it by my own people! And the Reds... And that Scheidemann... I didn't abandon the Army! The Army abandoned me!... No road to Berlin... Every last Rhine bridge handed over... The risk of a civil war... Or falling into enemy hands... An ignominious end... Or putting a bullet through my... No choice but to cross the border..."

And so on, sir, day after day. His Imperial Highness would seem to be tireless. Though lately he has taken to chopping in silence. Nor am I bound to keep count any longer. But as the years go by, young trees are coming up in the deforested area around Doorn, new trees HIH will fell when their time comes.

1927

MAMA DIDN'T DELIVER ME till the middle of golden October, but if you look closely you'll see that the year I was born was the only year with any glitter to it: the rest of the twenties, before and after, flickered at best, trying to inject some color into an otherwise drab existence. What made my year golden? Was it the new, stable Reichsmark? Or was it *Being and Time,* a book appearing on the scene in such linguistic frippery that every cub columnist felt bound to heidegger it up?

Granted, after war, hunger, and inflation—which a cripple

on every corner and the widespread destitution of the middle class let no one forget—it was tempting to celebrate life as "thrown-ness" or dismiss it as "being toward death" in the chitchat over champagne or just one more martini. But there was nothing golden about those fancy words blown up out of proportion into an existential finale. Now Richard Tauber's tenor—that was golden. Mama, the moment she turned on the record player, worshiped him from afar, and from the day I was born till the day she died (she did not live long) she was wont to sing *The Tsarevich,* much acclaimed on operetta stages at the time: "On the Banks of the Volga a Soldier Stands" or "Now That You're Gone Do You Still Think of Me?" or "Alone, Once More Alone" or the bittersweet finale "I Sit Here in My Golden Cage."

But that was all gold leaf. The only genuine articles were the chorus girls. Even in Danzig we could see touring companies of them, spangles and all. If not in the Municipal Theater, then in Zoppot's Casino. But Max Kauer—who'd made a name for himself and his medium, Susy, in music-hall circles with a fortune-telling and magic act (his valises were covered with hotel stickers from all the European capitals) and whom I later called Uncle Max because he was a school friend of Papa's brother Fiedel—Max Kauer pooh-poohed any reference to "the chorus girls on tour here" with a wave of the hand: "A cheap imitation."

While Mama was still pregnant with me, he'd shout, "The joint's always jumping in Berlin. You really should take a gander," imitating the Tiller Girls, or, rather, their endless legs with his spindly magician fingers and doing his Chaplin impersonation. He liked giving "leg reports" and maintained it was "all in the exercises." He would talk of their "rhythmic precision" and his "unforgettable experiences at the Admiral's Palace." He would drop the names of the floor show's stars— "You should have seen that frisky Trude Hesterberg and her company jazz up Schiller's *Robbers*; you'd have laughed your heads off"—and rave about the Chocolate Kiddies he'd seen at the Skala or the Wintergarten. "And soon Josephine Baker is coming to Berlin. That wolf in woman's clothing. 'Thrown-ness' on the dance floor, as the philosopher might say."

Mama, who didn't mind letting her longings out into the open, must have conveyed Uncle Max's enthusiasm to me. "People in Berlin—they just dance and dance," he'd say. "You've got to go, really. You've got to see the one and only Haller Revue with La Jana dancing against a gold lamé curtain." And out came the long-legged magician fingers again. Mama, who was still carrying me, must have smiled and said, "Later maybe. When business picks up." But she never made it.

Once, in the late thirties, when not a flicker of the twenties' gold was left, she put the grocery in my father's care and went on a Strength-through-Joy excursion to the mountains, the Salzkammergut. There they danced and danced. The Bavarian shoe dance.

1928

YOU CAN READ EVERY WORD of it. I wrote it all out for my great-grandchildren. For when they're grown up. Nobody'd believe what went on here in Barmbeck and everywhere. It sounds made up, I know, but it's my life. I was left with three kids and a tiny income when an orange crate came down on their father in front of Shed 25 on the waterfront. He was a stevedore. The company said it was "negligence on the part of the claimant," so there were no damages or any kind of recompense. My oldest was with the Police by then, Station 46. You can read it all here: "Herbert never joined the Party, though he always voted for the Left...." We were Social Democrats, the whole family. My father and my husband's father too. Then, suddenly, when all the fuss and bother started up here, Jochen, my second, he went Communist. Member of the Red Front and all. He was a quiet boy before that. Beetles and butterflies were all he cared about. And his job: taking lighters out to the Kehrwiederfleet or other places in the Warehouse District. And all at once here was this fanatic. The same as Heinz, our youngest. But what did *he* do when the time came to vote in the Reichstag elections? He turned Nazi. A real little Nazi. And never a word to me about it. One day there he was in an SA uniform making speeches. He worked in the Warehouse District too. Coffee-bean distribution. He'd smuggle some home from time to time for roasting. You could smell it all over. Out to the stairs. Then all of a sudden...

Things were pretty quiet at first. Even Sundays, when they were all together at the kitchen table and I was at the stove. The two of them'd just needle each other. And when things got a little loud—a fist on the table or something—my Herbert'd calm them down. They'd both listen to him even when he was off duty, when he wasn't in uniform. But then the trouble started up. You can read all about it here. What happened on May the 17th. Two of our comrades—both in the Republican Militia, who were the Social Democrats that kept order at meetings and elections—anyway, they were killed, murdered. One here in Barmbeck, the other nearby in Eimsbüttel. Comrade Tiedemann was shot by the Communists from their propaganda truck and Comrade Heidorn by the SA when he caught them pasting their posters over ours on the corner of Bundesstrasse and Hohe Weide. So anyway, there was this big blowup at the kitchen table. "No!" Jochen shouted. "It was those Social Fascists! They were firing at us and hit Tiedemann by mistake; they killed their own man!" And my Heinz shouted, "It was self-defense! Self-defense, pure and simple! It was those Reich bastards started it!" But my oldest knew what was what from the police report, and he had the newspaper too, the *Volksblatt,* and he banged it on the table, and this is what it said. Here, you see? I pasted the article in. "… that Tiedemann, a carpenter by trade, was shot in the side of the head and since the exit wound is lower than the entrance wound the bullet must have come from above.…" So it's clear the Commies shot him from their truck, and the SA shot first in Eimsbüttel too. Not that it helped in the slightest. No, the argument just kept going, because now Heinz, the SA man, turned on Herbert, my oldest, and called him a "dirty cop," and Jochen, the middle boy, joined in and shouted that really ugly insult, Social Fascist, right in Herbert's face. But he kept his cool, did Herbert. He was like that. All he said was what I wrote down here: "Ever since your Moscow masters have rotted your brains with their Comintern resolutions, you can't tell Red from Brown." No, he said a few more things too. Like "There's nothing that makes your capitalist happier than to see workers bumping each other off." "You can say that again," I called over from the stove. And let me tell you, that's exactly what happened. In any case, the killings in Barmbeck and Eimsbüttel marked the end of peace and quiet in Hamburg. But things calmed down a little at our kitchen table because even before Hitler came to power my Jochen parted ways with the Communists and then, only because he suddenly lost his job, joined the SA in Pinneberg and found work in a silo. My youngest, who stayed a Nazi on the surface, started making less of a show of it and lost all his enthusiasm, and when the war came he went to Eckernförde and joined the Navy. Lost his life in a submarine. Jochen, the middle boy, he died in the war too. Ended up in Africa, never came back. All I've got are these letters. The ones pasted in here. My oldest stuck it out with the Police and came out alive. They sent him to Russia, the Ukraine, with a Police battalion, so he must have been mixed up in some dirty business. Never said a word about it. Not even after the war. And I never asked. But I could tell what was wrong and stayed wrong till the end, in '53, when he quit the Police because he had cancer and just a few months to live. He left his Monika, my daughter-in-law, three children, all girls. They've been married forever and have children of their own. The children—they're the ones I put all this down for, painful as it was. Putting it on paper, I mean. Everything that happened. But you can read it too.

1929

AND FROM ONE MINUTE TO THE NEXT, what do you know, we're all Americans! Right, they bought us up. 'Cause old man Opel, Adam, was dead and gone, and the young blood they didn't want us. Anyways, the assembly line was old hat for the likes of us. We were all on group piecework. And I'd worked piece rates even before that. On the Frog. Know why they called it that? 'Cause the kids in the street, when they saw that two-seater all shiny and green, which is how it came on the market, whenever they saw it they'd shout, "Froggy!" Anyways, in '24 it was, the Frog went into production. I worked on the brake system, the front axle. But when they made us Americans, all of us, in '29 it was, all there was was group piecework, even with the Frog, 'cause then the Frog came off the conveyor belt too. Thing was, some of us didn't last long, 'cause they fired a bunch and right before Christmas, which was a pretty low-down thing to do. Our newspaper at work, the *Opel-Prolet,* said the Americans use the "Ford system," which means every year you kick out your old people and hire new people cheap. You can do that easy if you're on an assembly line with piecework. But to get back to the Frog. It was the greatest. Sold like hotcakes. Sure the industry people bad-mouthed it something awful, said Opel copied it from Citroën, except the Citroën was yellow, but when the French tried to sue and get some money out of it, they lost. Anyways, the Frog you'd see it everywhere, all over the country, 'cause it was cheap, lots of people could afford it, not only big shots and people with drivers. No, not me. With four kids and a house to pay off? But my brother—a sales rep in sewing goods, haberdashery—he switched from his motorcycle, which he had to ride in all kinds of weather. The Frog had twelve horsepower, believe it or not, and it did sixty an hour and went a hundred kilometers on only five liters! Went for 4,600, but my brother got his for 2,700, 'cause prices were falling and things getting tougher with the unemployment and all. Anyways, my brother and his sample case they drove all over the place in that Frog. Even Konstanz. Always on the road. Elsbeth—they were engaged—he took her on day trips to Heilbronn or Karlsruhe. He had a good time in bad times. And bad they were, 'cause a year after they made us all Americans it was my turn to go on the dole like those people in Rüsselheim and places like that. Anyways, my brother took me along with him on his business trips a few times, and once we went all the way to Bielefeld, where his company was, and I got to see the Porta Westfalica and what a beautiful place Germany is. Know where the Cherusci gave it to the Romans in the Teutoburg Forest? We had a picnic lunch there. Real nice. But there wasn't much to keep me going otherwise. A little gardening for the city, a day here and there at the cement factory. But then came the coup and Adolf and things opened up some at Opel, so they took me on as a claim agent, first in purchasing, then in research, 'cause I'd put in all that time at the lathe back in the days of Adam. My brother, meanwhile, after his years on the road—and, later, the Autobahn—with the Frog, he got called up by the Army and the Frog spent the war in our shed. And there it stands to this day, 'cause my brother never came back from Russia and I can't bring myself to get rid of it. Me they sent to Riga for the war—we did repairs there—but the minute it was over I was back at Opel. It worked out good we were Americans. We hardly got bombed during the war and weren't dismantled after it. Pretty lucky, eh?

1930

IT WAS IN BERLIN, NOT FAR FROM SAVIGNYPLATZ, just before the S-Bahn underpass at Grolmannstrasse. Though

merely an occasional customer at Franz Diener's Beer Hall, I was privy to the well-lubricated discussions of events great and small at the table occupied every evening by a stellar company of regulars. One would have thought that the regulars who chose Franz, the German heavyweight champion until he was dethroned by Max Schmeling after fifteen rounds, would be former or still active boxers. Such was not the case, however. In the fifties and early sixties he attracted a combination of actors, cabaret and radio people, and even writers and those rather dubious characters who call themselves intellectuals. So the topic of conversation was less likely to be Bubi Scholz's victories or his defeat in the Johnson match than stage gossip like animated speculations about the cause of Gustaf Gründigens's death in the far-off Philippines or a Sender Freies Berlin intrigue. And it all reached the bar at top volume. Hochhuth's play *The Deputy,* if I recall, was the subject of some debate; otherwise, politics, even though the Adenauer era was clearly drawing to a close, was off limits.

Much as Diener played the modest innkeeper, his face displayed a boxer's dignity and melancholy. People sought out his presence: he had a solid yet for some mysterious reason tragic aura about him. But there's nothing new here: artists and intellectuals have always been fascinated by boxing. Brecht wasn't the only one with a weakness for a fast fist. Before Max Schmeling went to America and made headlines, all kinds of famous figures—Fritz Kortner the actor, Josef von Sternberg the film director, even Heinrich Mann—flocked to see him and be seen with him. As a result, the walls in the front room of Franz's establishment and the wall behind the bar had pictures of more than boxers in standard poses; they boasted framed photographs of former or current cultural celebrities.

Franz was one of the few pros with enough savvy to turn his winnings into a profitable investment. His pub was always full to overflowing. The table where the regulars gathered was often occupied until well after midnight. He waited on them personally. But even if the conversation happened to turn to boxing, it as good as never touched on Diener's matches with Neusel or Heuser Franz was much too modest to allude to his victories; it was always and only about the first and second Schmeling-Sharkey bouts in '30 and '32, when Max became world heavyweight champion and then had to give up the title, or about Max's Cleveland victory over Young Stribling, whom he KO'd in the fifteenth round. But this look backward of mostly elderly gentlemen took place in a political vacuum: no one said a word about the Brüning regime and the shock people felt when the Nazis suddenly emerged from the Reichstag elections as the second strongest party.

I no longer remember who brought up the subject, whether it was O. E. Hasse, an actor who'd made a name for himself in *The Devil's General,* or the Swiss writer Dürrenmatt, who was well known by then; it may even have been me standing at the bar. Which makes sense, in fact, because the discussion that followed revolved around the sensational radio broadcast aired on 12 June 1930 and relayed to us by American shortwave transmitters so we could hear it starting at three the next morning, and I was the one in charge of the German end of the operation: it was my job as engineer at the Zehlendorf station of the Reich Broadcasting Company to adjust our newly constructed shortwave receiver for the best possible reception, as I had done earlier, though without the static-free results, for the Schmeling-Paolino bout. (I had also been assistant engineer for the broadcast of the landing of the Zeppelin in Lakehurst, when hundreds of thousands of listeners followed airship LZ-126 going through its paces above Manhattan.) But this time it was all over in a half hour: Sharkey, whose well-aimed left hook had kept him in the lead during the first three rounds, was disqualified in round four when he lashed out with a half hook, half uppercut that was aimed at the stomach but landed too low and sent Max sprawling. While Max writhed in pain, the referee pronounced him the new world champion. To the cheers of the crowd, by the way, because Schmeling was the darling even of Yankee Stadium.

Several of Franz Diener's regulars still remembered the broadcast vividly. "Sharkey was more than his equal!" "Come off it! Max was a late bloomer. Never got into his stride till round five." "Right. People were up in arms—the mayor of New York included—when he lost to Sharkey in '32 after fifteen heavy rounds, because Max had clearly beaten him in points."

No one had much to say about his later encounters, with the "Brown Bomber," for instance,—Max KO'd Louis in the first bout after twelve rounds; Louis KO'd Max in the second, but in round one—or about the quality of our broadcasts, which kept improving. All they really cared about was the "Schmeling legend." In the end, they said during one discussion, he was less boxer than crowd pleaser: it was his personality that made him great, not his fists. Then too—through no fault of his own, of course—politics did its bit, the infamous politics of the time that made him the model German. No wonder he failed to make a comeback after the war, lost to Neusel and Vogt in Hamburg and Berlin.

Franz Diener, who rarely said anything about boxing and had remained behind the bar throughout the discussion, made the following comment: "I've always been proud to have lost my title to Max—even if all he's doing nowadays is running a chicken farm."

After which he went back to drawing beer, laying out portions of pickled eggs or meatballs and mustard, and keeping schnapps glasses filled, and talk among the regulars went back to theater gossip. At one point Friedrich Dürrenmatt called the assembled company to attention and delivered himself of a Bernese explanation of the universe, complete with galaxies, nebulae, and light-years: "Our earth, by which I mean everything that creeps and crawls and takes itself seriously, is nothing but a pile of crumbs!" Whereupon he called over to the bar for another round of beer.

1931

"'On to Harzburg!' was our call. 'On to Braunschweig!'..."

"They came from every *Gau,* every district. By train, most of them. But our comrades from the Vogtland—we came in a long line of motorcars...."

"An end to servitude! New flags flying! They came from as far as the coast, the beaches of Pomerania, from Franconia and Munich and the Rhineland. They came in trucks and buses, on motorcycles...."

"All proud to be dressed in brown..."

"The Second Motor Brigade set out from Plauen, twenty motorcars strong, singing, 'Their brittle old bones are trembling....'"

"It was dark when our unit left Crimmitschau and a glorious autumn morning by the time we reached Altenburg. Our destination—Leipzig...."

"Believe it or not, comrades, this was the first time I experienced the monument's full force. When I saw those heroic figures leaning on their swords, I heard the hour of liberation strike once more, today, over a hundred years after the Battle of the Nations.... Down with servitude!"

"Let me tell you, comrade, you won't find the nation, the new nation, sitting around in that jabberbin of a Reichstag. No, you'll find it out in Germany's streets...."

"But after we bade farewell to lovely Thüringen, after *Gauleiter* Sauckel led our column through Halle and Eisleben, Luther's birthplace, we came to Aschersleben in Prussia and had to take off our brown shirts and don the white of neutrality, so to speak...."

"Because the Social Democrats still hold sway there with their ban...."

"And their swine of a police chief. Severing. Mark the name!"

"But in Bad Harzburg we were on Braunschweig soil, back among our own: thousands and thousands dressed proudly in brown...."

"And a week later, in Braunschweig proper, where the police were ours too, and more than a hundred thousand brownshirts gathered in orderly ranks..."

"The Führer's eye met mine...."

"And mine! As we marched past..."

"And mine, though for no more than a second. Or was it eternity?..."

"Why 'mine,' comrades, when there was only 'us' marching past, hour after hour, arms raised high in the German salute. Each and every one of us will remember those eyes forever...."

"They seemed to be blessing me...."

"An army in brown marching past, his eyes resting on each of us..."

"But first he personally inspected the four hundred motorcars, omnibuses, and motorcycles stretching out one after the other, because the future belongs to motorized transport...."

"And then he consecrated the new SS and SA units, twenty-four in all, with words of steel...."

"His voice coming over the speakers was like the Germany of discipline and valor shining through the Great War's thunderclouds, like Destiny communing with us. It was the voice of Providence. It had the ring of bronze. It was entirely new...."

"Yet some say Mussolini's Fascists have beaten us to the punch. You know, with their black shirts, action squads, and storm troopers...."

"Don't be ridiculous! We've got nothing in common with those Latins! It's plain as the nose on your face: there's a German way of praying, a German way of loving, and a German way of hating. And anyone who tries to stop us..."

"But for the time being, at least, we need allies. Last week, for example, when the Harzburg front was created and that Hugenberg and his German national gang..."

"You mean those bourgeois plutocrats in bowlers and top hats..."

"Well, their days are numbered. They belong to the past. The Steel Helmets too..."

"Right. The future belongs to us and only us...."

"And as the endless columns of brown-clad masses followed the SA vehicles out of Leonhardsplatz and the city of Heinrich the Lionhearted, as each of us set off for our own *Gau,* we carried the flame the Führer's gaze had ignited in us. Long may it burn..."

1932

SOMETHING HAD TO HAPPEN. Things couldn't go on like that with emergency measures and one election after the other. But in the end things haven't changed much. Oh, I realize being unemployed looked a little different then than now. You didn't say, "I'm out of work"; you said, "I've gone on the dole." Which sounded like you were doing something about it. Nobody wanted to admit to being out of work. They were ashamed to. In any case, when they asked me in school or when Father Watzek asked me, I'd say, "Father's gone on the dole," while my grandson is perfectly comfortable telling everybody he's "on welfare." True, there were about six million when Brüning was chancellor, but do your counting right and you'll see we're back up to five. Which is why money's so tight nowadays and people buy only the bare essentials. Like I say, things haven't changed. Except that by the winter of '32, which was the third year Father was on the dole, his benefits had been slashed to a slim three marks fifty a week. And since both my brothers were receiving benefits too and my sister, Erika, was the only real breadwinner—she worked as a cashier at Tietz's—Mother had less than a hundred marks per week for household expenses. Nowhere near enough to make ends meet, but then everyone we knew was in the same boat. And woe betide you if you got the flu or something. You had to cough up fifty pfennigs just to get in to see a doctor. Having your shoes soled made a real hole in the budget. Coal was two marks a hundredweight, but the mines were piled high with it. Which of course meant they were guarded: barbed wire, dogs—the real thing. Winter potatoes were a big problem too. It couldn't go on like that. There was something fishy about the whole system. Just like today. Going for unemployment benefits, for instance. Father took me along once. "So you see how it works," he said. There were two policemen outside the office to keep order, and people standing both outside and inside, because there weren't enough chairs. But there was never any trouble outside or in, because everybody was wrapped in their own thoughts. They were so quiet you could hear the rubber stamps. The dry whack. There were five or six windows where they stamped your papers. I can still hear it. And I can still see the faces of the people they rejected. "Expired!" or "Missing documents!" Father was careful to take everything: registration form, most recent certificate of employment, proof of need, and money-order form. From the day he started getting benefits, they kept close track of his finances, even coming to the house. And woe betide you if you had a new piece of furniture or a radio set. Oh, something else: it smelled of wet clothes. Because they'd stand outside in the rain too. But there was no pushing, no disturbances. Not even political. Because everybody'd had it, everybody knew it couldn't go on like that, something had to give. And then he took me to union headquarters, where the unemployed had a self-help group with posters all over and appeals for solidarity and there was a pot of something, a soup or stew. I wasn't supposed to tell Mother we'd been there. "I'll get us through," she'd say, and laugh happily if she had some lard to spread on the bread she gave me to take to school, or joke sadly—"Bread sandwich today"—when all she had was dry crusts. Oh, it's not so bad today, but you never know. Anyway, even before the Nazis there was compulsory labor service for anybody on the dole. In Remscheid, where we lived at the time, that meant road construction at the new dam. Father too, because he got benefits.

What they'd do, because horses cost too much, was to hitch twenty men to this incredibly heavy roller and shout, "Heave ho!" I wasn't allowed to go and watch, because Father, who'd been in charge of machine maintenance in a factory, was ashamed to let his son see him. But at home I'd hear him crying in bed in the dark with Mother. She never cried, but just before Hitler took power she kept repeating, "It can't get any worse." "It couldn't happen now," I told my grandson the other day when he started bitching about things again. "You're right," the kid said. "No matter how many people are out of work, the stock market keeps going up."

1933

THE NEWS OF HIS APPOINTMENT reached us at noon in the gallery, while my young partner Bernd and I were having a snack and half listening to the radio. Not that I was surprised: after Schleicher's withdrawal He was the obvious candidate, the only possibility; even the venerable president of the Reich could only bow to His will to power. I tried to make a joke of it. "Now the housepainter will play the Old Master." But Bernd, who always claimed to care "not a fig" for politics, saw it as a personal threat and said, "We've got to get out of here!"

Much as I ridiculed his overreaction, I was glad I had taken the precaution of sending off most of the paintings that were likely to prove offensive in the event of the imminent takeover: a number of Kirchners, Pechsteins, Noldes, and the like. The only ones left in the gallery were a few of the True Master's late, stunningly colored garden pieces: they didn't belong to the "degenerate" category. The only reason he was in danger was that he, like his wife, was a Jew. "They won't dare touch him," I said to Bernd as much to make myself believe it as him. "He's over eighty. At worst he'll have to resign his post as president of the Academy. And in three or four months it will all have blown over."

Yet my anxieties remained, even increased. We closed the gallery. And once I'd managed to calm my dear Bernd somewhat—he was in tears actually—I went out into the fray. It was late afternoon by then. I soon had trouble making headway. I should have taken the S-Bahn. Columns converging from all directions, as far back as Hardenbergstrasse, advancing along the Siegesallee, one SA unit after the other, propelled by an undertow in the direction of their meeting place, their goal, the Great Star. If the columns piled up, the men would march in place, straining forward, impatient: anything but stand still. Oh, the monstrous solemnity in their straplined faces. More and more onlookers crowding the streets. The singsong chants rising over it all...

In the end I took to the bushes, so to speak, and wending my way through the by then pitch-dark Tiergarten I observed I was not alone in my desire to take a roundabout route. Having at last reached my goal, I saw that the Brandenburg Gate was closed to normal traffic, and it was only by enlisting the aid of a policeman—I no longer remember the story I made up—that I could get to Pariser Platz, which lies just beyond the Gate. How many times had we driven here full of expectation! The address so exclusive yet so familiar! The untold visits to the Master's studio! The scintillating conversation! The dry Berlin wit sparing of no one!

I found the janitor standing in front of the building, a typically *grand bourgeois* residence that had been in the family for decades. It was almost as if he'd been expecting me. "They're on the roof, sir," he said, taking me up the stairs. Meanwhile the torchlight procession, which seemed to have been planned for years and was in fact timed to the minute, had started: as I stepped onto the flat roof, I heard the cheers of the approaching columns. Revolting, that canaille! Yet the swelling roar was exciting. Today I can admit to being fascinated by it—if only for the space of a shudder.

There he stood with his wife, Martha, at the edge of the roof. Why did the Master wish to expose himself to that mob? Later, sitting in the studio, he had this to say: He'd stood up there watching the regiments return home victorious from France in '71, then in '14 the spiked-helmeted infantrymen and in '18 the battalions of rebel sailors. Why not risk a last glance from above? It was all perfectly absurd.

Yet only minutes before, on the roof, a cold Havana between his lips, he had been silent, both he and his wife bundled in winter coats and hats as if about to set out on a journey. Dark against the sky. A statuesque couple. For a while the Brandenburg Gate was only a black mass, scanned off and on by police searchlights. But then the torchlight procession arrived, spreading like a stream of lava which, separated for a short time by the pylons, eventually flowed together again, unremitting, unstoppable, solemn, portentous, lighting up the night, lighting up the Gate to the quadriga of stallions, to the goddess's sign of victory. We too on the roof of Liebermann's house were lit by that fatal glow, even as we were hit with the smoke and stench of a hundred thousand and more torches.

Much to my shame and much as I hate to admit it, this picture—no, this elemental painting—did more than horrify me: it gripped me deeply; it exuded a will that bade one follow. Nor did anything stand in its way. It moved on inexorably, a flood tide sweeping up everything in its path. The cheers coming up to us from below might well have elicited a *"Sieg Heil!"* from me—if only to see how it felt—had Max Liebermann not come out with the *mot* that was subsequently whispered all over the city. Turning from the historical scene as from a shiny historical panorama in oils, he berlined, "I couldn't eat enough to make me puke enough."

Watching Martha take the Master's arm as they left the roof, I began searching for words that might encourage the elderly couple to flee. None proved effective. They were not to be transplanted, not even to Amsterdam, for which Bernd and I immediately decamped. Within a few years all our favorite paintings, including a number from Liebermann's brush, were in the relative safety of our less than favorite country, Switzerland. Bernd eventually left me.... Alas... But that is another story.

1934

JUST BETWEEN THE TWO OF US, the matter should have been handled better. I let myself be carried away by personal considerations. The whole thing came about as a result of the sudden move we had to make after the Röhm putsch. We were sent from Dachau to take over the Oranienburg Concentration Camp on 5 July, that is, shortly after a pack of SA swine had been superseded by a commando of men who only several days earlier, in Wiessee and elsewhere, had made short work of Röhm's band. Still visibly exhausted, they gave us a report on the "night of the long knives" and dumped the whole thing in our laps along with several of Röhm's underlings, who were supposed to help us manage the bureaucratic end of things but proved totally incompetent.

One of these thugs—sporting the name Stahlkopf and the steel head to go with it—ordered the prisoners in our custody to line up for roll call and the Jews among them to form a special line.

There were only a dozen or so of them, one of whom stood out particularly. I would have recognized Mühsam anywhere. His face was unmistakable. Although the only representative of the Bavarian Soviet Revolution in the Brandenburg prison had had his beard chopped off and been put through the mill, there was plenty of him left. He was an anarchist of the sensitive type and a typical café intellectual. I remembered him as a rather comic figure from my early Munich days, a poet and propagandist of absolute freedom—free love first and foremost, of course. What I saw before me was a miserable wreck. I could hardly communicate with him, he was so deaf. He pointed to his encrusted, pus-infested ears with a broad, sheepish grin.

In my report to Brigade Leader Eicke—I am his aide-de-camp—I pointed out that Erich Mühsam, though harmless in some respects, could also be quite dangerous: even the Communists were afraid of his ideological tirades. "He would have been long since liquidated in Moscow," I said.

Brigade Leader Eicke assigned the case to me and, understandably enough, advised me to handle it with kid gloves. After all, Eicke had been personally responsible for doing

Röhm in. But immediately after roll call I made my first mistake: I decided to leave the dirty work to that SA imbecile
Stahlkopf.

Just between the two of us, I was leery of getting involved
with the Jew any more than necessary. Not least because of the
unusual way he handled himself during the interrogation: he
answered every question in verse, clearly his own in some cases
but quoting Schiller too: "... and is it not meet your life to
stake...." By then some of his front teeth were missing, but he
might have been performing on stage. It was amusing in a
way, still... I was bothered by the pince-nez perched on his
Jewish nose.... Even more by the cracks in both lenses... And
the smile he flashed at me after every line...

Anyway, I gave him forty-eight hours to do away with himself. It would have been the cleanest solution. Unfortunately,
he refused to do us the favor. So Stahlkopf stepped in.
Drowned him in a toilet bowl apparently. I didn't ask for the
details. But there was no way to make it look as if he'd hanged
himself: the fists were clenched uncharacteristically, and we
couldn't get the tongue out. Besides, the knots were too professional; Mühsam could never have made them. And then
that idiot Stahlkopf bungled it even worse: he made the whole
thing public at morning roll call by ordering the Jews to "step
out of line and cut him down." And you can be sure the two
doctors among them noticed what a sloppy job it was.

I promptly got a bawling out from Brigade Leader Eicke.
"My God, Ehardt, couldn't you have made cleaner work of it?"

He had every right to be upset, and, just between the two of
us, we'll be hearing for a long time about failing to make the
deaf Jew deaf and dumb. Rumors are rampant.... Mühsam's
being made a martyr abroad.... Even the Communists...

We've had to close the Oranienburg Camp and divide the prisoners up among other camps. I'm back in Dachau now. On probation, I presume.

1935

TEUTONIA, THE STUDENTS' SOCIETY to which I belonged and of which my father too was a member, an "Old Boy," afforded me the opportunity, once I had completed my medical studies, to do a residency with Dr. Brösing, another Teutonian, which meant that I assisted him in providing medical care for the labor camps set up to build the initial stretch of the Reich's Autobahn from Frankfurt am Main to Darmstadt. Prevailing conditions were extremely primitive, especially as the workers—those in the shovel brigades more than others—included many elements whose asocial behavior gave rise to constant conflicts. "Running amuck" and "going berserk" were everyday occurrences. As a result, our patients comprised not only the victims of work-related accidents but also numerous rowdies of disreputable origin wounded in brawls. Dr. Brösing treated stab wounds without inquiring after their provenance. At most he would utter his standard "Come now, gentlemen, aren't the days of the free-for-all behind us?"

But most of the workers behaved decently and were generally grateful for the Führer's momentous decision, dating from 1 May 1933, to build a network of motorways connecting the length and breadth of Germany and providing thousands of young men with work and wages. It also meant an end to the years of unemployment for the not so young, though many had trouble coping with the unwonted physical labor. Poor, unbalanced nutrition during the previous period may also have accounted for the various ills we came up against. But there was one heretofore unknown and hence unresearched occupational hazard Dr. Brösing and I encountered in the course of the rapidly progressing roadwork, a complaint that Dr. Brösing, who, though conservative, was not without a sense of humor, liked to call the "shovel malady" or even "shovelitis."

The case history would run as follows: a worker, young or advanced in years, would experience a sharp pain between the shoulder blades as a result of the intense pressure inflicted on them from the enormous loads of earth he was continually shoveling, a pain so severe as to disable him. X-ray plates enabled Dr. Brösing to pinpoint the ailment he had so appropriately named. It consisted of an avulsion fracture in the spinous process of the vertebrae on the cervical and thoracic border, the first thoracic and the seventh cervical spines being most typically affected.

In fact, the victims should have been declared unfit for work and dismissed, but Dr. Brösing, who had called the norms established by the site supervisory staff "irresponsible" and even—in private—"murderous" (though in other respects he appeared politically apathetic), kept putting off the dismissals, and the infirmary was constantly overcrowded. He seemed to be collecting patients either to document the course of the shovel malady or to point up an untenable situation.

As there was no dearth of free labor, the initial stretch of the Autobahn was completed on schedule. The opening ceremony took place on 19 May in the presence of the Führer and a number of high-ranking Party officials and with the participation of some four thousand road builders. Unfortunately the weather was miserable, rain mixed with hail, the sun breaking through only occasionally. Still, the Führer stood in an open Mercedes the entire way, greeting the hundred thousand on- lookers with his right arm either extended or bent. There was great jubilation. The "Badenweiler March" played over and over. Everyone from General Inspector Dr. Todt on down was aware of the event's monumental importance. After a brief speech by the Führer thanking the workers for "giving of both brawn and brain" a worker by the name of Ludwig Droessler addressed the following simple words to the honored guest on behalf of all the workers who had labored to make the Auto- bahn a reality: "By embarking on this venture, my Führer, you have set in motion an enterprise that will symbolize the vitality and greatness of our age for centuries to come...."

Later—by which time the weather had improved slightly— the stretch was cleared for a festive cavalcade that, to the pub- lic's great glee, included vehicles of not quite the latest vintage, including Dr. Brösing's ten-year-old hissing and sputtering Opel two-seater, which bore only the faintest trace of its origi- nal bright-green finish. But he had no intention of attending the official ceremonies, feeling the time would be better spent making his rounds at the infirmary. I could be on hand for the, as he put it, "poppycock in uniform."

Unfortunately, he was unable to place his report on the "shovel malady" in any professional journal. Even the Teuto- nia newsletter refused to publish it. No reason was given.

1936

OPTIMISTS WERE NEVER IN SHORT SUPPLY. In my camp, Esterwegen, which gained a certain notoriety from the "Song of the Moorish Soldiers" and its refrain about "the spades," it was rumored, starting early in the summer of 1936, that just before the Olympic Games opened there would be an amnesty putting an end to our wretched existence as harmful elements and peat cutters in the Ems region. The rumor owed its existence to the pious belief that even Hitler had to mind what the rest of the world thought and so the period of intimidation and terror was now over. Besides, peat cutting was an age-old German activity and would be taken over by National Socialist Labor Service volunteers.

But then fifty of us, all skilled craftsmen, were sent to Sachsenhausen, outside Berlin, where under the watch of SS men from the Order of the Death's Head we built a massive camp, one meant to house two and a half thousand inmates in a fenced-off area of three hundred thousand square meters. A camp with a future.

As an engineering draftsman I was included among the transferred peat cutters. Since the prefabricated materials for the huts were manufactured by a company in Berlin, we had some contact with the outside world, which was otherwise strictly forbidden, and therefore had an inkling of the to-do being made in the Reich's capital in connection with the Games, that is, we knew that the Ku'damm, Friedrichstrasse, Alexanderplatz, and Potsdamer Platz were swarming with tourists from all over the world. Little more leaked through, however. Not until a radio was installed in the guardroom of the by-then-completed hut for the commanding officers, where the site supervisory staff had set up shop. From morning till night it broadcast reports, first about the mood at the opening ceremony, then about the results of the early competitions, and since I often had reason to talk to the supervisors, either alone or with others, we would catch snippets of what was going on and were more or less up on things. When the results of the final events started coming in, however, they turned the volume up as loud as it would go and it was audible even out where we had roll call and on the adjoining construction sites. Many of us heard the awards ceremonies, which meant we also heard about all the international bigwigs on the celebrity rostrum: Gustav Adolf, the Swedish heir apparent; Crown Prince Umberto of Italy; an English under-secretary of state by the name of Vansittart; and a multitude of diplomats, including some from Switzerland. Many of us hoped that a massive concentration camp going up on the outskirts of Berlin would not remain hidden from so massive a foreign presence.

But the world paid us no heed. The world of sport had its own concerns. Nobody gave a damn about our lot. We didn't exist. So we went about camp business as usual. Yet there was still the radio. And that piece of battle-gray equipment, clearly borrowed from the military, brought us our only news from beyond the barbed wire. On 1 August there were German victories in the shot-put and hammer events. I was with Fritjof Tuschinski, a "green" (which is what the criminals among us were called on the basis of prisoner color coding), picking up blueprint revisions from the supervisors when the second gold medal came over the radio, and we heard the off-duty Death's Head SS men celebrating at the top of their lungs next door. Tuschinski started to join in, but the head supervisor, Haupt-sturmführer Esser, who had the reputation of being strict but fair, caught his eye. If *I* had joined in, I'd have been roundly punished, because I was a political prisoner—I had a red tri-angle—and they were tougher on us than on the greens. All Tuschinski had to do was fifty knee bends. I managed to gather my strength and stand stock-still, waiting for instructions, yet I rejoiced deep down at these and other German victories; after all, I'd been a middle-distance runner with the Magdeburg Spartakus Club only a few years before and even had some success in the three-thousand-meter category.

Even though we were forbidden to celebrate—Esser had made it amply clear we were unworthy to participate openly in German victories—it was impossible to prevent spontaneous if brief periods of affinity between prisoners and guards, for instance, when the Leipzig student Lutz Long entered an exciting broad-jump duel with the American winner of the hundred- and shortly thereafter two-hundred-meter races, Jesse Owens, a Negro—a duel Owens finally won with his Olympic record jump of eight meters six. He'd held the world record of eight thirteen in any case. But Long's silver was still celebrated by everyone within range of the radio: two SS Unterscharführer, who were known as bloodhounds; a green who worked as a guard, despised us politicals, and bullied us whenever he could; and I, a middle-ranking Communist functionary who experienced all this and more and is now chewing over the past with a set of poorly fitting dentures.

Perhaps the news that Hitler had deigned to shake hands with the victorious Negro was what brought about the short-lived camaraderie. Distance soon returned, however. Hauptsturmführer Esser made a report; prisoners and guards both were subjected to disciplinary measures. The radio, against the rules as it was, disappeared, which meant we missed the rest of the Games. I heard only rumors of the bad luck our girls had—dropping the baton in the final lap of the 400-meter relay. And by the time the Games were over, all hope was lost.

1937

OUR SCHOOLYARD GAMES didn't end with the bell; they ran from recreation period to recreation period under the chestnut trees and around the single-story lavatory building we called the piss hut. We fought. The piss hut, which was next to the gym, was the Toledo Alcázar. True, the event had taken place the year before, but in our schoolboy dreams the Falangists were still heroically defending the walls, the Reds storming them in vain. Part of the reason for the latter's failure lay in our lack of enthusiasm: nobody wanted to be a Red, myself included. All of us considered ourselves stalwart supporters of General Franco. In the end, a few of the older boys had us draw lots, and I, never suspecting the future significance of the draw, was one of several first-year boys who drew Red. Clearly the future starts making itself felt in the schoolyard.

And so we laid siege to the piss hut. We had to accept one compromise, however: during regular truces imposed by the teachers on schoolyard duty both neutral and combatant groups were to be allowed to obey calls of nature. One of the high points in the battle scenario was the telephone conversation between the commander of the Alcázar, Colonel Moscardó, and his son Luis, whom the Reds had captured and threatened with execution should the fortress refuse to surrender. Helmut Kurella, a third-year boy with an angelic face and the voice to match, played the role of Luis. My job was to hand the phone over to Luis in the person of Caballo, the Commissar of the Red Militia. "Hello, Papa," said Luis in a voice that rang out clear as day over the schoolyard. "What's wrong, my lad?" "Oh, nothing. They say they're going to shoot me if the

Alcázar doesn't surrender." "If that is so, my son, then commend your soul to God, cry 'Viva España!' and die a hero's death." "Farewell, Father. I embrace you warmly."

That was the angelic Helmut as Luis. Whereupon I as the Red Commissar, coached by an older boy, cried out "Viva la muerte!" and shot the brave boy to death under a blossoming chestnut tree.

Actually, I'm not sure I'm the one who was charged with the execution, though I may have been. In any case, the battle went on from there. During the next recreation period the tower was blown up. We did it acoustically. But the Falangists refused to surrender. What was later called the Spanish Civil War played itself out in the schoolyard of the Conradinum in Danzig-Langfuhr as a single event repeatable ad infinitum. The Falange was eventually victorious, of course, the encirclement being pierced from without by a horde of overly zealous fourth- and fifth-year boys. Embraces all around. Colonel Moscardó greeted the liberators with his by then famous "Sin novedad," which means something like "Nothing to report," and we Reds were liquidated forthwith.

By the end of recreation the piss hut could be used as usual again, but on the next day of school we were back at our game. And so it went until the summer holidays. It was 1937. We could have acted out the bombing of the Basque town of Guernica. The German newsreel had shown it to us, this strike by our volunteers, before the feature film. On 26 April the town was turned into a rubble heap. I can still hear the engines and the background music. But all I got to see were our Heinkels and Junkers approaching, diving, departing. They might as well have been on maneuvers. There was no heroic feat for us to reproduce in the schoolyard.

1938

THE TROUBLE OUR HISTORY TEACHER GOT INTO started after all of us watched the wall coming down in Berlin on television and everybody, including my grandma, who lives in Pankow, could cross over to the West. I'm sure Herr Hösle meant well, but instead of talking only about the wall, he asked all of us, "Do you know what else happened in Germany on a November the 9th? Fifty-one years ago, to be precise."

And then, because all of us had some idea but nobody really knew the details, he told us the story of *Kristallnacht,* which took place all over the Reich and was called "Crystal Night" because a lot of dishes and china belonging to Jews were broken and a particularly large number of crystal vases. Also all the windows of shops owned by Jews were smashed with paving stones. And a lot of other valuable things were destroyed for no reason.

Maybe one of the problems was that Herr Hösle couldn't stop and spent history period after history period going on about it and reading out reports that said lots of synagogues were burned down and ninety-one Jews were killed. It was all very sad, and in Berlin—no, all over Germany—people were jumping with joy because it meant all Germans could finally unite. But Herr Hösle stuck to what went on then and how it came about, and I must admit it did start to get on our nerves hearing all those terrible things.

Anyway, he really got it from almost everybody at the next Parent-Teacher Association meeting for what they called his "obsession with the past." Even my father, who enjoys talking about the old days, I mean, about fleeing the Soviet occupied zone before the wall went up and coming here to Swabia and feeling out of place here for so long—even my father said more or less this to Herr Hösle: "Of course I've got nothing against my daughter learning about the atrocities the SA hordes committed all over the place and unfortunately here in Esslingen too, but there's a time for everything. And that time is not now, when we finally have reason to rejoice and the whole world wishes us well...."

All of us kids had already been interested in what went on in our town at the time, in Wilhelmspflege, a Jewish orphanage, for instance. The children all had to go outside, and the schoolbooks and prayer books and even the Torah scrolls were thrown into a pile and set on fire. And the children, who were forced to look on, they stood there crying because they were afraid they'd be set on fire too. But the only thing that happened was they beat the teacher, Fritz Samuel, beat him unconscious with Indian clubs from the gym. Thank goodness there were people in Esslingen who tried to help. For example, there was a taxi driver who offered to take some of the orphans to Stuttgart. In any case, what Herr Hösle told us got us all worked up. Even the boys in our class raised their hands, the Turkish boys too, and my friend Shirin (her family comes from Iran).

Herr Hösle did a good job of standing up for himself at the Parent-Teacher Association meeting, my father said. He said Herr Hösle told the parents that no child could understand the end of the wall without knowing when and where things started going wrong and what actually led to Germany being divided. And nearly all the parents agreed. But in the end Herr Hösle had to stop talking about *Kristallnacht,* for the time being at least. I'm really sorry.

Still, we learned a lot. For example, that nearly everybody in Esslingen just stood and watched, or turned the other way, while the thing at the orphanage took place. That's why a few weeks ago when Yasir, a Kurdish boy in our class, was going to be sent back to Turkey with his parents we came up with the idea of writing a letter of protest to the mayor. All of us signed. But on Herr Hösle's advice we didn't bring up the fate of the Jewish children from the orphanage. We all hope Yasir will be allowed to stay.

1939

THREE DAYS ON THE ISLAND. Once assured that there would be rooms for rent in and around Westerland and that the hall–cum–living room would provide enough space for our group palaver, I accepted the offer of our host, who was very much one of us and had made it big in publishing, big enough to be able to afford one of those thatched-roof Frisian houses on Sylt.

Our get-together took place in February. More than half of the potential guest list showed up, including a few big shots who run things in radio or—well, well, some things never change—the press. A few bets were made about one of them, the editor in chief of a high-circulation glossy, and, sure enough, there he was, though late and for a flying visit only. After the war most of us had found jobs on small papers or magazines or gone in for freelance work. I was one of the lat- ter. But we all bore the stigma—and stamp of quality—that came with the legend of having been war correspondents and therefore members of one or another propaganda unit, and may I take this opportunity to point out that roughly a thousand of our colleagues lost their lives flying over England in He-111 bombers, reporting from the front lines, and the like.

In any case, those of us who survived took to making more and more of a noise about getting together, and after some hesitation I consented to set things up. We agreed to exercise restraint: no naming of names, no personal revenge, just the sort of friendly gathering that took place shortly after the war among former Knight's Cross holders or members of one or another division, or inmates of a concentration camp, for that matter. Having started out as a whippersnapper in the Polish campaign and never having held or been suspected of holding a desk job in the Ministry of Propaganda, I enjoyed a certain standing. Besides, a lot of the men remembered my reports on the early days of the war: on the Second Tank Division's Seventy-ninth Engineer Battalion during the battle on the Bzura, on building bridges under enemy fire, and on our tanks' advance to just outside Warsaw, in which the use of dive-bombers from a foot soldier's point of view set the tone. In fact, I always wrote about common soldiers, cannon fodder, and their quiet bravery. The German infantryman. His daily marches along Poland's dusty roads. Combat-boot prose. Tanks constantly pushing from behind, men crusted with mud, burned by the sun, but spirits high, even when brief skirmishes left villages ablaze, showing the true face of war. Or my less than dispassionate depiction of the endless columns of utterly broken Polish prisoners...

The occasional contemplative tone in my reports must have lent them credibility, though the censor did a good deal of clipping: when I gave the encounter of our tanks with the

Russians at Mosty Wielkie too much of a "comrade-in-arms" flavor, for example, or when my description of the beards of elderly Jews in caftans came out a bit too jovial and sympathetic. At any rate, several of my colleagues at the get-together confirmed that the vivid quality of my Poland articles made them very much like what I'd been doing lately in Laos, Algeria, or the Near East for the big-name glossies.

Once the billeting issue was settled, we fell into collegial chitchat. The only problem was the weather: a stroll along the beach or to the mudflats was out of the question. Though accustomed to all sorts of climates, we turned out to be passionate stay-at-homes, sitting around the fire over the punch and grog our host kept plying us with and working our way through the Polish campaign, the Blitzkrieg, the Eighteen Days.

After the fall of Warsaw into a rubble heap, one of us, who had evidently done well in business and become an art collector, went off on another tack, dishing up long-winded and increasingly stentorian quotes from the articles he had written on a submarine and later published as a book under the title *Hunters in the Ocean* with a foreword by the Admiral of the Fleet. "Tube five ready! Hit amidships!" "Reload the torpedo!" Of course that was a lot more exciting than my infantrymen trudging Poland's endless dusty roads....

1940

I DIDN'T SEE MUCH OF SYLT. As I mentioned, the weather limited us to short walks along the beach in the direction of List or in the opposite direction, toward Hörnum. But our odd assemblage of old-timers, as if still plagued with foot troubles from the days of the retreat, stuck to the fireplace, drinking and smoking and rummaging around in our memories. One recalled victories in France; another, exploits in Narvik and the Norwegian fjords. We each seemed obliged to go over every article that had appeared in *Adler,* the Luftwaffe magazine, or *Signal,* a Wehrmacht publication known for its color illustrations and up-to-date layout and distributed throughout Europe. A man by the name of Schmidt had determined the course taken by *Signal*; after the war he did the same—under a pseudonym, of course—for Springer's *Kristall.* And now, having been granted the questionable pleasure of his constant presence, we were forced to listen to his sermon on what he called "platter victories."

He meant Dunkirk, for instance, to which the entire British Expeditionary Force had fled with their French allies, and there were more than three hundred thousand men waiting to be embarked. Schmidt—his former name, the more recent one being best left unsaid—was still bursting with indignation: "If Hitler hadn't stopped Kleist's tank division at Abbeville, if he'd let Guderian's tanks and Manstein's tanks push through to the coast, if he'd given orders to scour the beaches and round up what he found, then the English would have lost their whole army rather than a few pieces of matériel, and the war would have been over early: the Brits could never have resisted an invasion, believe me. But no, the commander in chief handed them their victory on a platter. He felt obliged to spare England, I suppose, or believed in negotiating. Believe me, if our tanks had..."

Thus the lamentations of the once and former Schmidt, after which he sank into a deep reverie and stared into the fire, totally uninterested in what others might have to offer by way of pincer movements and daring battle tactics. One of us, for example, who had kept his head above water during the fifties with war-story potboilers for Bastei-Lübbe and now sold his soul to those dubious publications known as the pulps, had made a splash during the war with his Luftwaffe stories for *Adler*. Today he was detailing the advantages of the Ju-88 over the Ju-87, a.k.a. the Stuka, using his hands to show the way it dropped its bombs at the end of a nosedive and served as its own targeting device by letting them go just before it started to climb, the short intervals it used in serial bombing, and the "outside curve" attack it used for ships trying to dodge it snakelike. But he'd flown more than Junkers, he'd flown the He-111, with its "glass pulpit" and unobstructed view of London and Coventry. He was quite matter-of-fact about it. We could believe it was pure chance he came out of the air strikes on England alive. In any case, he managed to demonstrate serial bombing by closed formations so convincingly—making use of Hitler's expression "rub out," for example—that we could all relive the period of the reprisals, the terrorist attacks on Lübeck, Cologne, Hamburg, and Berlin.

After that the energy around the fire threatened to flag, and the group resorted to the usual sort of trade gossip: which publisher had ousted which editor in chief, whose job was in jeopardy, how much Springer or Augstein paid this or that reporter. We were finally rescued by our art-and-submarine expert. Either he went on in an appropriately colorful style about Expressionism and the paintings he'd managed to hoard or frightened us with sudden booming cries like "Ready to dive!" Soon we thought we were hearing depth bombs. "Sonar contact, sixty degrees!" Then "Periscope, mark bearing!" And only then did we spy the danger: "Destroyer starboard." What

a relief to be nice and dry with gusts of wind serving only as
background music.

1941

IN THE COURSE OF MY WORK as a correspondent in Russia
and later in Indochina and Algeria—war never stops for
us—I rarely had anything sensational to report. In the Polish
and French campaigns and then in the Ukraine I spent most
of my time with infantry units behind the tanks in one battle
of encirclement after another, from Kiev to Smolensk, and
later, when the mud season set in, with an engineering division
that laid log roads for supplies and reinforcements and did
general repair work. As I say: combat-boot prose, footcloth
prose. My colleagues were much more vainglorious and eloquent. One of them, who later—much later—sent articles
from Israel to our mass-circulation tabloid about "blitz victories," as if the Six-Day War were a continuation of the Bar-
barossa Campaign, boasted of having jumped over Crete with
our parachutists in May '41 ("Max Schmeling sprained his
ankle"); another, on the cruiser *Prinz Eugen,* had watched the
Bismarck sink the British battleship *Hood* three days before *it*
sank with its thousand-man crew: "And if an aerial torpedo
hadn't hit the rudder and knocked her out of commission, the
Bismarck might well be afloat today...." But there were all
kinds of "what if" stories.

They were the basis for the millions our fireside strategist
Schmidt made from the *Kristall* series he turned into a tome, a
blockbuster, for Ullstein. His latest discovery was that the

Balkan campaign cost us our victory over the Russians: "Only because a Serb general by the name of Simović led a coup in Belgrade did we have to clean up down there, and that took five costly weeks. What if our armies had been able to start their push east on 15 May instead of 22 June, what if General Guderian's tanks had been positioned for the final attack on Moscow before 15 November, five weeks before, before the mud hit and Father Frost took over..."

And on he went, in mute communion with the fire, about "platter victories," winning battle after battle—Stalingrad and El Alamein were next—after the fact. No one supported his speculations, but no one, including me, dared to contradict him: there were two or three other dyed-in-the-wool Nazis in our presence, editors in chief then as now and highly influential in our circle. Who is willing to bite the hand that feeds him?

Finally I escaped the HQ back-room atmosphere with an old pal, who like me had reported from the standpoint of the common soldier, and we made fun of the "what if" philosophy in a local pub. We'd known one another since January 1941, when the two of us—he a photographer, I a cub reporter—received our orders to accompany Rommel's Afrika Korps to Libya. His pictures of the desert and my reports of the recapture of Cyrenica made a big splash in *Signal*. Now we sat at the bar reminiscing and pouring schnapps after schnapps down our gullets.

Pretty far gone, we walked along the Westerland beach promenade into the wind. For a while we sang: "Hurrah for the storm and the thundering waves..."; then we just stood and stared mutely out at the sea. When we started up again, I tried my hand at a parody of the former Herr Schmidt:

"Think what would have happened if Churchill had changed his mind early in World War I and landed on Sylt with three divisions. Wouldn't things have come to an end a lot sooner? Wouldn't history have taken a completely different turn? No Adolf and the dirty mess that came after. No barbed wire, no wall down the middle. We'd still have a kaiser and even a colony or two...."

1942

WE GATHERED SLOWLY the next morning, in dribs and drabs. The sun had poked a few holes in the cloud cover, making a stroll in the direction of Keitum possible, but in our meeting room, whose rustic timberwork projected a solidity that would last for centuries, the fire was burning again—or burning still—and our host kept filling our cups with tea out of bulbous China canisters. The talks were muted, even when about current events, and it took patience to pick out the references to the Volkhov encirclement, the Leningrad blockade, or the Arctic Sea front. One speaker might have been on holiday in the Caucasus; another made equally touristlike comments about the occupation of southern France. Yet Kharkov was taken, the great summer offensive was begun. One communiqué after the other. Slowly, however, things turned critical: one correspondent had had the frozen soldiers cut from his dispatches; another, the absence of replacement troops at Rostov. It was then, during a chance pause, that I spoke up.

Until that point I'd refrained from putting myself forward. The bigwig editors may have intimidated me a bit. But since

they and the art-and-submarine expert hadn't drifted in yet
(they'd probably found themselves a more attractive audience
in the posh communities on Sylt), I seized the opportunity and
said, or, rather, stuttered—I am more at home with the written word—my piece. "I'd made my way from Sebastopol to
Cologne for a home furlough. I was staying with my sister
near the Neumarkt. Things looked more or less peaceful, almost as before. I went to my dentist and had him drill one of
my left molars. I was supposed to go back two days later and
have it filled. It was not to be. In the night between the 30th
and 31st of May... A full moon... Like a hammer... More
than a thousand Royal Air Force bombers... Raking our flak
with gunfire... Then streams of firebombs, high-explosive
bombs, aerial bombs, phosphorus canisters... Right over the
center of town... But the outlying areas too... Deutz and
Mühlheim on the other side of the Rhine... Carpet bombing,
no targets... Whole districts in flames... Only roof fires where
we were, but you should have seen what went on next door...
Things you can't imagine... I helped two old women in the
apartment above ours. The curtains and both beds had caught
fire. No sooner did I get the fire out than one of the women
asked me, "Who's going to find us a cleaning lady?"... But
it's not something words can tell.... People buried alive...
Charred corpses... I can still see the tram wires along Frie-
senstrasse strewn over the smoking rubble like streamers at
Carnival. And Breite Strasse's four huge office buildings—
reduced to steel skeletons. The Agrippa Building with its two
cinemas—burned to the ground. The Café Wien on the Ring,
where I used to take Hildchen, my wife now—gone... The
upper floors of Police Headquarters—gone... And Sankt
Aposteln—it might have been split with an ax.... The Cathedral was still standing, smoking but standing, while every-

thing around it, even the bridge to Deutz... The building where my dentist had his practice, it simply was no more.... Apart from Lübeck, Cologne was the first terrorist attack. I know: we started it all with Rotterdam and Coventry, if you leave out Warsaw, that is. But a thousand bombers, including seventy or so four-motor Lancasters... True, our flak brought down more than thirty of them.... But they just kept coming.... It took four days to get the trains running.... I cut my furlough short. Even though my tooth had started acting up again. I wanted to get back to the front. There at least I knew what was what. I bawled—broke down and bawled—when I saw my Cologne from Deutz. Everything in smoke... Only the Cathedral still standing..."

They listened to me, which doesn't happen often, and not only because I'm more at home with the written word. This time your humble servant had set the tone. Others started in about Darmstadt and Würzburg, Nuremberg, Heilbronn, and so on. And Berlin, of course, and Hamburg. Rubble heaps all... The same stories over and over... But it's not something words can tell....

At about noon, when our ranks had filled out somewhat, we moved on to Stalingrad, and from then on it was Stalingrad and only Stalingrad, though none of us had been in the encirclement. Lucky bastards that we were...

1943

EVEN THOUGH OUR GODFATHER of a host made a point of leaving us to our own devices, he did see to it that our palaver followed more or less the sequence of events, which meant that after Stalingrad and El Alamein all we could talk about was retreat or, as it was called at the time, "front straightening." Most of us had had trouble writing, not so much because the censors cut or rewrote texts as because it was a lot easier to give a stirring account of the destruction of convoy ships in the Atlantic and the victory parade along the Champs-Élysées than of chilblain, the evacuation of the Donets Basin, or the capitulation of the remnants of the Afrika Korps in Tunis. The defense of Monte Cassino offered a modicum of heroic material. "Granted, the liberation of the Duce could be turned into a feat of sorts, but what else?" So we considered it embarrassing—if not downright out of place—when yet another of our number reported on the uprising of the Warsaw Ghetto and tried to make the massacre look like a victory.

He hadn't opened his mouth before, this plump little man decked out in loden—I later learned he delighted amateur hunters with brilliant animal stills and illustrated safari features—but he'd been on the spot with his Leica in May '43 when more than fifty thousand Jews were liquidated by artillery fire and flamethrowers in the walled district. The Ghetto later disappeared almost without a trace.

He'd been posted there as a member of a Wehrmacht propaganda unit: only for the length of the campaign. On the side—during his free time, that is—he had put together three copies of an album bound in grained leather: one for the Reichsführer of the SS, Himmler; one for the commander of the SS and Police in Cracow, Krüger; one for the Warsaw commander, SS Brigadeführer Jürgen Stroop. It eventually surfaced as the "Stroop Report" at the Nuremberg Trials.

"I shot in the neighborhood of six hundred pictures," he

said, "though only fifty-four went into the album. All neatly mounted on bristol board. A quiet, precise kind of work. But the handwritten captions are only partly my doing. Stroop's aide-de-camp, Kaleske, talked me into them. And the text on the front page in Gothic script—"There is no more Jewish district in Warsaw"—came from Stroop himself. At first it was only a matter of evacuating the Ghetto, ostensibly to prevent the outbreak of an epidemic. So I wrote, "Out of the factories!" in my best calligraphy. But our men met with opposition poorly armed boys, some women too, and members of the infamous Halutz Movement. So in went the Waffen-SS and a company of engineers with flamethrowers and also a group of volunteers from Trawniki—Latvians, Lithuanians, and Poles. We had our losses, you can be sure, but I didn't go around snapping them. I steered clear of corpses altogether. More group shots. One of the pictures that later became famous I called "Pulled from the Bunkers by Force"; another one, just as famous, "To the Transfer Point." They all went to the loading ramp. And from there to Treblinka. That's when I first heard the name Treblinka. A hundred and fifty thousand or so were packed off there. But I have pictures with no captions too, pictures that speak for themselves. One is pretty funny—our men having a friendly chat with a group of rabbis. But the one that became world-famous after the war was the one showing a group of women and children with their hands up and our men on the right and in the background pointing their guns at them. And a nice little Jewish kid out in front. In knee socks. With a peaked cap sliding off his head. You've seen it, I'm sure. It's everywhere. It's been reproduced thousands of times. All over the world. Book covers even. Made a real cult figure out of the kid. And not a word of credit to the photographer. Not a penny have I earned, not a single measly mark. Forget the copyright convention. Forget royalties. But I once estimated that if I'd got fifty marks each time it came out, I'd have chalked up... No, never fired a shot. And always out in front. You remember.... Nothing but pictures... And the handwritten captions, of course... Old-fashioned, in the German script... Crucial documents, anyone will tell you..."

On he went, long after people had stopped listening. Meanwhile the weather had cleared, and everyone felt in need of fresh air, so we risked a stroll—some in groups, others alone—though the wind was still strong. Across the dunes. I'd promised to bring my son back some shells. I did too.

1944

SOONER OR LATER THERE HAD TO BE A SHOWDOWN. Not that there was something in the air. It's just that this sort of get-together brings it on. When all we could talk about was retreat—"Kiev and Lvov in enemy hands, Ivan marching on Warsaw..."—when the Nettuno front caved in, Rome fell without a battle, and the Normandy invasion made a mockery of the impregnable Atlantic Wall, when one city after another was bombed to bits and there was nothing left to eat, when the reaction to the "Steal No Coal" and "Even the Walls Have Ears" posters was reduced to a bemused smile at best, when most of us veteran reporters had sunk into "hold-out" jokes, somebody—one of those Propaganda Campaign types who'd never seen action, who'd sat out the war in a cushy office job and gone on to churn out best-sellers in an only slightly modified diction—pulled the phrase "miracle weapon" out of his sleeve.

There was an immediate and raucous outcry. The big boss of the country's leading magazine shouted, "Don't be ridiculous!" Some even booed. But the man in question, now well on in years, refused to be daunted. He smiled a provocative smile and predicted a great future for the "Hitler myth." Calling on Charles the Saxon-Slayer, Frederick the Great, of course, and—who else?—that "predator of a Napoleon" as his witnesses, he constructed a monument to the "Führer principle" to come. Not one word of the "miracle weapon" article that appeared in the *Völkischer Beobachter* in the summer of '44, caused a sensation, and, let's face it, reinforced the nation's will to hold out—not one word did he repudiate.

And here he was, standing with his back to the fire, stiff as a ramrod. "Who had the vision to show Europe the way? Who rescued Europe by stemming the tide of the Bolshevik flood? Who made the first, pioneering step on the path from remote-control weapons to carrier systems with atomic warheads? He and he alone. He alone has the grandeur to stand up to history. As for my article in the *Völkischer Beobachter,* let me ask all those gathered here: Are we not needed again as soldiers, be it only in our own mockery of an army? Are we not both spearhead and bulwark? Is it not clear by now that Germany actually won the war? The world looks on with envy and admiration as we make our comeback. After total defeat our inexhaustible energy is generating economic strength. We are 'somebody' again. Soon we shall be back in the forefront. Japan, having enjoyed similar successes..."

The rest was lost in roars, guffaws, arguments, and counter-arguments. Someone shouted "Deutschland über alles!" in his face, thereby plugging his eponymous longtime best-seller.

The big boss removed his hulking presence from our midst by way of protest. But the orator was overjoyed at the effect of his provocation and took his seat with as seerlike a gaze as he could muster.

Our host and I tried in vain to bring the discussion back on track. Some insisted on rehearsing more retreats, the encirclement disaster at Minsk, for instance; others started rehashing the attempt on Hitler's life—"Had it worked, an armistice with the Allies would have stabilized the eastern front and made a common campaign, the Yanks and us, against Ivan something of a..."—but most bemoaned the loss of France, recalling the good times they'd had in Paris and the superiority of the French way of life, and were so far removed from the Battle of Normandy that I had the feeling they'd learned of the Allied landings on the beaches from American wide-screen extravaganzas years after the fact. Of course some regaled us with their sexual exploits—our art-and-submarine expert, for instance, who lamented his French harbor bride only to switch back to secret missions and navigable depths.

The old fogey so enamored of the "Hitler myth" felt the need to remind us that in 1944 a German had been awarded the Nobel Prize for chemistry. His pronouncement came from the fireplace, where he appeared to have dozed off. "And the news arrived, gentlemen, shortly after Aachen had fallen and only days before our last offensive, in the Ardennes. Yes, neutral Sweden honored the great German scientist Otto Hahn for his work on splitting the atom. Too late for us, of course. But had we been able to beat America to the punch, had we been able to develop so crucial a miracle weapon..."

No uproar this time. Everyone just sat there, deep in thought over the consequences of a missed opportunity. Sighs.

Heads shaking. Throats clearing with no weighty statements forthcoming. Even our submarine man, a hale-fellow-well-met with a stentorian bent, ceased spinning his yarns.

But then our host proposed a round of Frisian grog, and lifting our glasses lifted our spirits and brought us together. No one felt like venturing into the early night. Bad weather was forecast.

1945

ACCORDING TO OUR HOST there was a low-pressure area moving from Iceland in the direction of Sweden. He'd been listening to the weather reports. The barometer was dropping rapidly, and there were winds with a force of twelve on the Beaufort scale. "But have no fear. This house can weather any storm."

That Friday, 16 February 1962, at eight o'clock in the evening, the sirens began to wail. It was war. The hurricane hit the island head on. Not surprisingly, the open-air theater had an invigorating effect on some of us: our years in the theater of war had trained us to be game for everything, at the forefront, if possible. We were still pros, myself included.

So despite our host's warnings a contingent of former war correspondents set out from what we had been assured was a safe haven. Hunched over, we made our way, crawled our way from Alt-Westerland to the beach, where we found flagpoles down, trees uprooted, thatched roofs torn asunder, benches and fences hurtling through the air, while through the spray we could intuit more than see a series of waves the size of houses ramming the west coast of the island. Later we learned what the storm surge had meant on the upper Elbe and into Hamburg, particularly the Wilhelmsburg district: a water level three and a half meters above normal, dikes breaking, not enough sandbags, over three hundred casualties, the army called in. A man who later became chancellor took over and kept the worst at bay....

No, there were no casualties on Sylt. But the west coast was washed back a full sixteen meters. "Land under water!" could be heard even on the lee side of the island. The rocks at Keitum were completely submerged; List and Hörnum were in danger. Trains could not pass the Hindenburg Dike.

Once the storm had abated, we took stock of the damage. We had a need to report. It was what we'd learned to do, what we knew best. But as the war drew to an end and the only things to report would have been damage and defeat, we were told to write "hold-out appeals," exhortations to stay the course. I did a piece on the East Prussian refugees and their trek from Heiligenbeil over the frozen Haff in an attempt to reach the spit called Frische Nehrung, but nobody—least of all *Signal*—would publish my tale of woe. So although I saw ships overladen with civilians, wounded soldiers, and Party bosses casting off from Danzig-Neufahrwasser, although I saw the *Wilhelm Gustloff* three days before she sank, not a word did I write. And when Danzig could be seen blazing far and near, I wrote no heartrending elegy; I made my way to the Vistula with a few scattered soldiers and civilian refugees. And when I saw the Stutthof Concentration Camp evacuated and inmates who had survived the march to Nickelswalde crammed first onto barges, then into ships anchored at the mouth of the river, I wrote no horror stories, no warmed-over

Götterdämmerung. I saw it all and wrote nothing. I saw the corpses stacked and burned after the concentration camp was evacuated, I saw the empty huts taken over by refugees fleeing with bag and baggage from Elbing and Tiegenhof, but I saw no more guards. There was an influx of Polish farm laborers and occasional plundering. There was fighting as well, because the bridgehead at the mouth of the Vistula held until May.

The weather couldn't have been nicer. I lay among the pine trees, sunning myself, but could not put pen to paper even though all sorts of people—the peasant woman from Masuren who had lost her children, a venerable couple who had made their way here with great difficulty, a Polish professor who was one of the few survivors of the camp—poured out their misery to me. Describing misery was something I hadn't been trained to do. I lacked the words. So I learned silence. I left on one of the last coast-guard ships heading west from Schiewenhorst. Despite several low-flying bomber attacks we made it to Travemünde on 2 May.

And now here I was among others who had made it back and who like myself had been trained to report advances and victories and gloss over the rest, and I like all the others was putting the damage down on paper with the plaints of the storm victims ringing in my ears. What else could we do? Reports were our stock-in-trade.

The following day our crowd dispersed. The big shots had left earlier for the massive beach houses of the island dignitaries. I experienced an indescribable sunset after a brisk, sunny day. Then, as soon as the trains were back in operation, I made my way home over the Hindenburg Dike. No, we never got together again.

My next report was from Algeria, where after seven years of nonstop carnage the war had abated, though refused to end. What is peace, anyway? For us war never ends.

1946

BRICK DUST. BRICK DUST everywhere, let me tell you. In the air you breathe, the clothes you wear, between your teeth—you name it. But don't think that got us down. Not us women. Main thing was, the war was over. And now there's talk of building a monument to us even. I'm not kidding! A citizens' initiative: The Berlin Rubble Woman! Back then, though, when the city was in ruins and there was rubble everywhere you stuck your foot, all we was worth was—I'll never forget—sixty-one pfennigs an hour. Still, you got this better ration card—Number Two, they called it—a worker's card. And for a housewife's card you got only three hundred grams of bread a day and a measly seven grams of fat.

It was hard work, shoveling rubble. Me and my daughter—Lotte's her name—we did column work, right in the middle of town, where just about everything was bombed flat. Lotte had to take the baby along. Felix, she called the kid, but he got TB, from the brick dust, I guess, and died on her in '47 before her husband—he was a POW—came home. Practically strangers they were. It was one of those war weddings—by proxy, you know—'cause he was off fighting. First in the Balkans, then on the eastern front. Didn't last long, the marriage. They had nothing in common. And he wouldn't lift a finger. Wouldn't even gather wood in the Tiergarten. Just lay there in bed and stare up at the ceiling was all he'd do. 'Cause he saw some pretty bad things in Russia, I guess. Forever beefing about what he'd been through, as if those nights in the bomb shelters were nights on the town for us women. Well, we didn't beef. We dug. And dug some more. And sometimes we cleared bombed-out attics, whole floors of buildings, dumping the rubble in pails and running down five flights with them 'cause we didn't have none of them slides yet.

And once—I'll never forget—we was rummaging through this room that was so bombed out that even the wallpaper was hanging from the walls, and what do you know, Lotte runs across this teddy bear off in a corner, all covered with dust. A few whacks, though, and it's good as new. 'Course we could all imagine what'd happened to the kid it belonged to, so nobody in our column wanted it, but then Lotte took it for her Felix, who was still alive at the time. But mostly we just shoveled rubble into these huge carts on tracks or knocked plaster off bricks that were still whole. At first they emptied the rubble into bomb holes, then onto dump trucks that made whole mountains out of them, which are all green now and look real nice.

Right! And the bricks that were still whole we stacked up nice and neat, me and Lotte. Piecework they called it. We were a great group, our column. Some of the women had seen better days—officials' wives, that kind of thing. Even a countess. The genuine article. Von Türkheim, her name was. She had some big estate, in the east, I think. And you should've seen us! Overalls out of old army blankets, sweaters from wool scraps, and kerchiefs round our heads, tied tight on top, you know, to keep the dust out. Fifty thousand rubble women there was in Berlin. Rubble *women*. Not a man in the bunch.

Wasn't enough of them. And them that was, they just stood around and did nothing or else ran the black market. No dirty work for them!

But once—I'll never forget: we was starting a new pile and had an iron girder to dig out and I came up with this shoe. You guessed it! It had a man attached. Wasn't much left of him. All you could tell was he was in the home-front troops: he had one of their armbands on his sleeve. But the coat looked perfectly usable. Pure wool. Prewar. So "Off you come," I said to myself and filched it then and there. Still had all its buttons. And a harmonica in the pocket. A real Hohner. Gave it to my son-in-law. Thought it'd buck him up. He never played it, though. Or when he did, he made it sound real sad. Me and Lotte, now, we were different. We looked on the bright side of things. And things did get better. Little by little…

Right. I got a job at Schöneberg Town Hall, in the kitchen, and Lotte, who'd been a signals operator during the war, she went back to school after the rubble was out of the way. Took steno and typing. So by the time she was divorced she had a job as a kind of secretary. But I'll never forget how Reuter— he was the mayor right after the war—Reuter praised the rubble women. And whenever I can, I go to our reunions— coffee and cake at Schilling's. I always get a kick out of it.

1947

DURING THAT UNPRECEDENTED WINTER, when we had temperatures of twenty degrees below zero and major water-

ways like the Elbe, Weser, and Rhine froze over, making shipping coal from the Ruhr district to numerous parts of the
Western Zone impossible, I was the Hamburg city senator in
charge of energy. As Mayor Brauer stressed in his radio talks,
never, not even in the war years, had the situation been so
acute: eighty-five people froze to death during the cold spell. I
have no idea how many died of influenza.

Some relief was provided by the "warming halls" that the
City Senate set up in major districts like Eimsbüttel and
Barmbek, Langenhorn and Wandsbek. Since the coal supplies we had accumulated the previous year were confiscated
for military use by the British occupation forces and the supplies of the city's electric power stations sufficed for only a few
scant weeks, drastic reductions were in order. All districts
were subject to power cuts. S-Bahn service was curbed, then
tram service. Restaurants closed at seven P.M., theaters and
cinemas ceased operation. Over a hundred schools had to can-
cel classes. All but the most vital industries shortened their
workweek.

Things got worse, however: even hospitals experienced
power cuts. The Public Health Department had to call a halt
to X-ray screening at its Brennerstrasse clinic. Nor did it help
that as a result of the previous year's poor harvest, production
of vegetable oil was down, which reduced the already low
caloric intake of the population: individuals were allotted only
seventy-five grams of margarine per month. And since the
British authorities rejected the German request to take part in
international whaling expeditions, there was no hope that the
local margarine factories of the Dutch firm Unilever would
help. No one helped! And people were starving and freezing
to death.

Yet if you ask me who suffered most, I would have to say—not without pointing a finger at those who even then managed quite well, thank you—that it was the people whose houses had been bombed and who had to live amidst the rubble in roofless cellars and the refugees from the East camping in allotment gardens or Nissen huts. Even if my responsibilities did not extend to housing, I made it my business to inspect both the former—the Waltershof garden, for example—and the latter, emergency shelters thrown together out of corrugated iron over cement floors. I saw unspeakable things: icy winds would blow in through the cracks, but the iron stoves went unlighted; old people would take to their beds and never leave them. Was it any wonder if the poorest of the poor, who had nothing left to trade on the black market—where four pieces of coal went for an egg or three cigarettes—fell into either despair or bad ways? Homeless children were especially likely to be involved in plundering coal trains.

I am proud to admit that I refused to judge them according to the regulations. I was once taken to the Tiefstack shunting yard by a group of high police officials to observe their illegal activities. A risky business it was. Under cover of darkness they came, adolescents and children many of them; they came bearing sacks and hods, ducking into every shadow, yet caught now and then by the arc lamp's beam. Some tossed the coal down from the train, others ran and picked it up. And in a flash they were gone, heavy laden and—I presume—happy.

I asked the head of the Railway Police to refrain from intervening this time, but the operation was already under way. Searchlights lit up the terrain; speakers amplified the commands; police dogs barked. I can still hear the whistles, see the horror on the children's faces. If only they could have cried, but they were beyond that.

No, please don't ask what I felt. All you need for your report is: There seems to have been no way around it. City officials—the police in particular—could not simply stand by and watch.

The cold did not let up until March.

1948

IT WAS ACTUALLY THE FIRST TIME my wife and I could think of having a real holiday. We lived on a small pension and had to scrimp and save, even though the Reichsmark was worth hardly anything. But since neither of us smoked, we could use our cigarette cards—there were ration cards for everything—on the black market and even lay small sums aside.

So we went to the Allgäu Alps. But it just rained and rained. My wife later made up a poem about what we went through up there in the mountains, a real poem, with rhymes and in our Rhineland dialect: we're both of us from Bonn, you see. Anyway, this is how it began:

It poured three long days an long nights through, I ween,
An nary a star or the sky could be seen....

But all anyone in our boardinghouse or anywhere else talked about was the new currency we knew was coming. And then we heard for sure: it was two days away.

Now sure an it was a fine kettle of fish!
First the rain, then the currency. Holiday? Pish!

was the way my wife rhymed it. Well, I rushed down to the village barber with my old Reichsmarks and had my hair cut, had it cut shorter than usual, and my wife she had her hair dyed a nice chestnut color and—since cost was no object— got a permanent wave as well. But then we went and packed. No more holiday for us! Well, it turned out everybody wanted to get home, and the trains were jammed, all of them, but especially the ones heading for the Rhineland. It was almost like panic-buying just after the war. Here's how Anneliese put it into verse:

> Seats on the train? There were none to be had:
> Every man Jack had gone currency mad.

Anyway, the minute we got into Bonn, we rushed to our savings bank to take out what little we had left, because the coming Sunday, the 20th of June to be exact, was the day set for the switchover. Well, you should have seen the line! And in the rain! It was raining everywhere, not only in the mountains. We had a three-hour wait—that's how long it was. Each of us got forty marks and a month later another twenty. New marks, German marks, because Reichsmarks, like the Reich, were a thing of the past. That was supposed to take care of us, but it didn't. At least not people on small pensions. Besides, what we saw from one day to the next, why it made our heads spin. All of a sudden—it was like somebody had said, "Hocus-pocus"—the shop windows were full: wurst, ham, radios, shoes (the genuine article, with leather soles), and suits (worsted!) in all sizes. Things people had hoarded, of course. Currency sharks, you might call them. Saved up their valuables till the real money came. Later people said it was all Erhard's doing. Erhard and his thick cigar. But it was the Americans who printed up the new money, in secret, and the Americans who kept the new German mark out of the Soviet Zone. That's why the Russians went and printed up their own marks and closed off Berlin, which led to the airlift and a Germany divided by currency as well. So things were tight all over again. At least for people like us. As you can tell from Anneliese's poem:

The banks they took all and gave back a wee mite.
When the wolf's at the door, there's nought as looks bright.

No wonder that, at a local meeting of the Social Democrats, Comrade Hermann said, "Why do you think we've got all those luxury items on the market? Because business doesn't care about our needs; all business cares about is profit." And right he was, even if things did improve in time. Less for people like us on a pension—we couldn't do anything but gape at the shop windows—but at least there was fresh fruit and vegetables: cherries at fifty pfennigs a pound, cauliflower for sixty-five a head.... Affordable if you stuck to a budget.

Fortunately my wife submitted her poem—"The Flight from the Alps" she called it—to a contest run by the *Kölnische Rundschau*. It was for poems about "A Holiday I Shall Always Remember." Well, believe it or not, she won second prize. Twenty new marks plus ten for publication in the *Rundschau*. They went right into our savings account. We saved everything we could. But in all these years we've never quite managed to save enough for a holiday. I guess we were what they called at the time "currency victims."

1949

YOU'LL NEVER GUESS what happened the other day, Ulli, and to a graybeard like me. I had an uncanny encounter. With

Inge the Fair. She still exists. Inge the Fair, whose cool presence (*in natura et figura* and in days of yore, or should I say
days of Adolf?) was enough to inflame us Stettin youths,
make us quiver or stutter or at the very least turn and stare. I
can even claim to have got closer than arm's length to her. No,
not while camping on the Haff. The two of us served as or-
ganizers of winter aid for the freezing eastern front, and one
day while piling and packing underpants, sweaters, wristlets,
and suchlike items we simply fell on each other. Nothing came
of it other than some clumsy gropes on a bed of cardigans and
fur coats, after which we stank of mothballs.

But to go back to the present-day Inge, she is no less subject
to the ravages of time than you or I, but wrinkled and grizzled
as she is, Frau Doktor Stephan still radiates the kind of forti-
tude that catapulted her into the upper echelons of the movement. You remember, I'm sure. Promotion after promotion.
By the end she was a group leader in the Alliance of German
Maidens. We never made it to those heights in the Hitler
Youth, I rising only to the rank of junior platoon leader,
you to junior troop leader. By the time they put us in Luftwaffe auxiliary uniforms, the days of brown shirts and kerchiefs and braids were long past. But Inge, as she whispered
to me shamefully, kept her "maidens" together to the bitter end—caring for Pomeranian refugees, singing for the
wounded in field hospitals—and did not abandon the Alliance until the arrival of the Russians, who, by the way, did
her no bodily harm.

So as not to try your readerly patience any further, let me
state that we chanced upon each other on the occasion of the
Leipzig Book Fair, the program of which included a meeting
of the Duden Lexicographical Society, the workers-and-

peasants state being obliged to tolerate such a meeting given that said Society numbers both brands of Germans among its members. Now although I, like you, am soon to join the ranks of university *emeriti,* I have been assured that Duden-West will continue to exploit my linguistic acumen for the foreseeable future, and Inge is a representative of Duden-East (with which we have a not always peaceable collaborative arrangement) and hence likewise of the Community of Linguistic Meddlers, which encompasses even the Austrians and the Swiss. As I have no desire to bore you with our disputations in the matter of spelling reform, I will simply point out that the mountain has long been in labor and—as per Aesop—will bring forth its mouse in due time.

Much more interesting is my tête-à-tête with Inge. We made a date for cake and coffee in the Mädler Arcade. It was all prim and proper: she wanted me to partake of a local pastry. After a brief interval of shoptalk, however, we shifted to our Stettin years. She dished up the usual schoolgirl stories at first, then, leery of stirring the embers of our common Hitler youth, fell back on clichés like "in those dark years of seduction…" and "How they sullied our ideas and abused our good faith." But when we came to the immediate postwar period, she was perfectly at ease explaining her switchover from one system to the other—after an eighteen-month grace period—as a "painful conversion to anti-Fascism." She made a speedy career for herself in the East's Free German Youth movement, being highly qualified after all. She also told me about her role in the ceremonies marking the founding of the German Democratic Republic, which you may recall took place in 1949 in the building that had once housed Göring's Ministry of Aviation. She took an active part in world youth festivals, May Day parades, and collectivization campaigns, diligently exhorting recalcitrant peasants to give up their land. Yet it was these campaigns with their "loudspeaker coercion tactics" that provoked her first doubts. Not that she ever left the Party. And as a stalwart member she assures me she is doing everything possible "to confront the Party's errors with constructive criticism."

Next we wandered onto the routes our families had taken once forced to flee. Hers had settled in Rostock, where her bona-fide working-class background—her father had been a welder in the shipyards—gained her entrance into the university and paved the way for her Party career. My parents, you remember, ended up first in Denmark, then in Schleswig-Holstein, or, to be more precise, Pinneberg. As I put it to Inge, "I was fortunate enough to be washed ashore in the West and to be picked up by the British." I then listed my stations of the cross: the stint in a Munster POW camp, the aunt in Göttingen, the belated secondary-school certificate and first few semesters at the University there, the first teaching job at Giessen, the Fulbright to America, and so on and so forth.

As we chatted, I saw that our Western route had its disadvantages: we had lost our brown shirts but were given no blue shirts in exchange. "The blue shirts were merely a symbol," Inge said. "What mattered was that we believed in something, whereas you in the West lost any ideals you might have had." I naturally countered by saying, "There were plenty of ideals around when I wore my brown shirt and you your lily-white blouse!" "But we were children, we were deceived!" she replied, stiffening. She'd been good at that back then as well. She certainly didn't let me put my hand on hers. She only confessed, more to herself than to me, "Somewhere something went wrong." Which obviously made me respond, "On our end too."

From then on, our talk was all business: the Duden Society and its debates over what was still, after all, one language. We eventually arrived at the spelling reform, agreeing that it had to be radical to be at all effective. "Nothing halfhearted!" she cried, a little color coming to her face. I nodded and thought of my first love.

1950

I'D WORKED IN A BAKERY BEFORE THE WAR, and the people of Cologne nicknamed me "The Goofy Crumb Bun." They didn't mean anything bad by it, though: after the great Willi Ostermann, I wrote the best um pah pah waltzes. In '39— the last time we held our famous carnival, the last time we shouted the famous "Up Cologne!"—"You Sprightly Little Fawn" was number one, and you can still hear "Ahoy There, Captain!" the song that put the Mülheim ferry on the map.

Then came the grim years. I didn't have another hit till after the war, when our much loved Cologne lay in ruins, the occupying army banned our carnival, and the future looked bleak. The song was called "We Are the Natives of Trizonesia," and it proved you couldn't ban the city's carnival spirit. No, a group of carnival diehards, all the kids, and even a few disabled ex-servicemen, decked out in prewar costumes, would make their way from the Hahnentor even through the debris. Then in '49 the first postwar carnival committee—traditionally made up of a "constellation" of three: prince, peasant, and maiden— took matters into their own hands and set to digging the rubble out of Gürzenich, seat of the carnival's most impressive events.

The next year we were official again. It was a jubilee year as well: the Romans founded our town as Colonia in the year 50. "Cologne As It Is and Has Been for 1900 Years" was our theme. Unfortunately, I didn't write the carnival hit that year, but then, neither did any of the other pros, like Jupp Schlösser and Jupp Schmitz. No, it came from a man by the name of Walter Stein, who got the idea for "Who Will Pay the Piper? Who's Got Money Now?" while shaving. It caught the mood of the times, I must say. But I must also say it was promoted by a radio personality, a certain Feltz, who turned out to be a slick customer, because he turned out to be the same person as Stein. Well, there was a big scandal, the kind Cologne is known for, but "Who Will Pay the Piper..." kept being played and played. Clearly this Stein or Feltz or whoever he was had struck the right note. After the currency reform everybody was hard up—the man in the street, at least. Now the "prince" of the carnival, Peter III, he'd never wanted for money: he was in potatoes! Our "peasant" owned a marble quarry in Ehrenfeld. As for the "maiden," Wilhelmine, who according to the guidelines had to be a man, he was a jeweler—and a goldsmith to boot—and so, pretty well-heeled. In any case, the constellation spent money like water on the Shrove Tuesday Women's Night event in the covered market....

But what I really wanted to tell you about was the Rose Monday procession. It was a rainy day, and we had over a million people. They came from Holland and Belgium too. Even the occupying forces showed up. Just about everything was permitted again. It was almost like the old days, if you could imagine the city without the ghostlike ruins that were still all over the place. It was a historical procession—all ancient Romans and Germans, beginning with the Ubii, the Germanic tribe we come from. But then there was the usual leg-slap dancing by the men, accompanied by their "Maries," and a brass band out in front. And floats. Something like fifty of them. If in 1949 the battle cry was "We're back and doing all we can," in 1950 there were hundreds and hundreds of kilograms of sweets tossed to the kids—to everybody, actually— and a couple of thousand liters of genuine eau de cologne sprayed over the crowds from a fountain on wheels provided by the 4711 people. And you should have seen them, arms linked, swaying from side to side to the tune of "Who Will Pay the Piper?"

It held on for a long time, that song. And it was almost the only thing political about the procession. After all, the occupiers were keeping an eye on things. But two masks kept coming together; they would even dance together and kiss. Bosom pals, you might say, and obviously meant to be a bit wicked. Because one mask was the spitting image of Adenauer and the other of Comrade Goatee, you know, from Over There, Ulbricht. People had a good laugh over the slit-eyed Indian chief and the Siberian goat. But that was the only part of the procession with a pan-German twist. And it was more aimed at Adenauer, who was never partial to the whole carnival idea and had even spoken out against it before the war, when he was mayor of Cologne. I bet that when he was chancellor he'd have been glad to ban it. For good.

1951

VOLKSWAGEN GmbH
Wolfsburg
German Federal Republic
Gentlemen:

I am writing again because we have not yet received an answer from you. Is it because fate has decreed our place of residence to be in the German Democratic Republic? As it happens, our modest house is just outside Marienborn, not far from the border, but we can no longer cross it now that they have unfortunately had to build a protective barrier.

It is unfair of you not to answer. My husband worked for you from day one. I joined him later. In 1938 he was trained in toolmaking at the Braunschweig plant. Then he was a welder, and when the war was over he helped with the rubble removal, because nearly half the plant was destroyed by bombs. Later, when Herr Nordhoff took over and production started up again, he was promoted to the rank of inspector in Quality Control. He also served on the Factory Council. The enclosed picture shows him at the ceremony on 5 October 1951 when the 250,000th VW came off the assembly line and Herr Nordhoff gave a nice speech. It was not painted golden yellow the way the millionth Beetle was at the ceremony they had for it four years later. Still, it was a better ceremony than the one they had had three years earlier for the 50,000th Beetle, because back then they did not have enough glasses and gave us cups made of some artificial material and a lot of us, and the guests too, had terrible stomach pains and threw up right there in the factory building or just outside. This time they had real glasses. It was a shame that Professor Porsche (the real founder of Volkswagen, not Adolf) happened to die that year and so could not be present. He would certainly have answered our letter if he had seen our documents.

I went to work at VW-Wolfsburg during the war, right after Stalingrad, when everybody had to go to work. We were not making Beetles then, as I am sure you remember; we were making military vehicles for the Wehrmacht. My job was pressing sheet metal, and we had lots of Russian women working with us. They were unpaid, and we were not allowed to talk to them. Those were bad times. I went through the bombing too. But when the war was over, I got lighter work on the assembly line. That is when I met my husband. Then in 1952 my dear mother died and left us her little house and garden near Marienborn. I moved to the Soviet Zone, but my husband stayed on for a year. Then he had a serious accident and moved to Marienborn. Maybe that was a mistake, because now we are fated to be cut off from everything. We cannot even get an answer from you. That is unfair!

Last year we duly sent off the membership letter and the following documents relevant to the Volkswagen Savings Agreement:

1) a certificate stating that my husband, Bernhard Eilsen, deposited at least five Reichsmarks a week starting March 1939 and pasted the stamps in his book for four years with the understanding that he was saving for a blue-and-black Strength-through-Joy automobile, as the Nazis called it. He deposited a total of 1,230 marks, the selling price for factory delivery;

2) a certificate from the local Strength-through-Joy Society official in charge of motor vehicles.

The reason my husband came away empty-handed was that the few Volkswagens produced during the war were given to Party bigwigs. Because of that and because he is now on a disability pension, we feel we are entitled to a Beetle, our choice being model 1500 in lime green with no extras.

Now that more than five million Beetles have come off the assembly line and you have even built a plant for the Mexicans, we feel you should be able to fulfill your part of the Volkswagen Savings Agreement even if we do reside permanently in the German Democratic Republic. Or don't we count anymore as Germans?

According to an agreement your Supreme Court has recently concluded with the Committee to Assist Former Volkswagen Savers located in Karlsruhe, we are eligible for a reduction of six hundred marks. We will be glad to pay the remainder in our currency. That will be possible, won't it?

We look forward to hearing from you soon.

Yours sincerely,
Elfriede Eilsen

1952

WHENEVER OUR CUSTOMERS ASK, I still say, "It was the 'magic mirror,' as they used to call television in its early days, it was the 'magic mirror' that brought us together; love followed, a little at a time." It all began on Christmas Day in 1952, when groups of people crowded in front of radio-shop windows all over Lüneberg to watch the first bona-fide TV broadcast. The one where I was had only one set.

The show itself was no great shakes: first a story about the carol "Silent Night" and a teacher and a man by the name of

Melchior who whittled crucifixes then a kind of ballet in which Wilhelm Busch's Max and Moritz romped about to the music of Norbert Schulze, the composer the former soldiers among us were indebted to for both "Lilli Marlene" and "Bombs Over England." Oh, yes, it opened with some ceremonial claptrap by the head of the Northwest German Broadcasting Company, a man named Pleister, who soon became the butt of TV critics. But then there was a newscaster who managed to look both alluring and retiring in her flowered dress and who, when she smiled, smiled at me.

Her name was Irene Koss, and it was thanks to her that Gundel and I got together. Gundel happened to be standing next to me in the crowd. She clearly loved everything the magic mirror had to offer: the Christmas story moved her to tears; every prank Max and Moritz played made her clap in delight. But when I screwed up my courage, turned to her after the news—I can't remember what there was besides the Pope's message   and said, "Has it occurred to you, Miss, that you look amazingly like Irene Koss?" She replied with a pert "Can't say that it has."

Without having exchanged another word, we met again the following day in front of the same crowded shop window, this time early in the afternoon. She stayed on, though she must have been bored by the soccer match between St. Pauli and Hamborn 07. That evening we watched the news again, mostly because of Irene Koss, but before that I tried my luck and invited her to warm up over a cup of coffee. She accepted. She was a refugee from Silesia, she told me, and sold shoes at Salamander's. I had lofty plans to become a theater director or at the very least an actor—"And they're no pipe dreams," I assured her—but was forced to admit I was helping out in my father's less than booming restaurant; in other words, I was unemployed.

After the news we watched what we both thought to be a clever program about the preparation of the traditional Christmas stollen, the stirring of the batter being accompanied by the witty remarks of Peter Frankenfeld, who later hosted the hit talent show *There's Nothing to It*. We also enjoyed Ilse Werner and her whistling and singing, but most of all Cornelia Froboess, the child star from Berlin, who had made a name for herself with the catchy "Don't Forget Your Swimming Trunks."

And so it continued: we kept meeting in front of the shop window. Before long we were watching hand in hand. For a few days things went no further, but by the time the new year was upon us I'd introduced her to my father. He liked the spitting image of Irene Koss; she liked the restaurant on the edge of the woods. To make a long story short: Gundel brought new life to the ailing Meadow Inn. She found a way to persuade my father, who'd been despondent since my mother's death, to take out a loan and buy a TV set for the main dining room. And not one of your puny table models, no. A console. Philips' finest. And did it pay off! By May there wasn't an empty table or chair in the place. People came from far and wide, because the number of those who could afford TV sets was, and long remained, minimal.

We soon had a large group of regulars who not only watched TV but also consumed great quantities of food and drink. And when Clemens Wilmenrod, the TV chef, became the rage, Gundel, who'd stopped selling shoes to be my fiancée, used his recipes to spice up the formerly nothing if not monotonous Meadow Inn menu. Starting in the autumn of 1954, by which time we were married, the *Schölermann Fam-*

ily series attracted an even broader clientele, and we would follow the ups and downs of the TV family together. In the end it was as if the Schölermanns had rubbed off on us somehow, as if we *were* the Schölermanns, the "average German family," as people put it disparagingly at the time. Well, yes, we are average. We're blessed with two children, and a third is on the way. We both could lose a little weight. I've had to put my lofty plans in mothballs, but I'm perfectly content with my supporting role. Because Gundel has taken a leaf out of the Schölermanns' book and turned the Meadow Inn into a small hotel. Like so many refugees who had to start from scratch, you can't stop her. As the regulars are wont to say, Gundel— she knows what she wants.

1953

IT HAD RAINED ITSELF OUT. When the wind came up, we could feel brick dust in our teeth. That's Berlin for you, people said. Anna and I had been living there for six months at the time. She'd come from Switzerland, I from Düsseldorf. She was studying modern dance, the barefoot kind, with Mary Wigman in a large private house in Dahlem; I still wanted to join Hartung's Steinplatz studio and become a sculptor, but couldn't stop writing poems, long and short, wherever I stood, sat, or lay alongside Anna. And then something happened, something that went beyond art.

We took the S-Bahn to the Lehrte station—its steel skeleton was still standing—past the Reichstag ruins and the Brandenburg Gate, which was without its usual red flag, but it wasn't until we got to Potsdamer Platz, on the west side of the border, that we saw what had gone on and was now going on again after the rain. There was smoke pouring out of the Columbushaus and the Haus Vaterland. A kiosk was in flames. Singed propaganda, mixed with smoke by the wind, was snowing down in black flakes. Swarms of people were milling about aimlessly. No police. But Soviet tanks—T-34s, I recognized them instantly—were wedged in among the crowds.

"Attention!" the sign warned. "You are leaving the American sector." A few young people ventured across, some on bikes. We stayed in the West. I don't know if Anna saw more or other things than I did. We both saw the baby faces of the Russian soldiers who had dug themselves in along the border. And farther along we saw the stone throwers. There were plenty of stones, stones everywhere. Stones against tanks. I could have sketched the stance of a stone thrower or written a poem, long or short, about the stone throwing, but failed to draw or write a line. Yet the motions involved have remained with me.

Ten years later, when Anna and I were beset by children and in our parents' stage and Potsdamer Platz had become a walled-up no-man's-land, I wrote a German tragedy entitled *The Plebeians Rehearse the Uprising* that upset the temple guards of both states, a play in four acts about power and the powerless, about revolutions planned and spontaneous, about the possibility of altering Shakespeare, about rising production norms and a red rag, about proposals and counterproposals, about the hard-hearted and the fainthearted, about tanks and stone throwers, about a rained-out workers' revolt which, almost before it had been put down, was falsely termed a popular uprising, dated the 17th of June, and proclaimed a national holiday, thereby leading to more deaths in the West each time it was celebrated. Traffic deaths.

The deaths in the East came from shootings, lynchings, and executions. There were prison terms imposed as well. Bautzen was packed. But all that came to light much later. The only thing Anna and I saw at the time were the powerless stone throwers. We kept our distance: we loved each other and art; we were no workers throwing stones at tanks. But from then on we knew it was a never-ending battle. Sometimes, even if decades after the fact, stone throwers *do* prevail.

1954

I WASN'T THERE, IN BERN, but I did experience it over a radio besieged by a group of budding economists in my student digs in Munich. Schäfer's center pass to the Hungarian penalty zone. Yes, even today, the aging yet still enterprising head of a consulting firm based in Luxembourg, I can see Helmut Rahn, the player everyone called "The Boss," catching the ball on the run or kicking on the run, no, dribbling around two players who have flung themselves at him, slipping past another few, and slamming the ball into the lower left corner of the goal with his left foot at a distance of a good fourteen meters. Grosics can't possibly reach it. Five or six minutes from the end the score is 3–2. The Hungarians attack. Kocsis sets the ball up for Puskás, Puskás is right there, but no goal. All protests are in vain: the *honvédmajor* was offside, claims the ref. In the final minute of play Czibor comes up behind the ball and, seven or eight meters from the goal, aims at the near corner. But Toni Turek makes a flying save with both fists. The Hungarians have barely enough time to put the ball back into play before Mr. Ling blows his whistle. We're the world champions! We've shown the world what we're worth, we're back, losers no more, we can sing "Über alles in der Welt" under our umbrellas in the Bern stadium and around the radio in my Munich room.

But my story does not end here; it actually begins here. Because my heroes on that July day in 1954 were neither Czibor nor Rahn, Hidegkúti nor Morlock; no, in my capacity as investment broker and general financial adviser I have for decades looked after the economic well-being of my idols Fritz Walter and Ferenc Puskás, and a thankless task it's been: all my attempts at bridging the nationality gap have been in vain. After that famous match they became archenemies, the Hungarian decrying the German's Teutonic delusions of grandeur and hinting at drug abuse. "Their mouths foamed as they played," he supposedly once said. Years later—by which time, though still banned from German playing fields, he was under contract to Real Madrid—Puskás brought himself to make a written apology, as a result of which nothing stood in the way of a business deal between the two, and my consulting firm immediately stepped in to set something up.

No luck! Fritz Walter was awarded medal after medal, hailed as "the king of Betzenberg," but his potential as an advertising come-on for Adidas or a vineyard that toyed with the idea of naming its sparkling wine after him was underrated and underpaid. It wasn't until his best-sellers about the invincible eleven and their coach beefed up the old income a bit that he was able to buy an unpretentious movie theater in Kaiserslautern near the castle ruins, the kind of place where you can buy lottery tickets and soccer coupons in the foyer. It actually turned out to be more trouble than it was worth: it brought in next to nothing. And he could have made a killing in Spain in the early fifties, when Atlético Madrid tried to woo him away with a quarter of a million. But the modest—much too modest—Fritz turned them down. He loved his Rhineland. There and only there would he be king.

Not so Puskás. After the bloody Hungarian uprising, which found him on tour with his team in South America, he stayed in the West, giving up his successful Budapest restaurant and eventually taking Spanish citizenship. He had an easy time of it with the Franco regime, because, coming from a country where the ruling Party had made him—like the Czech Party their Zátopek—a "hero of socialism," he knew the rules of the game. For seven years he played for Real Madrid, raking in millions, most of which he plowed into Salchichas Puskás, a sausage factory that did a brisk business at home and abroad, but saving some, gourmand that he was (he had a perennial weight problem), for his gourmet eating establishment Pancho Puskás.

So that, while of course my two idols did market themselves, they lacked the insight to combine their interests, sell themselves as a package, a "two-for-one" deal. Not even my company, which specializes in mergers, had any success turning the former working-class youth from a Budapest slum and the former Rhineland bank teller into business partners—for example, advertising a Fritz Walter Vintage as a natural complement to Major Puskás's salami and thus reconciling the provincial hero and the citizen of the world and turning a profit into the bargain, so to speak. No, they were both wary and rejected the idea—or had others reject it for them.

The *honvédmajor* still maintains that his goal was valid, in other words, that it tied the score 3–3. He may think that Mr. Ling, the referee, was getting back at the Hungarians for meting out England's first defeat at home, in holy Wembley Stadium. The Magyars trounced them 6–3. And Fritz Walter's secretary, whose job it is to run interference for the King of Betzenberg, refused even to accept a Puskás salami I offered him as a personal gift. It was a defeat I'll never quite get over.

Which is probably why I occasionally find myself wondering what German soccer would have become if the referee hadn't blown his whistle and we'd fallen behind in overtime or lost our nerve at the sudden-death play-off, that is, if we'd left the field defeated yet again....

1955

OUR HOUSE WENT UP THE YEAR BEFORE, partly financed by a building and loan association—Wüstenrot, I believe it was—and the good civil servant in my father was satisfied that the papers had been signed "under relatively stable conditions." The thing was that, while not only my two sisters and myself but also my mother and grandmother soon felt perfectly at home in its five and a half rooms, it was without an air-raid shelter, and that despite the fact that my father had assured the architects he was willing to lay out whatever additional funds it might entail. During the planning stages he had written letter after letter to both the architects and the powers that be, enclosing pictures of mushroom clouds over American testing grounds and of the "relatively undamaged shelters" in Hiroshima and Nagasaki. He even made some rather awkward sketches of a basement room big enough for six to eight people with an air lock and reinforced door and of a similarly fashioned emergency exit. He was therefore terribly disappointed when these "precautionary measures mandatory in our atomic age for a relatively large segment of the civilian population" were ignored. There were no governmental standards, the building authorities informed him.

Not that Father was particularly opposed to the bomb. He accepted it as a necessary evil as long as the Soviet Union presented a threat to world peace. But he certainly would have found fault with later efforts on behalf of the Chancellor to squelch all discussion of civil defense. "It's all just a game," I can hear him saying. "He's afraid he'll lose votes if the population gets uneasy, so he pretends the 'atomic cannons' are just extensions of the artillery. Pretty clever, the fox."

In any case, there it stood. People in the neighborhood started calling it the "House of the Three Goldilocks." When the time came to put in the garden—our job was to plant the fruit trees—we all of us remembered that Father had made a point of setting off a large square in a shady section, but it wasn't until Grandmother, as was her wont, subjected him to serious cross-examination that he confessed he had been studying the latest Swiss civil defense literature and was planning to build a "relatively economical" underground bunker. When several newspapers reported a simulated joint maneuver on the part of the Western Powers on 20 June 1955 under the code name Exercise Carte Blanche with Germany, East and West, as the theater of war, atomic war, estimating the number of deaths at two million and the number of wounded at three

and a half million—not including East Germans, of course—
Father got down to work.

Unfortunately he let no one help. He was so annoyed with
the building authorities that he decided to do the job single-
handedly. Not even Grandmother could stop him. When it
came out that the earth was in great peril from ominous clouds
packed with radioactivity called "fallout" just waiting to de-
scend, and, even worse, that as early as 1952 these contaminated clouds had been discovered directly above Heidelberg
and the surrounding areas, in other words, right over our
heads, he grabbed his shovel and started digging. By now even
Grandmother was convinced, so much so that she financed
more than a few sacks of cement.

Single-handedly and after work (Father was a department
head at the Land Registry Office) he dug the four-and-a-half-
meter pit; single-handedly and over a single weekend he managed to lay the foundation. He also worked out how to cast the
entrances and exits as well as the air-lock chambers in concrete. Mother, usually a woman of few words, was lavish in
her praise. Perhaps that was what made him continue going it
alone when he reached the point of building a formwork for
the dome of our—as he called it—"relatively bombproof
family shelter" and filling it in with concrete. That too seemed
to have gone well, and he was standing in the rotunda check-
ing the inside when the accident occurred: the formwork gave
way and down came the concrete. By the time help arrived, he
was beyond help.

No, we didn't go through with his plan. Grandmother
wasn't the only one opposed to it. But from then on—not that
it would have made Father happy—I marched in the Easter
antinuclear demonstrations. Did it for years. And even though

I'm getting on now, I take my sons to demonstrations like the ones in Mutlangen and Heilbronn against the Pershing missile. Not that they've done much good.

1956

IN MARCH OF THAT MORBID-MOURNFUL YEAR, when one died in July, shortly after his seventieth birthday, and the other, not yet sixty, died in August, when the world I had known seemed a wasteland to me, the stage a void, I, a student of German literature making his own first attempts at poetry in the shadow of two giants, encountered them both in Berlin at the grave of Heinrich von Kleist, a remote spot with a view of the Wannsee, the site of many an uncommon encounter both fortuitous and contrived.

I assume they agreed upon the time and place in secret, possibly using women as go-betweens, the only fortuitous element thus being myself, the modest student in the background, who recognized one by his Buddha-bald pate and the other, racked with illness, by his frail demeanor. I was hard put to keep my distance, but as there was no wind to speak of on that radiant yet nippy March morning, their voices—the one now tender, now surly, the other ringing and rather shrill—carried well. They did not speak much; they were comfortable with pauses. At times they stood so close they might have been on a single pediment, but they also moved apart, concerned to maintain the presumed gap between them, the one famed in the western sector of the city as literary— and consequently uncrowned—king, the other the readily quotable authority of the eastern sector. Since the city was then divided by a war—if only of the cold variety—the two men had been pitted against each other, and it took ruses on both sides to arrange for them to meet *au-dessus de la mêlée,* so to speak. They must have been gratified, my idols, to escape their assigned roles if ever so briefly.

That was how it looked; that was how the duologue proceeded. Nothing in their wanderings or at least in the bits and pieces I put together betrayed any sense of enmity. Each quoted from the other's works rather than from his own and took pleasure in the ambiguity of the selection process. One chose to recite the terse poem "The Coming Generation," rendering the final verse with particular relish, as if he had composed it himself:

> When all errors are exhausted
> The last companion to sit down with us
> Is nothingness.

The other gave a rather blasé rendition of the verse that closes "Man and Woman Walking through the Cancer Ward," an early poem:

> The fields are swelling round each patient's bed,
> Flesh smoothed to soil, heat surging forth;
> The juice begins to flow. Earth calls.

Connoisseurs, they delighted in quoting each other and lauding each other between quotations, making lavish and derisory use of buzzwords all too prevalent among us students: "No one can be so phenotypically alienated as you," one cried. "Your morgue of Western civilization has both a monologic and a dialectic relationship to my epic theater," the other screeched. And so on, all mutual barbs and mirth.

Next they set upon the recently deceased Thomas Mann, whose "heavy-duty leitmotifs" they lampooned. Then came Mr. Beaker (Becher) and Mr. Fountain (Bronnen), whose aqueous names and political deeds they naturally turned into puns. Their own political sins they dealt with rather cursorily: one gave a mocking reading from a hymn to the Party written by the other ("... the great reaper-leader of the Soviet land, / Joseph Stalin, / Spoke of millet, spoke of dung and arid wind..."), whereupon the latter pointed out the connection between the former's onetime enthusiasm for the Nazi propaganda organ *Dorische Welt* and a speech he once gave in honor of the Fascist Futurist Marinetti; one praised the other's play *The Measures Taken* ironically as "the verbal universe of a true Ptolomean," then immediately exonerated both of them, sinners that they were, with a quotation from his own great poem "To the Coming Generation":

> You who shall emerge from the flood
> We have drowned in
> Recall
> When you think on our frailties
> The dark times
> You have escaped.

The "you" I took to refer to me, a member of the "coming generation" currently listening in on them in the shadows. I had to be content with this admonition: I had expected my idols to give me more insight into their pioneering errors, but none was forthcoming. Well trained in silence, they now turned to matters of health. One, a physician, was concerned about the other, who, pounding his chest by way of explanation, reported that a Doctor Brugsch had proposed a series of tests at Charité Hospital. One was concerned about the "hullabaloo" attending the upcoming celebration of his seventieth birthday—"A nice cold beer would do just fine"—while the other insisted on stipulating in his will that no one, not even the authorities, might force him to lie in state in public, no one might deliver an oration at his grave. Which was all well and good, said the one, but "stipulations or no, who will protect us from our epigones?"

Nothing about the political situation. Not a word about rearmament in East or West. And still quipping over the quick and the dead, they left the grave of the immortal Kleist without ever having quoted or so much as mentioned him. At the Wannsee station the West Berliner, who lived in Schöneberg near Bayerischer Platz, took the S-Bahn, and the East Berliner climbed into the chauffeur-driven vehicle waiting to take him, presumably, to Buckow or the Schiffbauerdamm.

When summer came and the two men died, one after the other, I decided to burn my poems, give up German literature, and switch to the Technical University, where from then on I diligently devoted myself to mechanical engineering.

1957

Dear Friend,

After all the times we once shared I feel moved to write you this letter. Granted, we have gone our separate ways, yet I feel I can count on our ongoing cordial relations and hope my confidential note reaches you even if our divided Fatherland necessitates certain precautions.

But let me apprise you of the occasion for my friendly

words. Now that we may consider the reconstruction phase of both your Federal Armed Forces and our National People's Army to be complete, I was awarded a bronze medal on 1 May of this year. During the review of my work I came to the realization that the honor belongs in no small part to you as well: the two of us labored together to produce the German steel helmet.

It is lamentable (though certainly understandable) that the history of the M-56 was passed over in silence at the ceremony, but during the war we were of course equally responsible for the helmet at the Thale Iron and Steel Works, developing, as we were, the B and B-II helmets originally designed by Professor Fry and Doctor Hänsel and later tested under fire. As you surely recall, the Chief Command forbade us to "invalid out" the M-35, though its faults—the overly abrupt sides and an angle of fall of up to ninety degrees—had been demonstrated by sizable human casualties. The new helmet, tested as early as 1943 at the Döberitz Infantry Camp, provided increased protection under fire as a result of a reduced angle of inclination; it also proved compatible with two-centimeter bazookas and eight-centimeter mortars (a.k.a. the "stovepipe") and with binocular periscopes and Dora walkie-talkie sets. As a number of reports made clear, it turned out to have additional advantages as well: it was light, it allowed the head greater freedom of movement with all weapons and equipment, and it enhanced audibility by dampening background noise.

Unfortunately, as you know, the M-35 remained in use to the bitter end. With the buildup of the National People's Army, however, I was allowed to go back to the tried and yet again tested B and B-II helmets at the Thale Iron and Steel Works, now nationally owned, and use them as the basis for the new People's Army M-56 helmet, which is currently in production. We are planning a first run of a hundred thousand. The lining was made by the Taucha Leather and Saddle Manufacturers, also nationally owned. We are proud of the helmet, and I reject as unfounded the malicious claim one encounters here and there that it resembles certain Czech models.

On the contrary, dear friend! As you can see, in both helmet and uniform design our Republic has acknowledged its debt (though not openly, of course) to *Prussian* models, even taking over the reliable combat boot for common soldiers and jackboot for officers, while your "Blank Bureau" in Bonn seems bent on breaking with tradition entirely: it has obediently accepted an American helmet model and toned down the standard battle-dress gray-green to a slate color. I hope you will not be offended if I point out that despite its absurd-looking uniforms, that is, despite its attempts to look as informal, even civilian, as possible, Bonn's army cannot hide its aggressive stance, having decided, as have we, to use Wehrmacht generals of outstanding merit to lead the troops.

Now, however, let me return to the honor accorded me (and you, in principle, as well). Do you know who popped into my head as I was handed the bronze medal at the May Day festivities? Professor Schwerd of the Technical University in Hannover. You remember, the one who designed the steel helmet introduced in 1915, first at Verdun and then on all fronts, to take the place of the wretched spiked variety. We all considered ourselves his disciples. In any case, I felt a great debt of gratitude to him for the honor I (and you, in secret) had just received. And yet my joy was tempered by the thought that two German armies now stand facing each other. Our Father-

land is split. Foreign powers have willed it so. One can only
hope that in the not too distant future we shall once more
be united. Then, as in our youth, we shall go walking in the
mountains, in the Harz. Then *all* our soldiers will wear the
helmet that evolved during the Second World War into a max-
imally bulletproof descendant of pure German lineage. And
to that, dear friend and colleague, the two of us were privi-
leged to contribute our mite.

Best wishes,
Erich

1958

THERE'S NO DENYING IT: after the food craze and the travel
craze, the economic miracle gave rise to the German Fräulein
miracle. But which cover girls were the first? Who graced
magazines like *Stern* as early as '57? Which of the up-and-
coming generation of beauties were known by name when the
Fräulein miracle swept across the Atlantic and *Life* heralded
"the sensation from Germany"?

As a voyeur of recent vintage I fell in love with the twins
back in the early fifties, soon after their arrival from Saxony for
a summer visit with their father, who had jilted their mother.
They stayed on in the West, though shedding a few tears for
their Leipzig ballet school after I got them their first dance-
hall engagement at the Palladium: Alice and Ellen had higher
aspirations; they'd dreamed of the Düsseldorf Opera—*Swan
Lake* and so on.

I laughed to hear their Saxon jabber as I paraded them

along the Königsallee shop windows in purple stockings, first attracting attention, later creating a sensation. Before long they were picked up by a group of Lido talent scouts and, after I'd had a little talk with their father, packed off to Paris. Well, I packed myself off too. I'd had enough of dry-as-dust Düsseldorf. And when, after Mother's death, I made noises about pulling out of our flourishing detergent business, I was quickly offered so astronomical a sum for my shares that ever since I've been able to travel, stay at top hotels, maintain a Chrysler and driver and a chalet near Saint-Tropez—in other words, lead a typical playboy existence. But they were the real reason I slipped into the role, which seems amusing only from without. I was attracted by their double beauty. I'd fallen prey to two plants from a Saxon hothouse. Their divinely outlandish long-leggedness gave my futile existence a goal, though a goal I never achieved: Alice and Ellen, Ellen and Alice took me for no more than a lapdog—well, a perennially solvent lapdog.

In Paris it was nearly impossible to come near them. "Miss Bluebell," a veritable monster whose real name was Leibovici, kept the sixteen long-legged wonders of her revue safely cloistered: no male visitors in the dressing rooms, no contact with the Lido clientele, and only cabdrivers over sixty to take them back to the hotel after the performance. Word went round in my circle—which at the time was made up primarily of globe-trotting lechers—that "a safe was easier to crack than a Bluebell girl."

Still, I did find opportunities—or, rather, their strict disciplinarian granted me opportunities—to take them for walks along the Champs-Élysées. She also set me the task of comforting them: they were ignored by the dressers and viciously attacked by the other chorus girls as a result of their Teutonic origins, their tall, slim appearance making them answerable for all manner of "*boche*" war crimes. It was agony! And it was heartbreaking to see their tears. I dabbed them like an obsessed collector.

The attacks subsided once they became popular, however, and in America admiration for the "sensation from Germany" was completely unmarred by abuse. Even Paris eventually lay at their feet. From Maurice Chevalier to Françoise Sagan, from Princess Grace of Monaco to Sophia Loren—everyone went gaga the moment I introduced the Kessler twins. Only Liz Taylor seemed a bit envious when gazing upon my Saxon lilies' waists.

O Alice! O Ellen! Coveted though they were, even the randiest of studs failed to make headway with them. During the shooting of *Trapeze* both Tony Curtis and Burt Lancaster made continuous advances—to no avail. I didn't even need to stand guard. They were all just one happy family. As soon as Ellen and Alice appeared at the end of a break, Tony and Burt would tease them, shouting, "*Ice* cream! *Ice* cream!" To which my little darlings would reply, "*Hot* dogs! *Hot* dogs!" And even though Burt later boasted of having bedded one of them, I don't imagine he got much out of it or even realized which of them he was with.

They were good only to look at, which was just what I could do—whenever and wherever I pleased. And I was the only one until they went their separate ways. Their brilliance outshone everything, even the much acclaimed miracle most people associate exclusively with the German economy: Alice and Ellen embody the miracle of the Saxon Fräulein, which is every bit as miraculous today.

1959

BECAUSE WE'D FIRST FOUND EACH OTHER, Anna and me—it was 1953 in January-cold Berlin—on the Egg Shell dance floor, we decided to go dancing (and because our only salvation was to leave the Book Fair premises, with its umpteen thousand new publications and umpteen thousand blithering insiders) at the publisher's expense (Luchterhand's—or was it S. Fischer's?—brand-new beehive building, in any case it certainly wasn't Suhrkamp's polished parquet; no, it must have been a place rented by Luchterhand), hot to trot, seeking and finding each other, Anna and me, as always, by dancing, this time to a tune with the rhythm of our youth— Dixieland!—as if only dancing could save us from the brouhaha, the flood of books, the self-important people, remove us, tripping the light fantastic, from their twaddle—"It's Böll, Grass, and Johnson comin' round the bend!"—and at the same time riding out our inkling of something coming to an end, something getting off the ground, now we have a name, getting over it in a quick spin and on rubber legs, up close or touching fingertips, because the only way we could deal with the Book Fair babble—"*Billiards, Speculations, Tin Drum*"—and party buzz—"German post-war prose has made it at last!"—and military intelligence— "Forget Sieburg and the *Frankfurter Allgemeine,* this is the breakthrough!"—was to turn a deaf ear, let ourselves go, step to a combination of Dixieland and heartbeat, which drowned them out, made us light and airy, gave us wings, so that the weight of the tome—seven hundred and thirty pages fat— was offset by the dancing and we went from printing to printing, fifteen, no, twenty thousand, till all at once, just as somebody cried out, "Thirty thousand!" and started listing possible contracts with France, Japan, and Scandinavia, up we went, outbidding the new success by dancing aboveground, and Anna lost her petticoat with its embroidered mouse-tooth hem and three levels of frills when the elastic gave up or, like us, lost its inhibitions, whereupon Anna, released, floating up over the fallen linen, tossed it with the tip of one foot in the direction of a group of onlookers, Fair people, with even a reader or two among them, who were celebrating at the publisher's (Luchterhand's) expense what was by now a best-seller and shouting "Oskar!" and "Oskar's dancing!" but it wasn't Oskar Matzerath on the floor doing "Jimmy the Tiger" with a telephone operator, it was Anna and me going at it with great gusto, having left Franz and Raoul, our baby boys, with friends and taken the train all the way from Paris, where I had shoveled coal into the stove to heat our cold-water flat and written chapter after chapter staring at the oozing walls, while Anna, whose fallen petticoat was an heirloom from her grandmother, sweated it out daily at Madame Nora's barre, Place Clichy, until I typed up the last pages, sent the proofs off to Neuwied, and finished painting the dust jacket with a blue-eyed Oskar, whereupon the editor (Reifferscheid, his name was) invited us to Frankfurt and the Book Fair so we could experience, no, savor the acclaim together, from foretaste to aftertaste, but mostly what we did was dance, later too, after making a name for ourselves, though having less and less from dance to dance to say to each other.

1960

IT WAS A CRYING SHAME! The German team entering the Olympic Games in Rome was one and united, but Adidas was permanently split. And it was all Hary's doing. Not that he intended to provoke further arguments between us, though he did bring our quarrel to a head. Still, we'd broken off business relations much earlier, when my brother set up a company to compete with me right here, near Fürth—Puma, he called it. And even though Puma never came close to my production figures, the two of us together basically cornered the world market for running shoes and soccer boots.

But Armin Hary did play the two of us off against each other by switching between Adidas spikes and Puma spikes for his record-breaking sprints. Both companies paid heavily as a result. In Rome he used my brother's spikes, but wore mine on the podium when receiving the gold for his legendary performance. At the same time I put his running shoes in our museum after the ten-second world-record run in Zurich, and I designed the 9.9 model for Hary to wear to the starting line in Rome.

It was a shame he let my brother woo him away, and it was typical of our family feud that right after the gold—Hary was also part of the winning 400-meter relay team—the press were shown eight Puma models with his name, starting with Hary Start and Hary Spurt and ending with Hary Victory. I have no idea how much Puma had to shell out for them.

Now that the time for compromise and reconciliation has passed—the company is sold, my brother dead—I can see only too clearly that neither of us should ever have let ourselves be taken in by the crook, as he has rightly been called. The price we had to pay was soon plain for all to see. No sooner had he set the world record than the scandals came fast and furious. Right there in Rome the brat got into an argument with the relay officials, and within a year his career as a sprinter was as good as over. After a meteoric rise. No, the car accident had nothing to do with it; it was his flagrant flaunting of the amateur rules. And people say that we at Adidas and Puma—we're the ones who put him up to it. Well, that's nonsense, of course, though I must admit my fine upstanding brother would spare no expense to steal a runner: Fütterer, Germar, Lauer—he wooed them all. But with Hary he fell on his face, even if from today's vantage point I feel the court's ruling was petty, totally excluding the possibility, for this unique phenomenon in short-distance running—in recognition of which even black man Jesse Owens shook the hand of white man Armin Hary—of gaining another victory or breaking another record.

Let me repeat: a crying shame! Even though, brilliant as it was, his athletic career was a clear sign of the rifts in his moral fabric, and his later occupations—he worked in real estate and various businesses—often ended in scandal (in the early eighties he was involved in the machinations of the "New Home" trade-union savings racket and the Munich archbishopric and was sentenced to two years in prison for fraud), I can still see the tall young man, as my brother must have seen him, setting a world record by covering the hundred-meter distance in forty-five strides, the longest stride measuring two meters twenty-nine.

And what a start the man had! Almost before his feet left the block he was out in front, in front of even the black runners. And that white man's record lasted for years. What a shame he was never able to beat his own famous 10.0. If Armin Hary had stuck with Adidas instead of going in with Puma and my brother, he would definitely have made 9.9. Jesse Owens even thought him capable of 9.8.

1961

EVEN IF NO ONE PARTICULARLY CARES anymore, I always
say to myself looking back, Those were the best days of
your life. You were given a job to do. You risked your life daily
for more than a year. You were so scared you practically bit
your fingernails off, but you met the danger head on, trying
not to think about whether you were in for another disastrous
semester. The thing was, I was a student at the Technical University—and even then interested in district heating—when
from one day to the next the wall went up.

People made an enormous fuss, rushed to rallies, staged
protest marches in front of the Reichstag and elsewhere. Not
me. First thing, in early August, I got Elke out. She was at a
teacher-training college over there. All you needed was a West
German passport, which was no problem because we had the
personal data on her and a picture. But by the end of the
month we had to start fiddling with the entry permits and
working in groups. I was the contact. My passport, which was
issued in Hildesheim, where I actually come from, worked for
the next few weeks, but starting some time in September you
had to hand in your entry permit as you left the eastern sector.
We might have been able to make our own if somebody had
smuggled out the kind of paper they used.

Not that people are interested nowadays. My kids certainly
aren't. They either turn a deaf ear or say, "We know, Dad. You
were real noble, your generation." Well, maybe my grandchildren will listen when I tell them how I got their grandma
out and how she took an active part in "Operation Travel Bureau," which was our cover name. We were experts at getting
the official stamps right. Some used hard-boiled eggs; others

swore by finely sharpened matches. We were mostly students and mostly leftist, but we had our dueling society types and a few like me who couldn't get excited about politics. It was election time in the West, and our Berlin mayor was a candidate for the Social Democrats, but I didn't vote for Brandt and the comrades or for old man Adenauer either, because fancy words and ideologies didn't mean a thing to me; what counted was what you did. And our job was to "transfer," as we called it, passport pictures into West German or foreign passports— Swedish, Dutch. Or find contacts to bring us passports with pictures and personal data—hair color, eye color, height, age— of the kind we needed. We also needed the right kind of newspapers, small change, used bus tickets—the odds and ends that, say, a Danish girl would be likely to have in her bag. It was tough work. And all of it free or at cost.

Nowadays, when nothing is free, nobody can believe we didn't make a penny from it. Oh, a few held out their hands when we started digging our tunnel. It had a crazy history, the Bernauer Strasse project. What happened was that without our knowing it an American TV company put up over thirty thousand marks for the right to make a documentary about the tunnel. We'd dug for four long months and through that Mark Brandenburg sand—it was a hundred meters long, the tunnel—and when they filmed us smuggling thirty or so people, including grandmas and grandkids, into the West, it never occurred to me they'd put it on the air there and then. But that's what they did, and the tunnel would have been discovered in no time if it hadn't flooded—despite our expensive pumping equipment—shortly before the film was shown. No matter. We carried on elsewhere.

No, we had no casualties. I know. The papers were full

of reports of people jumping from the third story of border buildings and landing on the pavement a hair's breadth from the safety net. A year after the wall went up, a man by the name of Peter Fechter was shot barging his way through Checkpoint Charlie; he bled to death because nobody would come to his aid. We didn't need to worry, though, since we stuck to sure things. Still, I could tell you stories people didn't want to believe back then even. About all the folks we took through the sewers, for instance. It stank to high heaven down there. One of the routes leading from the center of East Berlin across to Kreuzberg we called "Glockengasse 4711" after the cologne, because all of us, the refugees and our people, had to wade knee-deep in raw sewage. I served later as a cover, but not in the sense you might think. It was my job to wait until everybody had disappeared down the manhole and then pull the cover back in place: the refugees themselves were so panic-stricken they'd forget to do it. We had a similar problem at the Esplanadenstrasse runoff canal in the north of the city, when a few refugees let out a mighty cheer the moment they crossed over to the West: the East German police standing guard caught on and threw tear-gas canisters down the hatch. Then there was the cemetery that had one wall in common with *the* wall, so we dug a subterranean passageway up to the graves for our clientele, harmless-looking mourners with flowers and suchlike paraphernalia, to vanish into. It worked just fine until a young woman, who was taking her baby with her, left the pram at the camouflaged entrance to the passageway, which gave things away immediately....

Slips like that had to be factored in. But now let me tell you about a time when everything worked. Had enough, you say? I understand. I'm used to it. Things were different a

few years back when the Wall was still up. I'd be having a
Sunday beer with my co-workers from the district heating
plant, and one or another of them would ask me, "What was
it like, Ulli, when the Wall went up and you had to smuggle
Elke into the West?" But nowadays nobody's interested, not
here in Stuttgart at least. Because the Swabians never really
grasped what it meant back in '61. So when the Wall came
down all of a sudden... Actually, they liked having it there
better. Because now that it's gone, they've got the solidarity
tax to pay. So I'll shut up about it, even though it was the best
time of my life, wading knee-deep through the sewage,
crawling through the subterranean passageway.... My wife is
right when she says, "You were another man back then. We
had a real life...."

1962

IT WAS LIKE THE POPE when he goes on his trips to see
his people in Africa, say, or Poland, and nothing bad can happen to him: the great deportation king, when they finally
hauled him into court, he sat there in this cage, this glass cell,
but it was closed on three sides only. On the side where the
judges had their bench it was open. That's what Security ordered, so I made glass plates for only three sides of the box, but
I used special bulletproof glass. We were lucky to get the job,
my company, but then we're old hands at customers with
unusual requirements. We've done banks all over Israel and
Dizengoff Street, jewelers who have all kinds of fancy tsatskes
in their show windows and want to make sure no burglars can

get at them. My father before me, he was the foreman of a glass factory in Nuremberg, which was a real nice city back then, and they had customers as far away as Schweinfurt and Ingolstadt. There was plenty of work to go around till '38, when things fell apart all over. I don't need to tell you why. God, did I curse Father when I was a kid. He was so strict; he put me on night duty for days on end.

We were lucky, me and my kid brother, we got out in time. We were the only ones. Everybody else was still there when the war broke out and all of them, including my sisters, both of them, and every last cousin, they were all sent to Theresienstadt and from there how should I know? To Sobibor or Auschwitz maybe. Only Mama died—how do you say it again?—a natural death, of heart failure, I mean. Gerson—he's my brother—couldn't find out anything more, and he went poking around in Franconia and all over the place when the war was finally over. All he found out was the day deportations took place and that there were whole trainfuls from Nuremberg, which is where my family had lived forever.

So anyway, there in my glass box he sat, the man our papers called the mastermind of deportation. They wanted bulletproof, I gave them bulletproof. Sorry if my German's a little off—I left Germany age nineteen with my kid brother and we managed to get to Palestine by ship—but that guy in the box fumbling with the headset, his German was worse. The judges all said so, and they talk good German; his sentences went on forever, they said, and you couldn't make head or tail of them. But one thing I could understand, sitting there in the audience with ordinary people, was that everything he did he did because he was following orders. And that there were plenty of others who did things because they were following orders. But they were lucky: they were running around scot-free, earning good money even, Adenauer's secretary of state, for instance, the guy our Ben-Gurion had to negotiate with about the money.

So I said to myself, "Jankele," I said, "you should have made a hundred—what am I saying?—a thousand of those glass boxes. With a few more people you could have handled it easy. Another thing you could have done is whenever a new name came up—like Alois Brunner, say—you could have taken a tiny little glass box with just his name and put it like a kind of symbol between Eichmann's glass box and the judges' bench. On a special table. And by the end of the trial it would have been full, the table.

They wrote a lot about him and about evil and how evil is kind of ordinary—"banality" was the word they used. They stopped writing so much after they strung him up, but as long as the trial dragged on, the papers were full of him. His only competition was Gagarin, that Soviet guy in the space capsule, which made the Americans jealous as hell. But I remember saying to myself, "Jankele," I said, "looks like they're in the same boat, the two of them. Each in a box by himself." Only Gagarin's much more by himself. Because Eichmann's got people to talk to, at least since our side brought him back from that chicken farm in Argentina he owns. And he likes to talk. Most of all he likes to talk about how he'd rather have sent us Jews to Madagascar than to the gas chambers and that he never had anything against the Jews. He even admired the Jews for coming up with the idea of Zionism and doing such a good job of making it work, he said. And if he hadn't been ordered to take charge of the deportations, the Jews might even have been grateful to him for personally initiating the mass migration.

Well, I said to myself, "Jankele," I said, "maybe you should be grateful to Eichmann for letting you and your kid brother Gerson take part in the mass migration. But for the rest of the family you shouldn't be so grateful. Not for Father and all your aunts and uncles and your sisters and your pretty little cousins, about twenty all told." I wouldn't have minded talking to him about that, because he was certainly in the know about who went where and how my sisters and our hard-nosed father ended up. But I couldn't. There were witnesses enough without me. Besides, I was glad to take charge of his safety. I think he liked his bulletproof cell. Why else would he have smiled the way he did?

1963

AN INHABITABLE DREAM. An apparition come to stay. I was *so* taken with it! A ship, a salmon-pink music-steamer of audacious design lying at anchor hard by the hideous, all-dividing wall, grounded on a wasteland, thumbing its nose, its towering bow, at the barbarians, rising up—as we came to see when comparing it with other nearby buildings, modern as they were—beyond reality.

People called my praise a schoolgirl's effusions, but I wasn't ashamed of my enthusiasm. I bore the gibes of the elderly cloakroom attendants with forbearance, or, perhaps, arrogant equanimity, though I realized that as the daughter of a farmer from the North Sea bogs of Wilstermarsch and earnest music student occasionally supplementing her scholarship by hanging coats I had no business making loud and sanctimonious pronouncements. Besides, the gibes of my mature cloakroom colleagues were quite good-natured actually. "Our first flute is practicing her high notes again," they would say. I played the flute at the time.

And in fact it was Aurèle Nicolet, my much esteemed maestro, who encouraged enthusiasm in me (and, I imagine, many other schoolgirls inclined to effusion and rapture), the enthusiasm to make eloquent pleas for an idea that serves humanity, for the good ship *Philharmonie* run aground, because he too was a fireball, with a shock of flaming curly locks that, as I thought at the time, made his face seductively attractive. In any case, he immediately translated my image of the ship run aground into *le bateau échoué*.

Berliners, on the other hand, called upon their legendary wit, combining the tentlike elements in the construction with the centrality of the conductor and reducing the ingenious design to the "common" denominator of the Karajani Circus. Others praised and niggled at once. Professional jealousies came to the fore. The only person who really had something to say was a man I respect, Professor Julius Posener, and he made the following point: "Scharoun's job was to create a Piranesi-like space and turn its prisonlike character into something festive." But I still maintain it is a ship—a floating prison, if you will—whose inner life is inhabited, infused, dominated by music—the music captured in its space and immediately set free, if you will.

What about the acoustics? They were praised by everyone, nearly everyone. I was there, allowed to be there, when they tested them. Shortly before the official opening—for which occasion Karajan had naturally taken on the Ninth—I slipped into the concert hall. It was so dark I could scarcely make out the seats. The only shafts of light fell on the podium down in front. All at once a gruff but good-natured voice called to me out of the dark: "Don't just stand there, girl! Make yourself useful. Up on the podium! Double time!" And I, the hardheaded farmer's daughter always ready to answer back, did as I was told: rushed down to the front, clambered up into the light, and had a revolver thrust into my hand by a man who was later introduced to me as the acoustical engineer. Then the gruff voice emerged again from the dark of the honeycomb-encrusted concert hall: "All five bullets. One right after the other. Don't worry, girl! They're just blanks. Now! Now, I say!"

So I raised the revolver and pressed the trigger fearlessly. They later told me I "looked like an angel." Anyway, I stood there pressing the trigger five times in quick succession for the acoustics man to take his readings, and I could tell it had gone well. The gruff voice coming out of the dark turned out to belong to the architect, Hans Scharoun, whom I respect as much as I did my flute teacher. Which is why—though also following an inner voice—I've given up music and am now studying and am very much taken with architecture. From time to time—because I have no scholarship now—I go back to the Philharmonie in my capacity as cloakroom attendant. And so I have the chance to experience many times over how much music and architecture complement each other, especially when a naval architect both captures the music and sets it free.

1964

REALLY. I DIDN'T LEARN ABOUT all the awful things that happened there and everything that went with them until much later, to be precise, when we had to have a speedy wedding because I was pregnant, and we got lost in the Römer, which is where you go for your civil ceremony here in Frankfurt. Right. All those steps and the excitement of it all. Anyway, "You're in the wrong place," they told us. "You want to go two stories down. This is the trial."

"What trial?" I asked.

"Don't you read the papers? The Auschwitz trial!"

So we go downstairs. The witnesses are waiting. Not my parents—they were against the marriage at first. No, Heiner's mother, all nervous, and two friends of mine from the telephone company. Afterward we went to the Palmengarten—Heiner had reserved a table—for the real celebration. But I couldn't get that trial out of my mind, so I kept going back, even after I was in my fifth or sixth month and they moved it to the Frankenallee, the Gallus Haus, where there was a bigger room and more space, mostly for the public.

Heiner never went, not even when he had night duty at the freight depot where he works and could have come with me. But I told him what there was to tell. All the awful things and the numbers—they went into the millions. You couldn't keep track, because they kept coming up with new ones. Really. First they said three, then only two million at most—three or two million people gassed or killed in other ways. But the other thing that went on in the courtroom was just as bad, if not worse, because you could see it, and I kept telling Heiner about it until he said, "Lay off, will you? I was four, maybe five at the time. And you'd just been born."

Right, but Heiner's father and his uncle Kurt, who's this real nice guy, they were both soldiers and in Russia too. Heiner's mother once told me. But when the family finally all got together at Beate's christening and I tried to bring up the subject of the trial and Kaduk and Boger, all they would say was, "We didn't know a thing about that. When did you say it was? 'Forty-three? All we could think about then was retreat." And Uncle Kurt said, "When we had to get out of the Crimea and could finally go home on furlough, what did we find but our houses in ruins. What do you hear about the Yanks and the Brits and their terrorist bombings? Not a word. And why? Because they won, and the losers are always to blame. So lay off, will you, Heidi?"

But Heiner had to listen. I forced him to, because I was sure it was no coincidence that we got lost in the Römer and found out about Auschwitz, and, even worse, Birkenau, where the ovens were. He didn't want to believe some of it at first, I mean, that one of the defendants ordered a prisoner to drown his own father and the prisoner went out of his mind and because of that, just because of that, the defendant shot him dead. Or what happened in the tiny courtyard between Block 10 and Block 11 at what they called the black wall: executions! Thousands of them. Nobody could give the judge an exact number. A lot of people seemed to be having trouble with their memories. When I told Heiner about the swing named after Wilhelm Boger, who used it to get the prisoners to talk, he refused to understand. So I took a piece of paper and drew what one of the witnesses had rigged up for the trial to show to the judges: a pole with a prisoner in those striped pajamas hanging from it like a puppet and tied in such a way that this Boger guy could hit him between the legs. Right, in the testicles. "And you know, Heiner," I said, "while the witness was telling the court what Boger did, Boger himself sat there off to the right, in the dock, behind the witness, sat there smiling, grinning...."

Really! Is he human? I asked myself. But there were witnesses who claimed this Boger behaved decently in other ways
and always took care of the flowers at headquarters. The only
people he really hated were Poles. Jews less. The gas chambers
and the crematorium in the main camp and in Birkenau,
where there were lots of Gypsies in special barracks and all of
them were gassed—that was even harder to understand than
the swing. What I didn't tell Heiner was that Boger looked a
little like his uncle Kurt, especially when he smiled, but that
wouldn't have been fair to Uncle Kurt, who was perfectly
harmless, your typical good guy.

Still, the Boger swing and all the rest—it kept coming back
to haunt us, especially when our wedding anniversary rolled
around and we remembered thinking, because I was pregnant
with Beate at the time, "Let's hope none of this has rubbed off
on her."

Then last spring Heiner said to me, "If I get some time off
this summer, maybe we can take a trip to Cracow. Mama's been
thinking about it for quite some time. She actually comes from
Upper Silesia. I've been to Orbis, the Polish travel agency...."

But I don't know. Maybe it's not for us; maybe it won't
work out. Though it's a lot easier to get a visa now. Really.
Auschwitz isn't far from Cracow. They even have sightseeing
tours, the brochure says....

1965

ONE EYE ON THE REARVIEW MIRROR, but full speed ahead.
All the way from Passau to Kiel. Scouring the provinces.

Canvassing for votes. Glued to the wheel of our borrowed DKW, Gustav Steffen, a student from Münster who, because he's not from the best of families (he has a Catholic proletarian background; his father voted for the Center Party) worked as an apprentice to an automobile mechanic while taking academic courses at night school, and now (the two of us are campaigning for the Social Democrats) he is deftly, efficiently—"We're not like the other side; we're on time"—ticking off the stops on our itinerary: "Yesterday Mainz, today Würzburg. Churches and bells. A conservative stronghold with liberal incursions along the edges...."

We pull up in front of the hall. Since I am assigned to the rearview mirror, I read the text of a banner held high, like a holy message, by the always well-groomed Young Union boys first in reverse, then *in natura*—"What is an atheist doing in the city of Saint Kilian?"—and do not come up with an answer until I enter the jam-packed hall, the front rows occupied by students whose badges identify them as belonging to duel-fighting societies, but the answer—"I'm looking for Tilman Riemenschneider"—puts an end to the general hissing, invoking as it does the sculptor and mayor of Würzburg whose hands were chopped off during the Peasant Wars by the bishop and who now, explicitly present, informs my speech, "I Sing Thee, Democracy!" (Walt Whitman, slightly altered for purposes of the campaign)...

What the rearview mirror doesn't show must be sought in the memory. Our trip was organized by students from the Social Democratic Student League and the Liberal Student League, which in Cologne, Hamburg, Tübingen—everywhere—were collections of lost souls, but when it was all no more than a dream I cooked up a conspiratorial pot of lentil soup and things started moving. The Social Democratic Party had no idea of its undeserved good fortune (though at least it praised our poster with my rooster crowing the initials of the Party). The comrades were surprised that we managed to fill large halls even though we charged admission, but they were not particularly happy with much of what we said, for instance, my widely quoted demand that we should finally recognize the Oder-Neisse border, that is to say, renounce all claims on East Prussia, Silesia, Pomerania, and—painful as it was for me—Danzig. But that went beyond the Party platform, as did my polemic on 218, the abortion paragraph. On the other hand, they admitted, a good number of young voters responded. In Munich, for instance...

Today all 3,500 seats of the Krone Circus are occupied. I use my poem "The Steamboiler Effect" against the epidemic hissing of the extreme right wing, evident here too, and here too the poem makes an impression:

> Look at this people united in hiss.
> Hissophile, hissoplex, hissomaniacal.
> Hissing costs nothing and makes you feel good.
> But who pays to make this elite clan of hissers?

I was so happy to see friends looking back at me from the audience. Some of them are no longer with us—Hans Werner Richter, my literary foster father, who had his doubts before I went on the road, but then said, "Oh, go ahead. I've done my bit: the Grünwald Circle, the antinuclear movement. Now it's your turn for a little wear and tear...."

But it's nothing like that, Hans. I'm learning so much, uncovering long-standing mold, communities where the Thirty Years' War is still being waged. Cloppenburg, for example, our next destination and more Catholic than the Pope. On we drive through the Münster flatlands, Gustav whistling away. Cows, cows, and more cows; cows multiplying and being fruitful in the rearview mirror. Could even the cows be Catholic here? The closer we get to Cloppenburg the more tractors we see, tractors packed with large peasant families on their way to the hall we've rented, on their way to hear the devil incarnate....

It takes me two hours to make it through "The Choice Is Yours," which usually speeds along in less than half that time. I could have done a rip-roaring "Paean to Willy" or "The Emperor's New Clothes," but the tumult wouldn't have subsided if I'd read a passage from the New Testament. When they threw eggs, I responded with a reference to "agricultural subsidies squandered." This was not hissing country. People were more physical here. Some of the farm boys who pelted me with eggs invited me back to Cloppenburg four years later as converted Young Socialists, but this time I tried a little impromptu theology on them: "Quit it, boys, or you'll have to go to your confessor next week...."

We left the scene of the crime with a basketful of eggs: the area around Vechta and Cloppenburg is known for its thriving chicken farms. Gustav Steffen, who was to lose his young life in an automobile accident several years later, looked over at his bespattered front-seat companion and up at the rearview mirror and said, "We'll never win the election, but I bet we picked up a few votes here."

Back in Berlin, while I slept soundly, someone set fire to our front door and frightened Anna and the children. A thing or two may have changed in Germany since then, but not in matters of arson.

1966

SUDDENLY THEY STOPPED using the sublime word "being" in both the modern orthography, *Sein,* and the older one, *Seyn.* Suddenly, as if essence, reason, all being, and the all-nihilating nil were empty words, my very self was called into question and I was being called upon to bear witness. So after all these years—and because things going on at present bring back disjointed memories of, say, the German mark replacing the Reichsmark fifty years ago or that ominous year 1968 whose thirtieth anniversary is being celebrated like an end-of-season sale—I have decided to note down what happened to me one afternoon during the current summer semester. Suddenly, after giving my Wednesday contemporary poetry seminar a meticulous account of the textual correspondences between Celan's "Death Fugue" and "Todtnauberg" (though passing over in silence the memorable encounter between Celan and Heidegger at the latter's Todtnauberg cottage), I was deeply troubled by a series of questions that were too time-specific to be purely existential, to wit: Who was I then? Who am I today? What has become of the once "being-heedless" yet still radical sixty-eighter who only two years earlier just happened to be in Berlin when the first anti-Vietnam demonstration took place?

No, not five thousand, two thousand if that many, two thousand of us, duly registered as a political demonstration, marched arm in arm from Steinplatz down Hardenberg-strassse to the Amerikahaus, shouting as we went. All kinds of groups and subgroups—the League of German Socialist Students, the Social Democratic College League, the Liberal Student League, the Debating Society, and the Protestant Student

Community—called upon their members to take part. Some of us—myself included, if I remember correctly—had gone to Butter-Hoffmann and bought up large quantities of low-grade eggs to bombard what we called the imperialist establishment—egg throwing was all the rage then with both students and hidebound farmers—so I too threw eggs and chanted "Americans out of Vietnam!" and "Killer Johnson!" The demonstration was to have ended in a debate, and the head of the Amerikahaus, who seemed perfectly liberal, was ready to oblige, but the collective egg-throw took its place, and when it was over we marched down the Kurfürstendamm and Uhlandstrasse back to Steinplatz unhampered by the police. I can still remember the banners: "Leathernecks! Pack Your Bags!" and "United Against the War!" It was regrettable that some East German officials infiltrated our ranks, because even though they made no headway with their propaganda the Springer papers went to town with the story.

But how did *I* come to march in those ranks? Join arms with them. Throw eggs with them. Shout myself hoarse. I with my conservative, middle-class background, I who had studied religion and philosophy with Taubes, tried Husserl, enjoyed Scheler, inhaled Heidegger, and could easily have seen myself taking his lead. I was averse to anything that smacked of the real world, which I regarded as a mere "frame," and dismissed anything connected with it, like politics, as "being-heedless." And now here I was, joining a party, reviling the President of the United States of America and his ally, South Vietnam's dictator Ky (though I was not yet willing to let myself go and shout Ho! Ho! Ho Chi Minh!). Who was I, actually, thirty years ago?

The question kept eating away at me as the students gave

their papers. (There were only two or three, and they didn't require my full attention.) The students may have noticed that their professor was only half listening, but the question directed at me by one of them—namely, why Celan had abridged the line from the Todtnauberg poem "hope, today, for a thinker's coming (forthwith coming) word," deleting the two words in parentheses from the final version, which occurs in a volume entitled *Lightforce*—this central question brought me back to the reality of the university; however, because it was put so bluntly, it brought to mind a situation I had had to deal with at the time: just before the beginning of the 1966–67 winter semester I left the turbulent streets of Berlin, the scene of larger and larger demonstrations, to study in Freiburg.

From there I came here. I was much taken with Baumann in German literature. I tried to interpret my return as a Heideggerian "turn." The answer I gave to the student, her provocative question being meant to elicit a reply "forthwith," made reference to the controversial philosopher's temporary rapprochement with the National Socialist regime and his determination to enshroud any misdeeds in silence. It clearly begged the question and was in fact so unsatisfactory that I posed it to myself again immediately afterward.

That's right. It was to be near the great shaman that I fled to Freiburg, where he taught; it was he or at least his aura that lured me there. I became familiar with sublime words at an early age, because my father, who was chief physician at a Black Forest sanatorium and spent all his days off walking along trails in the woods, would take me from Todtnau to Todtnauberg and invariably pointed out the philosopher's modest cottage....

1967

MY WEDNESDAY SEMINAR DRAGGED ON, animated by little more than a butterfly that had flown through the open window, yet still involved in matters compelling enough to take me back to my long since nullified existence and make me pose such momentous questions as, What actually drew me away from Berlin? Shouldn't I have been there on 2 June and taken my place among the demonstrators at Schöneberg Town Hall? Wouldn't I, who claimed to hate the Shah of Iran, have been an appropriate target for the Shah's Iranian supporters, who attacked the demonstrators with slats?

The answer to all the above questions was, with only minor reservations, yes. I could have declared my solidarity with the cause and made myself known to the police by carrying a sign that said "Immediate Release of Iranian Students!" And since at the very time the Shah was visiting the Town Hall a parliamentary commission was studying the advisability of raising study fees, I might easily have joined the demonstrators and sung that idiotic old carnival chestnut "Who Will Pay the Piper?" And when the Shah and his Farah Diba went to the opera, accompanied in statesmanlike fashion by Albertz, the reigning mayor of Berlin, I might have been forced by the police into the passageway between Krumme Strasse and Sesenheimer Strasse and been bludgeoned to death during the performance. After all, I asked myself or something inside me asked, Why shouldn't I have been the one and not the literature student Benno Ohnesorg who was done in by Operation Foxhunt? Like me he considered himself a pacifist and belonged to the Protestant Student Community; like me he was twenty-six and enjoyed walking barefoot in summer. I could just as well have been the one they blotted out, polished off. But I kept my distance both physically and—with the help of a philosopher who after his "turn" gave himself up to serenity— ontologically. So he, not I, was the one they clubbed down; so his head, not mine, was the one a certain police detective in mufti by the name of Kurras struck with his PPK pistol, struck with such force over the right ear that his brain gushed out and his skull was smashed to bits....

All of a sudden I shattered the bliss of my students' inter- pretations of the two important poems by erupting with "It's a disgrace! Kurras sailed through two inquests and went on working in communications at Berlin Police Headquarters until he retired!" I said no more, but saw the provocatively mocking gaze of the inquisitive student trained on me, felt it penetrate my innermost being, my timorous being, which had been plagued by analogous questions since earliest childhood. When did it occur, my "turn"? What caused me to take leave from "merely being"? And precisely when during all those years did the sublime take hold of me, never—a temporary "turning away" notwithstanding—to let go?

It may have happened a month later, on 24 July, when the poet arrived in Freiburg after a rather long illness and, over- coming his initial misgivings, agreed to meet the philosopher, whose questionable past had given him pause, before the for- mal poetry reading for which he had been invited. He refused to be photographed with Heidegger, however, and although he later relented, the time for a picture worthy of the occasion had passed.

These anecdotes and more I told my afternoon seminar, be- cause I was now released from my inner questioning, the in- quisitive student's queries having adroitly led me to concentrate on relating my testimony of that complex confrontation. You see, I was the one Professor Baumann sent to reconnoiter the bookshop windows in Freiburg: at the philosopher's behest all available volumes of the poet's oeuvre were to be displayed with due dignity. And lo and behold, everything—from the early collection *Poppy and Memory* to *Speech Grille* and *The No One's Rose*—was physically if not always conceptually available. I even managed to come up with some rare special editions.

I was also the one assigned to arrange the poet's visit high in the Black Forest, where the philosopher's cottage awaited him, for the morning of the next day. But once more Celan took umbrage at Heidegger's comportment during the dark years and apparently went so far as to call him—quoting himself—a *Meister aus Deutschland,* thereby, if only tacitly, bringing death into play. It was therefore uncertain whether he would accept the invitation. He long seemed undecided and unapproachable.

In the end we did make the journey the next morning, though the sky was overcast, leaden. After the visit to the cottage and the momentous conversation or silence, at which no one, myself included, was allowed to be present, we met at a friendly café in Sankt Blasien. He did not seem at all out of sorts. Clearly the poet now found the thinker acceptable. Both were soon on the way to the Horbach Moor, from whose eastern edge we set off on a path of logs pounded into the dirt. Because the weather had remained nasty and the poet's shoes were, as he put it, "insufficiently rustic," we stopped before going very far, found an inn, took the table in the crucifix corner, and had a leisurely lunch. No, no. No mention was made of current events like the Berlin riots and the recently announced student death. One topic of conversation was the world of plants, and the poet turned out to know the names of as many herbs as the thinker—if not more. In addition, Celan could name a goodly number of them not only in Latin but also in Romanian, Hungarian, and even Yiddish. He was from Czernowitz, after all, in the multilingual region of Bukovina.

Although I imparted these and other reminiscences to the students, I could respond to the question posed by the inquisitive one among them about what I thought had or had not been spoken of in the cottage only by referring to the poem "Todtnauberg" itself. I pointed out many clues. The plant name "arnica," which the poet also calls *Augentrost*, "comfort for the eyes," allows of many interpretations. The well in front of the cottage with its three-dimensional star is likewise rich in associations. Then too there is the guest book, which plays a central role in the poem—serves as its heart, one might say— and which the poet signs, wondering fearfully "whose name it had before mine," yet surely full of "hope, today, for a thinker's coming word in the heart"; moreover, the words in parentheses, "forthwith coming," later deleted by the poet, lend a certain urgency to the wish, which, as we know, was never granted. What we do not know, what remains conjecture, can scarcely be surmised and therefore keeps the wound open is what was put into words or kept silent in the cottage....

Such more or less is what I told my seminar, though I never admitted to either the group or the inquisitive student how often I had imagined the conversation in the cottage, because between the rootless poet and the *Meister aus Deutschland,* between the Jew with the invisible yellow star and the former rector of Freiburg University with his perfectly round yet likewise invisible Party emblem, between the namer and the concealer, between the survivor constantly pronouncing himself dead and the harbinger of being and the coming God, the Un-utterable Words should have been found and were not, not a one.

And this silence kept its silence. I never told the seminar the reasons for my flight from Berlin, I shook off the inquisitive student's gaze and failed to reveal what had temporarily alienated me from the sublime the following year and, fleetingly again, driven me from Freiburg and into the turbulence of Frankfurt, the city where, immediately after leaving our university town, Paul Celan made the first draft of the poem "Todtnauberg."

1968

THE SEMINAR SEEMED PLACATED, but I was uneasy. No sooner had I used my carefully mediated authority to read the cottage poem as a late echo of the "Death Fugue" and challenge to the *Meister aus Deutschland,* death personified, than I found myself back on the spot: What made you leave Freiburg just after Easter in the following year? What "turn" turned you, who had always hearkened to the silence between words and felt at home in the sublimely fragmentary, in Hölderlin's gradual descent into muteness—what turned you into a radical sixty-eighter?

If it was not a delayed reaction to the murder of Benno Ohnesorg, then it was the attempt on the life of Rudi Dutschke that made you a revolutionary, verbally at least: you exchanged the jargon of "essentiality" for the jargon of the dialectic. Such was more or less the explanation I came up with, though I was uncertain of the deeper motivation for the shift and tried, for as long as my Wednesday seminar took care of itself, to quell the sudden uprising of past vagaries.

The first thing I did when I got to Frankfurt was to prove my new "turn" by ditching German literature in favor of sociology. And so I took courses with Habermas and Adorno. Although we (I soon joined the League of German Socialist Students) hardly let the latter get a word in edgeways, we considered him as much of an authority as the antiauthoritarian spirit of the times allowed. Since students were revolting against their teachers everywhere—and with particular vehemence in Frankfurt—we occupied the University, but then Adorno, the great Adorno, felt compelled to call the police, and it was immediately evacuated. One of our most eloquent spokesmen, a student named Hans-Jürgen Krahl, whose power of speech impressed even the master of negation and who had belonged to the Fascist Ludendorff League and reactionary Young Union several years earlier only to make the absolute "turn" to Dutschke follower and opposition leader— this Krahl was arrested, but released a few days later, and immediately took to agitating against the Bonn emergency laws and—recent events notwithstanding—his much revered mentor. On the last day of the Book Fair, 23 September, a panel discussion at the Gallus Haus, where the first Auschwitz trial had taken place a few years earlier, nearly ended in violence and in any case proved Adorno's downfall.

What turbulent times! In my sheltered seminar, disconcerted only by the provocative questions of a particularly intransigent young woman, I tried to bridge the thirty-year gap and work my way back into a discussion that soon turned into a tribunal of public opinion. Violent words were in fashion at the time, and I too shouted them from the crowd, I too came up with "far-out" comments, hoping to out-Krahl Krahl, thinking only, like him and everybody else, of exposing the egghead master of a dialectic that made a contradiction of everything, now standing there flustered and groping for words. And expose him we did. A number of women students crowding together at his feet had forced him to break off his remarks by baring their breasts to him, and in return they demanded to see him, the sensitive professor, naked. Stiff, plump, and clothed as always in good solid bourgeois attire, he was now to be, so to say, stripped of his authority; he was to divest himself piece by piece of the theory protecting him and hand the tattered results over to the Revolution—Krahl & Co. were adamant on that point—to make such use of them as it saw fit; in other words, he was to make himself useful. He was still needed, they told him. At the march on Bonn for starters. They had to squeeze what they could out of his prestige with the ruling class. But in principle he was done for.

I believe I was the one who called out that last remark. Or was it that something or somebody called it out of me? What caused me to support violence with words? The moment the faces of the moderately diligent Celan-seminar students plodding their way toward a degree came back into focus, I began to doubt I had ever been a radical. Maybe we, maybe I had done it all in jest. Maybe I was confused, misunderstanding precisely delineated phrases like "repressive tolerance" as I had earlier misinterpreted the Master's verdict against "being-heedlessness." Krahl, who was reputed to be Adorno's most gifted student, loved to set traps and take still raw concepts to extremes. True, there were other voices. Habermas, for instance. But once he started going on about the threat of leftist

Fascism—at the Hannover congress, say—we were through
with him. Then there was that writer with the walrus mustache who'd sold out to the Social Democrats and thought it
his duty to accuse us of "blind actionist tactics...."

The hall was in turmoil. As was I, I can only presume. So
what moved me to leave before it was over? Was I less radical
than I realized? Was I unable to tolerate Krahl's gaze? (He
had only one eye and consequently wore dark glasses.) Or was
I trying to escape the pitiful image of Theodor W. Adorno
humiliated?

Near the exit, which was crammed with people still trying to
get in, I was accosted by an elderly gentleman who had Book
Fair written all over him. "What nonsense you talk," he said
with a slight accent. "Prague is full of Soviet tanks for a month,
and you talk only about 'the collective learning process of the
people.' Come and see beautiful Bohemia and you will learn
collectively what is power and what is powerlessness. You know
nothing and think you know all...."

"Of course," I blurted out with no regard to my students,
who looked up shocked from their interpretations of the
poems, "there were other things going on in the summer
of '68: Czechoslovakia was occupied—and with the help of
German soldiers. Within a year Adorno was dead, of a heart
attack apparently. In February 1970 Krahl died in an automobile accident. And in the same year, never having received the
hoped-for word from Heidegger, Paul Celan flung what remained of his life from a bridge into the Seine. We don't know
the exact date...."

The seminar dispersed. Only the inquisitive student remained in her seat. Since she seemed to have nothing to ask, I
too held my tongue. She probably just wanted to be alone with

me. Neither of us said a word. But when she finally stood, she did come out with two sentences. "Well, I'll be going," she said. "You've got nothing more to give."

1969

IT MUST HAVE BEEN A GREAT TIME, even though I was classified as difficult. "Carmen is difficult," people would say, or "Carmen's a problem child." And not only because my parents were divorced and my father was mostly off doing construction work somewhere. But we had other problem children in our play group, grown-up problem children. I have in mind the students from Ruhr University who started the group in the first place—it was originally meant for kids of single-mother students—and wanted everything to be anti-authoritarian, even after they took in proletarian children, which is what they called us. That caused a lot of trouble, though, because we were used to strong-arm tactics, or, rather, our parents were. But my mother—who was the cleaning lady at the play group because the student mothers didn't want to dirty their hands—told the other neighborhood mothers, "Give the Reds a chance to do it their way." "Reds," she called them because the faction that wanted to open up the group to us "underprivileged" kids was on the extreme left, which meant there was all kinds of infighting, and the parent-teacher meetings would go on till after midnight and all but end in blows, or so my mother told me.

But chaos reigned pretty much across the board at the time, from what I can make out. There was trouble everywhere you looked. Elections coming up too. Though we had a sign at the play-group door, my mother tells me: Class Politics Over Party Politics. And we fought the class struggle on a daily basis. Because the leftist students had collected a bunch of toys for the play group, and all the kids—but mostly us proletarian kids—wanted them for themselves. I was one of the most aggressive, my mother tells me. We didn't have much to do with the elections, except that once the students took us to a demonstration at the University, which was this humongous concrete slab, and we had to march back and forth shouting, "Ax the new fat cats! Social Democrats!" But they won anyway, or at least their Willy did. Not that us kids knew anything about it, because that summer the TV was full of something else, namely, the moon landing, and there was nothing else we cared about watching—the other kids at home and me at our neighbor Frau Pietzke's. So we covered the walls with "antiauthoritarian" (we chose the subject matter) paintings and chalk drawings of the landing: the two men on the moon, their funny get-ups, and the lunar module, the *Eagle,* it was called. We had a lot of fun, I bet. But little problem-child me apparently made trouble for the parent-teacher crowd again, because in addition to the men—Armstrong and Aldrin, their names were—I drew and colored in something I'd seen very clearly on the TV screen, namely, the Stars and Stripes, the American flag, planted firmly on the moon in all its glory. Well, the students were real pissed off, the super-leftists especially. So they turned on the psychology. But no amount of cajoling seemed to work. My mother remembers that only a minority—the students who were just antiauthoritarian, not Maoist or part of some other revolutionary faction—voted against the resolution to wash my painting—"Stars *und* Stripes," as my mother still calls it—off the wall. And when one of the students—he's something like the secretary of state in Bonn now, you know?—when he tried to talk me into planting a bright red flag on the moon I wouldn't have it. I didn't cry. Not me. I stood up to him. I've got nothing against red. It just wasn't the flag I saw on television, that's all. So when the student kept at it, I threw a tantrum and trampled all the colored chalk and tubes of paint, including the ones the other kids were using, which made a terrible mess for my mother—who, as I say, cleaned up every day and was paid by the students, also mothers—to scrape up off the floor. Which is why when she runs into mothers from those days she still says, "My Carmen was a real problem child."

You can be sure I won't bring my kids up like that—if I ever have any, that is. No, I'll bring them up normal. Still, the year they put men on the moon and my mother got to vote for her Willy must have been a great time, and even now I have these real vivid dreams about the play group.

1970

MY PAPER WOULD NEVER PRINT IT. They want the goody-goody stuff: "He took all the guilt on his shoulders…" or "The Chancellor suddenly fell to his knees" or—to really lay it on thick—"went down on his knees for Germany!"

"Suddenly" my eye! It couldn't have been more calculated. And you can be sure it was that shady character who put him up to it—you know, his personal spy and negotiator, the one who's so good at selling the German population his disgraceful renunciation of ur-German territory. So now the big chief— the big drunk—is playing the Catholic. Genuflecting! What does that guy believe in? Nothing. It's pure show. Though you've got to hand it to him, from the publicity point of view it was a stroke of genius. Pow! Out of nowhere. And against all the rules. It looks like the same old routine: you lay down your wreath, you follow your predecessor, your head still bent, then you lift your chin and gaze boldly into the distance, and before you know it you're being whisked off to Wilanów Castle, where the cognac and champagne stand waiting. But no, he's got something up his sleeve: down he goes, down on the wet granite, with no support from his hands, no, he clasps his hands in front of his balls and puts a holier-than-the-Pope look on his face, holds out for a good minute or so till the shutters stop clicking, then picks himself up, but not the easy way, first one foot, then the other, no, in one go—he must've practiced it for days in front of the mirror—and then he stands there as if he'd just seen the Holy Ghost, as if to show the Poles—no, the whole world—how photogenic eating humble pie can be. Oh, he's got it down to an art; he even made the rain a part of it. But if I pull out all my cynical stops, the paper will never print it. And that despite the fact that not one of the editors can wait to see the last of the knee-bend Chancellor, bounced out or voted out, it doesn't matter. Just out!

So let me have another go at it. "Where the Warsaw Ghetto once stood, where in May 1943 it was so brutally and sense-lessly destroyed, the Chancellor of Germany knelt alone today at a memorial before which, on this cold, wet December day and every other day, the flames from two bronze torches flailed in the wind. He knelt to give expression to his remorse, re-morse for heinous deeds done in the name of Germany, thereby taking the guilt upon his own shoulders, though he did not in fact bear the guilt himself...."

That I can get printed anywhere. The man who bears his cross and suffers in silence! But why not throw in a little local color. Of the malicious variety. Can't hurt. A hint at the Poles' displeasure when he thumbed his nose at the Tomb of the Unknown Soldier, which is a real national monument, in favor of the Jews. All it takes is a few leading questions to bring out the anti-Semite in a Pole. Not so long ago the Polish students acted up the way the students in Germany and Paris did, but then the Minister of the Interior, Moczar, gave the word and the police started clobbering "Zionist provocateurs," and a few thousand Party officials, professors, writers, and other high-powered intellectuals, mostly Jews, were given their walking papers and ended up in Sweden or Israel. Well, you won't hear a word about that around here. And *we* think shouldering guilt is good form. People here make a big thing about the man's "Catholic stance, which gladdens the heart of every good Pole," but what really matters is that a man who betrayed his Fatherland, who fought in a Norwegian uniform against us, against Germans, has come here with his retinue— a Krupp executive, some leftist writers, and assorted intellectuals—to hand our Pomerania, Silesia, and East Prussia to the Poles on a platter, and then does his knee-bend number for them to boot.

But there's no point in trying. My paper would never print it. They'd keep it under wraps. They'd take the agency report. What do I care, anyway? I'm from the Rhineland, a happy-go-lucky type. And Breslau, Stettin, Danzig—what are they to me? I'll just do the mood thing: the Polish hand kiss, the magnificent restoration of the old town, Wilanów Castle and a few other showpieces while the economy is in a shambles... empty shop windows... queues for meat.... So Poland wants millions in credit, and I'm sure our knee-bend émigré Chancellor has promised same to his Communist pals. He makes my blood boil. It's not because he's illegitimate.... Those things happen.... It's just... It's everything about him.... When I saw him kneeling there in the rain... It was revolting.... I hate the guy's guts....

Will he be amazed when he gets home. They'll tear him limb from limb, him and his Commie contracts. And in lots of papers, not just mine. But it *was* a stroke of genius falling on his knees like that.

1971

YOU COULD MAKE A NOVEL OUT OF IT, really you could. She was my best friend. We would come up with the craziest things, the most hair-raising things, but never this. It all began when discos were opening up everywhere, and even though I was more into concerts and also had my mother's season the-ater tickets because her health was starting to go, I talked Uschi into coming to one with me. We'd just see what it was like, we said—and stayed all night.

She looked great with her curly ginger hair and freckles. And that Swabian accent! A little saucy but always a scream. I couldn't get over how she'd give a guy the come-on without really committing herself; it made me feel like a nerd, like I weighed every word I said.

Still, I really dug the music: "Hold That Train..." Bob Dylan of course. But Santana too and Deep Purple. And Pink Floyd—we really grooved on Pink Floyd. "Atom Heart

Mother…" It really turned us on. Though Uschi was more a Steppenwolf freak. "Born to Be Wild…" She really let herself go, something I could never quite do.

Things never went too far, though. Oh, we'd pass a joint around, two maybe, but who didn't back then? There was absolutely no danger involved, and my tolerance was pretty high anyway. Besides, my stewardess exams were coming up, and I was already working domestic flights, so I had less and less time for discos and pretty much lost track of Uschi, which was a shame but unavoidable. In August 1970 I switched to BEA's London flights and during the little time I spent in Stuttgart I had other problems, because my mother was going downhill fast, and my father… But that's another story.

Anyway, Uschi got into harder stuff while I was gone. Nepal shit, most likely. And then all of a sudden she was on the needle, shooting heroin. By the time I found out—and I found out from her parents, nice, unassuming people—she was too far gone. And what made things worse, she got pregnant and had no idea who the father was. No, it was a real tragedy, because she was still in school at the time, interpreters school, but what she really wanted was to be a stewardess like me. "Get out and see the world." God, if she knew how hard the job is, especially the long-distance flights. But she was my best friend, so I'd buck her up and say, "You can do it. You've got your whole life ahead of you…."

Well, what happened was this. At first she was all for having the baby, but then she decided against it because of her habit and went from doctor to doctor—with no luck, of course. I tried to help. I wanted her to go to London, because there she could have it done for the equivalent of a thousand marks before the third month and a bit more afterward and I had addresses from a woman I worked with—a Cross Road nursing home, for instance; I even offered to pay for her flight and room and board and incidental expenses, but she'd say yes sometimes and no sometimes, and got harder and harder to deal with on a personal basis.

In the end she had the abortion somewhere in the mountains, the Swäbische Alb. It was done by a couple—the husband had a glass eye—a couple of quacks. It must have been unreal. Really. A soap-and-water solution and a giant needle up the uterus. It didn't take long. The fetus and all went straight into the toilet bowl. One flush and it was over. A boy apparently.

That did her in more than shooting up. No, you probably have to say it was the two together—the habit she couldn't kick and the awful visit to the abortionists—that brought her to the edge. Not that she didn't put up a fight. But she was never a hundred percent clean until a charity provided me with an address in the country near Lake Constance, a halfway house kind of, something like a big farm run by a group of really nice anthroposophists, who were trying to come up with a drug therapy based on Rudolf Steiner's methods: medical eurythmics, painting, organic gardening, and stockbreeding—that kind of thing.

Anyway, I arranged for them to take her in. She liked it there. She started laughing a little, really came back to life, though in other ways it was unreal: the cattle kept getting loose and stampeding all over the place, and the toilets! They lacked the most basic things because the legislature in Stuttgart refused to give them a subsidy. They had internal problems too, with the group discussions especially. But that didn't bother Uschi. She just laughed. And she stayed on even after the main house burned down, which they later found out was due to some mice that had built a nest on a stovepipe hidden away somewhere and the straw began to smolder and eventually burst into flames. Anyway, she helped to set up emergency quarters in the barn and all, and things were going really well until this popular magazine came out with a cover story entitled "We've All Had Abortions."

Unfortunately I was the one who gave it to her. I brought it with me on a visiting day because I thought the flashy cover and all the pictures inside—there were passport pictures of several hundred women including film stars like Sabine Sinjen, Romy Schneider, Senta Berger, and so on—would cheer her up a little. The public prosecutor's office probably looked into the matter—abortion was against the law, after all—but nothing happened to the women: they were too well known. That's the way it always is. And Uschi got a real high, as she put it, from how brave they'd all been. She wanted to do her bit too, and sent a passport picture and a statement to the editors. She got a prompt rejection letter: the detailed account of her heroin addiction and the quack abortionists was too much for them. Calling attention to so extreme a case might do the cause more harm than good, they said. At a later date perhaps. The campaign against Paragraph 218 was not over by a long shot.

Can you believe it? A knee-jerk reaction. Cold as ice. Uschi couldn't handle it. She disappeared a few days after the letter came. We looked all over. Me and her parents. As soon as I could take time off I scoured the discos. There was no sign of her anywhere. They finally found her lying in the ladies' room at the Stuttgart station. She'd OD'd. The golden shot, they call it.

Of course I blame myself. To this day. She was my best

friend, after all. I wanted nothing more than to take her by the hand, fly her to London, deliver her to the nursing home, be there for her afterward, give her moral support—that's what you needed, wasn't it, Uschi? Actually I wanted to name our daughter Ursula, but my husband, who's really considerate and takes wonderful care of her—I still fly for BEA— thought it would be better if I wrote something about her instead....

1972

I'M HE NOW. He lives in Hannover-Langenhagen and is an elementary-school teacher. He—no longer I—never had an easy time of it. Unable to complete the secondary-school academic curriculum, he worked as an apprentice in business, but was forced to abandon that as well. He sold cigarettes, joined the army and rose to the rank of corporal, then enrolled in a private commercial school, but he was not allowed to take the examinations for the degree because he lacked the academic prerequisites. He went to England to improve his English and worked there in a car wash. He thought of studying Spanish in Barcelona. Finally a friend in Vienna tried something called success psychology on him and he plucked up the courage to go back to school in Hannover, where he managed to get into the teacher-training college without the formal academic prerequisites and eventually qualify as a teacher and where he is currently a member of the Union for Education and Research and even head of the Young Teachers Committee, a pragmatic leftist who believes in changing society step by step and dreams of doing so in a wing chair he picked up for a song in a junk shop. All at once he hears a ring at the door of his Walsroder Strasse second-floor apartment.

I—who is he—open the door. A girl with long brown hair asks to speak to me, to him. "Can the two of you put up two of us for a night?" She says "the two of you" because somebody must have told her that he or I live with a girl. He and I say yes.

Later, he says, I began to have my doubts, which my girlfriend echoed at breakfast. "We can only assume…" she said. But we went to school as usual. (She teaches too, but at a secondary school.) We had a class outing that day. We went to a bird sanctuary outside Walsrode. After school we still had our doubts. "They've probably moved in by now. I gave the girl with the long hair the key to the place."

So he talks it over with a friend—I too would certainly have talked it over with a friend—and his friend says what his girlfriend said at breakfast: "Dial 110…" He dials the number (with my consent) and asks to speak to the Baader-Meinhof Special Unit. The Special Unit people prick up their ears, say, "We'll follow the lead," and do so. Soon their plainclothesmen and the janitor are keeping an eye on the front door. They see a woman and a young man enter. The janitor asks who they're looking for. The teacher, they say. "Right," says the janitor, "he lives on the second floor, but I don't think he's in." A while later the young man comes back down, goes out and finds a telephone booth; he is arrested as he is dropping coins into the slot. He has a pistol on him.

The teacher is politically to the left of me, I'm sure. Sitting in his junk-shop wing chair, he is wont to dream himself into a progressive future. He believes in the "emancipation process of the underprivileged." The Baader-Meinhof position of a Hannover professor who, in leftist circles, is nearly as well known as Habermas—"The signals they are sending with their bombs are will-o'-the-wisps"—more or less coincides with his own: "These people have given the right the arguments they need to discredit the entire spectrum of the left."

That corresponds to my view of the matter. That is why he and I—he as teacher and union member, I as freelancer—dialed 110. That is why detectives from the District Criminal Investigation Department are now in an apartment that is the teacher's apartment and has a junk-shop chair in it. The woman with stubbly, unkempt hair who opens the door when the police ring the doorbell looks in poor health; she is so emaciated as to bear no resemblance whatever to the photograph in her police file. Perhaps she is not the one they are looking for. She has been pronounced dead many times. She is said to have died of a brain tumor. "Pigs!" she cries upon being arrested. Not until the detectives in the teacher's apartment find a magazine open to the page showing an X ray of the wanted person's brain are the detectives certain who it is they have apprehended. After that they find more in the teacher's apartment: ammunition, guns, hand grenades, and a Royal cosmetics case containing a four-point-five-kilo bomb.

"No," the teacher says later in an interview, "I had to do it." I agree, because otherwise he and his girlfriend would have been mixed up in the affair. "Even so," he says, "I felt uneasy about it. After all, I often agreed with her before she started throwing bombs, with what she said in the magazine *konkret* after the attack on Schneider's Department Store in Frankfurt, for example: 'The general argument against arson is that it can jeopardize the lives of people who have no desire to have their lives jeopardized....' Later, in Berlin, when Baader was released, she took part in an operation that left an innocent official severely wounded. After that she went underground. After that there were deaths on both sides. After that she showed up at my place. After that I ... But I really thought she was no longer alive."

He, the teacher I see myself in, wishes to use the considerable reward which is legally his for having dialed 110 to ensure that everyone captured thus far—including Gudrun Ensslin, who attracted attention while making a purchase in a fashionable Hamburg boutique—has a fair trial, which, as he puts it, "will make the social interconnections clear."

I would not do that. It is a waste of money. Why should the lawyers—Schily & Co.—profit? I think he should put the money into his and other schools to help the underprivileged he has made it his mission to help. But no matter to whom he gives the money, the elementary-school teacher is troubled about being labeled "the man who dialed 110" for the rest of his life. I am troubled too.

1973

A HEALTHY SHOCK? If that's what you think, you don't know my four sons-in-law. They're not married to my daughters; no, they're married to their cars. They're forever washing them, even on Sundays and church holidays, yammering over the tiniest dent, going on about pricier makes—Porsches and the like—leering at them like hot chicks they want to get into bed. And now—lines at every pump. The oil crisis! It's really hit home! A shock, yes; healthy, no. Oh, they stocked up all right. All four of them. And Gerhard, who talks like one of those health-food nuts—"No meat, for heaven's sake! No animal fats whatsoever!"—and swears by whole-grain bread, he sucked so long on the hose he fills his jerry cans with (he's stocked up on *them* too) that he nearly poisoned himself. Bellyaches, headaches, then carton after carton of milk. Heinz-Dieter went so far as to fill the bathtub, and the apartment stank so bad his little Sophie fainted.

Impossible, those two! And the others are no better. Beefing about the 100-kph speed limit. When they set the thermostat in Horst's office at nineteen degrees centigrade, he thought he'd come down with chilblain. You should have heard him curse the Arabs: "Those camel drivers! It's all their fault!" Though he had it in for the Israelis too, because they started fighting again and that upset the poor Saudis: "It's clear why they turned off the oil: they want to make things hard on us—and stay hard...."

Heinz-Dieter was close to tears: "What's the point of saving for a BMW if you crawl along the Autobahn at a hundred? Eighty on ordinary roads..."

"It's socialist egalitarianism, that's what it is," Eberhard, my oldest son-in-law, kept ranting. "Plays right into the hands of that Lauritzen, the guy who calls himself minister of transport." Which led to tiffs with Horst, who's every bit as car crazy, but a Social Democrat. "Just you wait," he says, "elections are coming, and..." They were constantly at one another's throats.

Finally I put my foot down and said, "Now you listen to me. Your independent mother-in-law, who's always been a great walker, has a great idea." I should point out that ever since their father's death, when my girls were virtually babes in arms, I've been head of the family, and if I've been difficult at times I've also kept the family together and am certainly the one to set them straight when, say, despite the urgent warnings of the Club of Rome an energy crisis takes them by surprise and they think they can behave like lunatics. So I said, "Now you listen to me. You all know I've seen the end of endless growth coming. Well, now's the time to face up to it. But that doesn't mean we have to go around in black, even though to-morrow is the Sunday of the Dead. What's more important is that it's Sunday, and like every Sunday from now on that means no driving. So I propose a family picnic. On foot, of course. First we take tram number three to the last stop and from there it's a hop, skip, and a jump to the beautiful woods surrounding Kassel. The Habichtswald, for instance."

You should have heard them wail.

"Supposing it rains?"

"If it really pours, we can make a run for Wilhelmshöhe Castle and wait it out looking at the Rembrandts and other paintings."

"Those old warhorses? We've seen them a million times."

"And who goes to the woods in November, when there's not a leaf on a tree?"

"Look, if it absolutely has to be a family day, we can all go to the flicks together."

"Or to Eberhard's and light a nice fire in the fireplace and sit around and..."

"Nothing doing," I said. "No excuses. The kids are looking forward to it. I can tell."

And so we all took the tram to the last stop, Druseltal, in our raincoats and rubber boots because it was drizzling at first,

and then spent two hours tramping up hill and down dale
through the Habichtswald, which has a special beauty when
the trees are bare. We even sighted deer from a distance,
watched them stare at us and bound away. And I identified the
trees for the children: "That's a beech tree. This one's an oak.
And the evergreens up there—see how they're being eaten
away on top? That comes from industry and all those many
too many cars. It's the exhaust that does it. The emissions,
understand?"

Then I showed them acorns and beechnuts and told them
about how we'd gathered them during the war. And we saw
squirrels scampering up and down the trunks. How sweet
they looked! But then it started raining more heavily and we
ducked into a restaurant, where I, the wicked mother-in-law
and good grandmother, treated the whole clan to cake and
coffee. The kids had their soft drinks, of course, and there
were a few schnappses too. "Even drivers can drink today," I
teased. Then I told the kids about all the things we had to do
without during the war. Not only gas. If you gathered and
shelled enough beechnuts, you could press them and make
real cooking oil.

But don't ask me about the aftermath. You don't know my
sons-in-law. Not a word of gratitude. Nasty remarks about
running around in the rain. And setting a bad example with
my "sentimental glorification of 'small is beautiful.'" "This
isn't the Stone Age!" Hans-Dieter roared at me. And Eberhard, who never misses an opportunity to call himself a liberal, had such a spat with Gudrun, my eldest, that he stormed
out of the bedroom, and guess where he slept, the poor thing.
Right. In the garage. In his old Opel, the one he washes and
washes, Sunday after Sunday.

1974

WHAT DOES ONE FEEL when one experiences oneself double before the television screen? If one makes it one's business to toe a double line, one cannot in fact be upset by finding one's "I" doubled under certain circumstances. Merely a bit surprised. One learns not only from rigorous training but also from life how to deal with oneself and one's double identity.

Having spent four years in a penal institution like Rheinbach and having managed, after a long-drawn-out procedure, to persuade the small prison board here to accord me access to my own television receiver, I am fully conscious of the implications of living a dual existence, but in 1974 I was still in detention at the Cologne-Ossendorf Prison awaiting trial, and when permission to install a television receiver in my cell for the duration of the world soccer championship was granted, the happenings on the screen rent my inner being in many respects.

Not when the Poles played a fantastic game in the pouring rain, not when Australia lost or the match with Chile ended in a tie—no, it happened when Germany faced Germany. Which side was one for? Which side was I or I for? Whom was I to cheer on? What conflict broke out in me, what forces pulled at me when Sparwasser shot his goal?

For us? Against us? Since I was being taken every morning to Bad Godesberg for interrogation, the Bureau of Investigation could scarcely have been unaware that these and similar ordeals were far from alien to me. But actually they were no ordeals at all; they were simply a behavior pattern in keeping with the duality of German statehood, that is, I was fulfilling a double obligation. As long as my duty consisted in making myself the Chancellor's most dependable aide, his dual-orientation conversation partner in off-the-record situations, I could handle the tension involved; in fact, I scarcely saw it as a conflict, especially since the Chancellor was clearly satisfied with my performance and, according to my contact people, the Berlin office was likewise, my activities having been praised in high circles there. The idea was that between the man who saw himself as "the Chancellor of peace" and myself, who pursued a mission as "the spy of peace," there should be a kind of synergy. It was a good time, one in which the Chancellor's biography fell in with his aide's agenda. We both took our jobs seriously.

But when on 22 June the referee blew the whistle opening the match between the German Democratic Republic and the Federal Republic of Germany before sixty thousand spectators at Hamburg's Volkspark Stadium, I was completely and utterly torn. Neither side scored during the first half, but when in the fortieth minute that lithe little Müller nearly put the Federal Republic in the lead, but in the end only hit the goalpost, I nearly screamed "Goal! Goal! Go-o-o-al!" in ecstasy and would have celebrated the lead of the West's separatist state just as I was ready to break out into a cheer when Lauck, outplaying Overath by far (he shook off the great Netzer later on in the match), nearly scored against the Federal Republic.

Back and forth, back and forth. One found oneself reacting even to the Uruguayan referee's decisions with tendentious commentary favoring now one, now the other Germany. I felt undisciplined, split, so to speak. Yet while Chief Detective Federau was examining me that morning, I had managed to stick to my prepared text. The questioning concerned my links to the rather extreme Hessen-Süd branch of the Social

Democratic Party, whose members saw me as a hardworking but conservative comrade. I enjoyed making them think I belonged to the rightist, more pragmatic wing of the Party. But then I was confronted with my darkroom equipment, all of which had been confiscated. The thing to do in such a case is to pooh-pooh the accusations. One points out one had been a professional photographer and pulls out one's holiday snapshots to show photography is still a hobby. But then the prosecution produced a sophisticated super-8 camera and two rolls of extremely fast film, claiming them to be "perfectly suited to undercover operations." I dismissed them as mere circumstantial evidence. Secure in the knowledge that I had not contradicted myself, I looked forward to returning to my cell and watching the match.

Neither here nor there could anyone have suspected I was a soccer fan. I myself had no idea that Jürgen Sparwasser had been a stalwart of our very own Magdeburg team. But now I kept my eyes on him after Hamann passed him the ball. He trapped it with his head, brought it to his feet, raced in front of the tenacious Vogts and, leaving even Höttges behind, rammed it past Maier into the net.

1–0 in favor of Germany! But which Germany? Mine or mine? Yes, I probably screamed "Goal! Goal! Go-o-o-al!" there in my cell, while at the same time lamenting that the other Germany had fallen behind. And when I saw Beckenbauer working to build up his team's offense, I cheered on the West German eleven.

As for my Chancellor (whose downfall was of course none of my doing—I would blame Nollau perhaps and most of all Wehner and Genscher), I sent him a postcard—and kept sending him cards on holidays and his birthday, 18 December—with my regrets for the outcome of the match. He didn't answer. But you can be sure that he too had mixed feelings about Sparwasser's goal.

1975

A YEAR LIKE ANY OTHER? Or a leaden time, when we were deafened by our own shouting? I have only the vaguest of memories, and they are of random unease under my own roof resulting from impending domestic disaster in both Friedenau and Wewelsfleth an der Stör, because Anna, because I, because Veronika, and consequently the children, wounded, leaving the nest, myself fleeing to—where else?— my manuscript, disappearing into the warm, bloated body of *The Flounder,* tripping down the staircase of the centuries, lingering off and on with nine and more cooks, who—now strict, now lenient—kept me under their rolling pins, while the present, paying my flight no heed, went on about its business, power refining its methods everywhere, at the high-security annex designed for the Baader-Meinhof prisoners at Stammheim or the much-contested site for the nuclear power plant at Brokdorf, though otherwise, once Brandt was gone and the new Chancellor, Schmidt, had objectivized us all, there wasn't much going on. The only place to find any action was the TV screen.

So I stand my ground: there was nothing special about the year, or if there was it was only that four or five of us West Germans had our papers checked at the border and then met five or six East Germans, all clutching manuscripts to their

breasts and some, Rainer Kirsch and Heinz Czechowski, having traveled all the way from Halle. We perched first at
Schädlich's place, then at Sarah Kirsch's or Sibylle Hentschke's
or somebody else's, having our coffee and cake (and exchanging the usual East-West barbs) before giving readings of
rhymed and unrhymed poems and short stories and overly
long chapters representing 1) work currently in progress on
both sides of the wall, and 2) the world in miniature.

Can this ritual—the more or less lengthy border proce-
dures; the ride to the meeting place (Rotkäppchenweg or
Lenbachstrasse); the now witty, now anxious squabbles, the
singing of pan-German songs of woe, the torrents of grapho-
maniac ink made oral text, the partly violent, partly taciturn
criticism of presented texts (an intimate but pale imitation of
Group 47), the hasty retreat just before midnight, the border
checkpoint at the Friedrichstrasse station—can this ritual be
the only lasting event this calendar year can muster?

Far off and close up, Saigon fell on TV. The last Americans
left Vietnam from the roof of their embassy in a panic, but it
was the finale to be expected and not a suitable topic of conversation over coffee, cake, and custard puffs. Ditto the terror
tactics of the Red Brigades as they played themselves out not
only in Stockholm, where they took hostages, but also among
themselves, among the prisoners at Stammheim, where the
next year Ulrike Meinhof hanged herself—or was hanged—
in her cell, though I can't say that even that long-lived issue
generated much interest among the assembled ink pens.
There were forest fires raging across the broad, flat Lüne-
berger Heide at the end of a dry summer, and five firemen lost
their lives after being surrounded by flames, but that was no
East-West topic either.

Perhaps—before Nicolas Born read from *The Side of History Turned Away from the Earth* and Sarah recited some of her Mark Brandenburg poems in dialect and Schädlich unnerved us with one of the stories that later appeared in the West under the title *Attempted Proximity* and I had a go at an excerpt from *The Flounder*—we took on an event that had made the headlines on the western side of the city that May: In Kreuzberg near the Oberbaumbrücke border crossing, a five-year-old Turkish boy named Cetin fell into the Spree Canal, and since the Canal constituted the border between the two halves of the city at that point, no one—neither the West Berlin police nor the soldiers in the patrol boat of the People's Army—would or could help the boy: in the West they didn't dare go into the water; in the East they had to wait for permission from above. So time passed, and soon it was too late for Cetin. When the fire department finally received orders to recover the body, the lament of the Turkish women on the west bank of the canal could be heard far into the East.

What else might have been discussed over coffee and cake in that year like so many others? In September, when we met again, manuscripts in hand, the death of the Emperor of Ethiopia—was he murdered or was it prostate cancer?—gave me the opportunity to tell everyone about an experience from my childhood. The film buff in me had seen the Negus Haile Selassie in the Fox Movietone News touring a typically drizzly port (Hamburg?) on a motor launch. There he stood—small, bearded, wearing a pith helmet a size too large for him, and standing under an umbrella held by a servant. He looked sad or troubled. It must have been 1935, shortly before Mussolini's soldiers marched into Abyssinia, as Ethiopia was then called. As a child I would have liked to have the Negus as a friend and accompany him when he was forced to flee Italy's onslaught.

No, I am not certain whether I brought up the Negus or even Mengistu, the latest Communist ruler, at our East-West meeting. I am certain, however, that we had to show our passports and entry permits just before midnight at the checkpoint known as the Palace of Tears. I am also certain that in West Berlin and Wewelsfleth, whenever I sought a roof over my head with my fragmentary *Flounder,* I found impending domestic disaster.

1976

NO MATTER WHERE IN EAST BERLIN we met, we thought we were bugged. We suspected carefully placed microphones everywhere—under the plaster, in the lighting fixtures, even in the flowerpots—and so we would go on ironically about the welfare state and its insatiable need for security. We would reveal top secrets slowly and clearly so as to make them easy to put down on paper, things like the basically subversive character of lyric poetry or the seditious intentions behind one or another use of the subjunctive. We advised "the firm"—which was how everyone referred to the security apparatus of the workers-and-peasants state, in private—to request official assistance from its Western competition (with centers in Pullach and Cologne) should our intellectual quips and decadent metaphors prove indecipherable on its side of the border and thus require a bit of pan-German cooperation. We were arrogant in our games with the Stasi, and as we presumed—half in earnest, half in jest—that our group had to have at least one informer, we would assure one another in the friendliest of terms that "in principle" we were each of us under suspicion.

Two decades later Klaus Schlesinger, whom the commission bearing the name "Gauck" had provided with all the documents Stasi diligence had seen fit to gather on him, sent me several reports made by informers to deal with our conspiratorial meetings in the mid-seventies. But all they said was who met whom in front of the Friedrichstrasse station bookshop, who kissed whom or gave what—a colorfully wrapped bottle, for instance—to whom, then in whose Trabant (license plate) and to what destination the parties drove, into what house (street, house number) and at what time the various people under observation disappeared, and at what time—after a more than six-hour watch—they emerged from the house (also referred to as "the object") and dispersed, the West Germans in the direction of the exit point, laughing and talking in loud voices, clearly affected by a large intake of alcoholic drink.

In other words, no bugs, no informers in our ranks, and not a word about our readings. Nothing—how disappointing!—about the explosive quality of rhymed and blank verse. No reference to the subversive chitchat over coffee and cake. So they never knew what the West Germans thought about the special effects in *Jaws,* which had just opened in a Ku'damm cinema. They never heard what we thought of the Colonels' trials going on in Athens. And when we gave our friends a report—firsthand, in my case—on the battles surrounding the Brokdorf atomic power plant, where the police used the American invention Mace for the first time and with immediate success, then hounded the thousands of protesters across

the flat fields of the Wilstermarsch with low-flying helicop-
ters, authorities in the East missed an opportunity to pick up
on the latest in Western crowd control.

Or maybe we never even mentioned Brokdorf. Can we have
spared our colleagues in their beyond-the-wall isolation, not
wishing to taint their rather idealized picture of the West with
discussions of Mace and descriptions of police brutality, police
clubbing down women and children? What probably happened is that either Born or Buch or I brought up the unpro-
nounceable gas (chloroacetophenone) that the spray cans in
Brokdorf were filled with by drawing a parallel with a gas
from World War I called "white cross" after the white cross
used to identify it on the can, whereupon Sarah or Schädlich,
Schlesinger or Rainer Kirsch expressed the opinion that while
the People's Police were not so well equipped technologically
at present, things would change once they had more Western
currency at their disposal: anything the West did could in principle be desirable in the East.

Though this is all idle speculation. None of it shows up in
Schlesinger's Stasi file. And what isn't there never existed.
Conversely every mention of time and place, every personal
description set down on paper represents a hard cold fact, the
truth. Schlesinger's gift (he sent photocopies) thus confirmed
that on one of my East Berlin visits—observed, as always,
from checkpoint to front door—I had been accompanied by
a tall female with fair curly hair who, as the border guards
added, was born on the Baltic Sea island of Hiddensee, had
brought along her knitting, and had been unknown in literary
circles until then.

That is how Ute got into the files. Since then she has been a
reality. No dream can take her from me: from that point on I

stopped needing to wander back and forth because of impending domestic disaster and started working away at the stonelike integument of the *Flounder* in her lee; I also went on reading excerpts to friends whenever we gathered—something Gothic about "Scania Herring" or a Baroque allegory entitled "The Burden of an Evil Day." But what Schädlich, Born, Sarah and Rainer Kirsch, or I actually read in our various venues does not figure in Schlesinger's file and, lacking the blessing of either the Stasi or the Gauck Commission, is less than real. At best we may presume that the year when Ute became a reality I read the fairy tale "The Other Truth" and either then or the year thereafter Schädlich read the opening of his "Tallhover," the story of the immortal informer.

1977

THESE THINGS LEAVE THEIR MARK. But what doesn't? Terror invents counterterror. Questions remain open. To this day I don't know how the two loaded revolvers Baader and Raspe supposedly shot themselves with made their way into the high-security wing at Stammheim and how Gudrun Ensslin was able to hang herself with a speaker wire.

These things leave their mark. But what doesn't? The expatriation of bard Wolf Biermann the year before, for instance. The moment he left the walled-in workers-and-peasants state, he felt its lack, because whenever he sang on a Western stage he felt the lack of a sounding board. I can still see him in my Friedenauer Niedstrasse house, where he visited us on an officially approved transit visa, talking wittily about himself, then about genuine communism, then about himself again and, later, trying out the program for his Cologne show, also sanctioned from on high, before a small audience—Ute, the many children, their friends—in my studio, that is, the show we saw televised live the next day with every outcry against the despotism of the Ruling Party, every sardonic chuckle the People's Own Snooping Service had wrested from him, every sob over communism run amok, led amok by its leading comrades—rehearsed, down to the pain-stricken caw heralding the onset of hoarseness, down to the wording of a spontaneous promise, every funny face, every tragic face, every batting eyelid—rehearsed, yes, rehearsed for months, years, for as long as the authorities had gagged him, forbidden him to appear elsewhere than in his lair (located just opposite West Germany's "Permanent Representation" in East Berlin), rehearsed, each number of the great show, because everything that bowled over mass audiences in Cologne our small audience had seen the day before. He knew exactly what he was after; he knew exactly how to get it. His courage made its way to the spectator tried and tested.

When they stripped him of his East German citizenship, we all hoped it would leave its mark and he would test his courage anew. In the West. Nothing came of it, however. Later, much later, he was insulted when the Wall came down because it had happened without his input. He has recently been honored with the National Prize.

Our group met one last time after Biermann lost his citizenship. We met in the Kunerts' house of many cats. We began with our readings (rehearsed in advance), but were then joined by a number of the people who had staged a public protest against the expatriation and now had to deal with the consequences. One of the marks that the protest left was that many (not all) of the participants felt obliged to apply for permission to leave the country. The Kunerts were taking their cats, Sarah Kirsch and Jochen Schädlich their children, books, and assorted goods and chattels.

That in turn left its mark. But what doesn't? Nicolas Born died suddenly some time thereafter. And later, much later, our friendships fell apart: reunification fallout. Our manuscripts, however, the ones we'd read to one another time after time, eventually came on the market. Even the flounder managed to swim himself free. Oh, yes, and toward the end of 1977 Charlie Chaplin died—waddled up to the horizon and vanished, leaving no successors.

1978

YOU'RE RIGHT, REVEREND FATHER, I should have come and poured out my troubles earlier, but I firmly believed things would take care of themselves. The children wanted for nothing—my husband and I felt certain of that—and we loved them both dearly. Ever since we moved to my father-in-law's beautiful estate—at his request, I must tell you—they seemed happy or at least content: the roomy house, the spacious grounds, the ancient trees. And although we are a bit isolated, it is not all that far—as you are aware, Reverend Father—from the center of town. Their school friends came to visit all the time. We had wonderfully cheery parties in the garden. Even my father-in-law, the grandpapa the children so adore, enjoyed seeing the young guests frolic on the lawn. And suddenly things went wrong....

It all began with Martin. One day the boy shaved his head bald except for a tuft over the forehead. And since Monika always has to do her brother one better, she dyed her beautiful blond hair partly purple, partly a pea green. Well, we could have looked the other way—which we did in fact—but then they started going around in the most frightful getups. I mean, really, we were shocked, my husband and I. Martin, who had actually been a bit of a snob until then, took to wearing blue jeans riddled with holes, a rusty chain for a belt, and a black leather jacket, the kind with studs, held together by a monstrous padlock over the chest. Moni wore leather too, old and cracked, and lace-up boots. And the music coming out of their rooms. If you can call that aggressive noise music, that is. The din would begin the moment they got home from school. With no regard for their poor grandpapa, whose only desire since retiring has been for peace and quiet. Or so we thought...

Yes, Reverend Father. Sex Pistols. That's what they call the caterwaul. They seem able to tell one kind from the other....

But we *have*. We've tried everything. Heart-to-heart talks, but no nonsense. My husband, who is otherwise patience personified, even threatened to cut off their allowances. Nothing helped. The children were always out somewhere and in bad company. And of course their school friends stopped coming: they were all from good families. What made it pure agony was that they brought those awful creatures, those punks, home instead. We'd run into them everywhere—squatting on the carpets, sprawling in the leather armchairs. And the language they used...

That's right, Reverend Father. And the "no future" things they said. Well, it finally got to Grandpapa and he—how shall I put it—went off the deep end. From one day to the next. We were completely beside ourselves, my husband and I, because my father-in-law...

You know what he was like. Well-mannered, well-groomed, a model of discretion, with the charm and quiet wit of a bygone era. After withdrawing from the banking world, he lived only for classical music, he hardly left his rooms except to sit on the terrace. Seeing him there, you would never dream he'd been—as I'm sure you are aware, Reverend Father—one of the pillars of the Deutsche Bank, but of course he never breathed a word about his many long years there—no, he was, as I say, discretion in pinstripes. Once, just after Erwin and I were married, I asked about his professional responsibilities during the terrible war years, and he answered, as was his wont, with a touch of irony, "That's a bank secret." And even Erwin, who is himself a banker, knows little about the circumstances surrounding his childhood and even less about his father's career....

But to return to the present and the change in Grandpapa which, as I say, took place practically overnight. Try to picture it, Reverend Father. He came down to breakfast in the most dreadful outfit. We were amazed, no, shocked. He'd shaved off his beautiful thick gray hair, leaving only a stripe running down the middle, and that he'd dyed a bright ginger color; moreover, he was wearing a sort of black-and-white smock he must have patched together in secret out of scraps of material and a pair of his old striped trousers, the kind he used to wear to board meetings. He looked like a convict. And everything—the scraps of material, even his fly—was held together with safety pins. Not only that. He'd managed—don't ask me how—he'd managed to stick two extra-large safety pins through his earlobes. And to top it all off, he'd come up with a pair of handcuffs, though he wore them only outside....

Certainly, Reverend Father, but no one could stop him. He

kept slipping out of the house. He made a fool of himself not only here in Rath but—or so people tell us—in Düsseldorf as well. The Königsallee! And soon he started going around with a gang of punks, terrorizing people all the way up to Gerresheim....

No, Reverend Father. Erwin could scold him till he was blue in the face and all he would say was, "Herr Abs is going out. Herr Abs must take over the Böhmische-Union-Bank and the Wiener-Kreditanstalt. Then he must go to Paris and Aryanize several major business concerns. Herr Abs has been requested to use the same discretion he used with the Bankhaus Mendelsohn. Herr Abs is known for his discretion and does not wish to be questioned further." We were subjected to that sort of thing daily, Reverend Father, and more....

Right. He'd identified with his former boss, Hermann Josef Abs. Their ties went back not only to the postwar reconstruction period but to the war itself. More recently Herr Abs had served as an adviser to Chancellor Adenauer on weighty matters of finance. And now Grandpapa saw himself called upon to act as the Chancellor's negotiator in thorny compensation cases like the I. G. Farben claim or demands on the part of Israel. "Herr Abs rejects all demands out of hand," he would say. "Herr Abs will see to it that Germany remains creditworthy." That's why those nasty punks shout "Papa Abs!" whenever Grandpapa leaves the house. And he always smiles and says, "Don't worry. Herr Abs is just off on a business trip...."

The children? You won't believe it, Reverend Father. Cured overnight. They were shocked too. Monika threw her leather outfit and those ugly boots away. She is now preparing diligently for her exams. Martin has rediscovered his silk ties and is thinking of going to London to study business, Erwin tells me. If it weren't for the tragic consequences, we should be grateful to Grandpapa for having made his grandchildren see reason....

Oh, yes, Reverend Father. It was terribly hard to come to what I realize seems a hard-hearted decision. We talked it over for hours, with the children too....

Yes, he's in Grafenberg....

Yes, it has a good reputation. We visit him regularly. The children too, of course. He wants for nothing. True, he still calls himself Herr Abs, but the orderlies assure us he gets on well with the other patients. And recently, we hear, he's made friends with a patient who calls himself, appropriately enough, Herr Adenauer. They enjoy playing bowls on the grass together....

1979

WILL YOU STOP BUGGING ME! What's "my great love" supposed to mean anyway? You're "my great love," though you're driving me crazy today, Klaus-Stephan, and you've never told me about "*your* great..."

All right, all right! Anything to stop this third degree. I assume what you mean by love is a throbbing heart, wet palms, and a stammer leading to delirium. Then yes, the sparks did fly once, when I was all of thirteen. You'll be surprised to learn that I fell hook, line, and sinker for a balloonist. Or to be more precise, the son of a balloonist, or to be absolutely precise, the older son. When was it now? Twelve years ago, in mid-September. Two men and their families flew from Thuringia to Franconia in a hot-air balloon.

What do you mean "pleasure trip"! Don't you get it? Over

the border. Over barbed wire, mines, and automatic firing devices, over the "death strip," and down to us. As you may recall, I come from Naila, a one-horse town in Franconia. And no more than fifty kilometers from Naila, in what was then a different country, there's another one-horse town called Pössneck, and it was Pössneck the two families were trying to get out of. In a balloon, and a homemade balloon at that. They put Naila on the map in all the papers and on TV even. Because it was all very picturesque: they landed in a clearing in the woods just outside town. Four grown-ups, four kids. And one of them was Frank. He'd just turned fifteen, and I really fell for him. Right there, on the spot, while we were standing behind the barrier and watching both families climb back into the basket and wave at the cameramen. All except my Frank. He just stood there. The whole thing was getting to him. He'd had enough. Of all the media hype, I mean. He wanted nothing to do with the basket. That was what won me over. I felt like running right up to him. Or running away in shame.

Right, it was completely different with us: things developed gradually, there was basically nothing spontaneous about it. With Frank it was love at first sight.

Did I talk to him? You bet I did. The second he was out of that basket. But he hardly said a thing he was so shy. Really nice. But talk about the third degree! I wanted to know everything, the whole story. Well, it turns out that both families had made an earlier attempt, but it was foggy and the balloon got wet and they landed on their own side of the border, though they didn't know it at the time. They were lucky they didn't get caught. But they refused to give in and went all over the country buying up bolts of raincoat material, which couldn't have been easy. Then the men and the women both stayed up nights sewing the pieces together with two sewing machines, so right after they made their successful flight the Singer people toyed with the idea of sending them two new state-of-the-art models, assuming that the balloon had been made with those old-fashioned pedal machines. But they were wrong: the machines weren't even Singer; they were East German and electric. So bye-bye super gifts. No publicity, no go. My Frank told me all that bit by bit during our secret trysts in the clearing where the balloon landed. Like I say, he was shy, completely different from boys in the West.

Did we kiss? Not at first. Later. By the way, I had an argument with my father about the whole thing. He claimed—and he wasn't totally wrong—that the fathers were irresponsible because they'd put their families' lives in jeopardy. But I saw it differently. I said—and *I* wasn't totally wrong—"You're just jealous, because they did something you'd never have the guts to do."

Well, well. Don't tell me *you're* jealous! I hope I'm not in for one of those scenes when you tell me we're through. Just because more than ten years ago...

All right, all right. I lied. I made the whole thing up. I was much too shy at the age of thirteen to say a word to him. I just stared and stared. Later too, when I saw him in the street. He would pass right by our house on his way to school, which isn't far from the clearing where the balloon landed. Then we moved away.

Yes, to Erlangen, where my father took a job in the Siemens advertising department. And Frank...

No, not just puppy love. The real thing. Deeply, with all my heart, whether you like it or not. And even though nothing

happened between us, I still think fondly of him, not that he
remembers me in the slightest.

1980

"IT'S ONLY A STONE'S THROW FROM BONN, really," his wife
told me over the phone. You have no idea how naive these
people are, Mr. Minister, though friendly too. "Do drop in and
see what we do here all day..." and so on. As head of the sub-
committee in charge of the matter, I thought it my duty to
have a look-see and report back to you if need be. She was
right: it was only a stone's throw from the Ministry of Foreign
Affairs.

Not at all, Mr. Minister. Their headquarters—or what they
call their headquarters—is in a perfectly ordinary row house.
And that is their base for intervening decisively in world history and putting us in a tight spot if need be. His wife assured
me that she took care of "all the organizational stuff," though
she also had the housework and three small children to tend
to. She did it with her left hand, she said, "it" meaning keeping in constant communication with the ship in the South
China Sea while seeing to the dispersal of contributions that
were still flowing in. Her only trouble, she said, was with us,
"with the bureaucracy." Otherwise, she stuck to her husband's
motto—"Be reasonable; attempt the unreasonable"—which
he had picked up some years back, in '68 it was, in Paris, when
students still had guts, and so on, and she advised me—meaning the Ministry of Foreign Affairs—to follow it as well, because without political guts more and more boat people would

drown, or else starve on that rat-infested island Pulau Bidong. In any case, it was high time that the ship for Vietnam her husband had been able to charter for several more months thanks to all those contributions, it was high time it be allowed to take on refugees from other ships, like the poor people who'd been fished out of the water by a freighter for the Danish Maersk Line. That was one of her demands. It was a moral imperative, a human imperative, and so on.

You can be sure I made that clear to the good woman, Mr. Minister. Over and over and precisely as instructed, of course. The Maritime Convention of 1910 is the only set of guidelines we can follow in this precarious situation, and it requires all captains, as I reiterated many times, to take the shipwrecked aboard directly from the water only, not from other ships, as would be the case with the *Maersk Mango,* which, sailing under a Singapore flag, had taken on more than twenty of the shipwrecked and now wished to be rid of them.

As soon as possible. We'd learned from a radio message that the ship had quickly spoiling tropical fruit on board, that it could not deviate from its course, and so on. Nonetheless, as I kept telling her, the direct transfer of the boat people to the *Cap Anamur* would violate the statutes of international maritime law.

She laughed at me, standing at the stove slicing carrots into her stewpot. "Your statutes date back to the *Titanic,*" she said. "Today's disasters are of a different order entirely. Three hundred thousand refugees have drowned or died of thirst—or so our sources indicate—and their number is growing. The *Cap Anamur* has rescued a few hundred of them, but we can't just sit here and pat ourselves on the back." When I questioned her figures and made a few of the usual objections, she countered

with "I couldn't care less if they include pimps and black mar-
keteers, or even crooks and U.S. collaborators!" All she cared
about, she said, was that people were drowning day after day
while the Ministry of Foreign Affairs and politicians in general clung to guidelines dating from the dark ages. "A year
ago, when the tragedy was just beginning, some local politi-
cos—in Hannover, in Munich—made a show of welcoming
a few hundred 'victims of Communist terror' in front of the
TV cameras; now all you hear is 'economic refugees' and 'flagrant violations of the right of political asylum.'"

No, Mr. Minister, there was nothing I could do. Not that
she was particularly upset. She was actually quite calm to
begin with, cheerful even, and always busy at the stove—
"vegetables with mutton gizzards," she called the dish—or on
the phone. She also had constant visitors—doctors and such
offering their services—and long conversations about waiting
lists, fitness for service in the tropics, vaccinations, and so on.
And of course the three children. As I say, I was in the
kitchen. I kept meaning to go and didn't even though there
was no place for me to sit down. Several times she handed me
her wooden spoon to stir the stewpot while she went into the
living room to make a phone call. When I finally took a seat on
the laundry basket, I landed on a rubber duck that let out a
pitiful quack, which made everybody roar with laughter. But
they weren't jeering or taunting. These people, Mr. Minister,
these people love chaos. It's what gets their juices going, she
told me. They're idealists who don't give a damn about rules
and regulations and so on. All they care about is their ability to
change the world, and the good woman in her row house is
convinced they can. Quite admirable, actually, though I can't
say I was happy to be the monster from the Ministry who had

to nix everything. There is nothing more unpleasant than to have to deny aid.

I was touched, but abashed as well, when one of the children, a girl, presented me with the rubber duck as I left. It can swim, she told me.

1981

IT WAS A REAL DRAG, Rosi, believe me. I'd never seen so many medals before. Knight's Crosses from the war. The kind my uncle Konrad has around his neck in one of the pictures. But there it was medals galore. The kind with the oak leaves too. Grandma explained it all at the cemetery and for all to hear, too, because she's hard of hearing. She's the one who sent the telegram: "First train to Hamburg stop. S-Bahn to Aumühle stop. Admiral of Fleet being laid to rest stop."

How could I say no? You don't know her. When she says "first train," you're on the first train. And I'm not one to take orders. You know what I've been through with the Kreuzberg squatters. We can expect Lummer to send his clearance commando to Hermsdorfer Strasse at any time. And was I embarrassed to show the telegram to my commune! They wouldn't let me hear the end of "the Admiral"!

But anyway, there I was, standing next to Grandma, while the grandpas parked their Mercedeses in front of the cemetery and formed a "guard of honor," as Grandma called it, from the brass band to the grave, every second one of them sporting a Knight's Cross over their civilian clothes. I was shivering—there was snow on the ground and it was freezing cold despite the sun—but almost none of them had coats on. They were all wearing their peaked navy caps, though.

As the coffin with the Admiral inside and the black-red-and-gold outside passed slowly in front of us, I saw from the caps of the men carrying it that like my father's two older brothers they had all served on submarines. (My father was only in the Territorial Army.) One of my uncles died in the Arctic, the other somewhere in the Atlantic or, as my grandmother always said, "They descended to a watery grave." One was a captain or something like that, the other, my uncle Karl, just a boatswain first class.

You won't believe it, Rosi, but about thirty thousand men went down in about five hundred boats, and all at the order of that man, the Admiral of the Fleet, who was actually a war criminal. Or that's what my father says. And most of them, he says, his brothers too, served on those floating coffins of their own free will. He's as uncomfortable as I am when Grandma starts in on her "dead hero" cult every Christmas; he's always arguing with her about it. I'm the only one who goes and visits her in Eckernförde in the little house where she venerates the Admiral to this day. But otherwise she's perfectly okay. I actually have an easier time with her than with him, because of course he can't accept our squatter situation. That's why Grandma sent the telegram to me rather than to him and to Hermsdorfer Strasse, where we've been living in perfectly comfortable quarters for months now with the help of a group of people sympathetic to the cause: doctors, leftist teachers, lawyers.... As I say, Herb and Robi were not particularly thrilled with the telegram. "You must be off your rocker," Herb said as I packed. "One old Nazi less." But I said, "You don't know my grandma. When she says 'the first train,' she means it."

And believe me, Rosi, I'm actually glad to have been there for the big to-do at the cemetery. Nearly everyone left over from the submarine war was there. It was funny and eerie and a little embarrassing all at once to watch them singing at the grave, looking for all the world as if they were still on a mission, scanning the horizon for a wisp of smoke or something. And don't think my grandma didn't sing along, loud and clear. First "Deutschland über alles," then "I Once Had a Faithful Friend." It gave me the creeps. Then a few of those radical right-wing drummer boys marched in in kneesocks despite the cold, and there were speeches about everything imaginable, but mostly loyalty. The coffin itself was a disappointment: nothing special. Couldn't they have made a kind of mini-submarine—out of wood, naturally—and painted it military gray? Wouldn't the Admiral have felt a lot more at home in something like that?

On our way out, as we waited for all the Mercedeses to whiz past, I asked my grandmother (who'd invited me to have a pizza with her at the station in Hamburg and given me more than enough to cover the train ticket), "What do you think? Was the watery grave Uncle Konrad and Uncle Karl went to really worth it?" I felt bad afterward for being so blunt about it, because for at least a minute she didn't say anything, and then only, "Well, my boy, there must have been *some* sense to it."

As I'm sure you've heard, Lummer's commando cleared us out not long after I got back. And a pretty truncheon-intensive operation it was too. Since then we've taken over a few other Kreuzberg buildings, and Grandma agrees it's a crime to leave the habitable quarters uninhabited. But if they clear us out again, how about coming and living with me in Grandma's nice little house. She'd be tickled pink. She said so herself.

1982

APART FROM THE MISUNDERSTANDINGS to which my quotation "perfidious Albion" apparently gave rise, I am perfectly satisfied, even now, with the report which I prepared for the Howaldt Shipyard and the Naval Technology Subdivision of General Power and Electricity in Wedel and which appeared under the title "Consequences of the Falkland War." Assuming that both the type-209 submarines Howaldt delivered to Argentina with their state-of-the-art electronic torpedo systems had been put into action against the British task force at the outset and had succeeded in sinking, say, the aircraft carrier *Invincible* together with the full-to-capacity troop transport *Queen Elizabeth,* the consequences for the West German government, despite its officially positive stance vis-à-vis the NATO Dual-Track Decision and the long overdue shuffling of chancellors taking place at the time, would have been disastrous. I can just see the headlines: "German Weapons Systems Prove Their Worth Against NATO Allies!" Unthinkable, I wrote, pointing out that even the sinking of the destroyer *Sheffield* and the landing craft *Sir Galahad* by Argentine planes of French provenance would scarcely have rendered a victory achieved by German-made submarines more palatable. Anti-German sentiment, barely concealed as it is, would have rushed to the surface. We would have been "Huns" again.

It is thus fortunate that when the war broke out one Howaldt ship, the *Salta,* was in dry dock undergoing repairs and the other, the *San Luis,* while it did see action, was manned by a crew so poorly trained that it proved incapable of coping with the complicated General Power and Electricity electronic torpedo-steering system. "As a result," I said in my report, "the British Navy and we as a nation got off 'scot-free,'" especially as neither the British nor we Germans have forgotten the first Falkland battle of 8 December 1914, when the all-conquering German Pacific Fleet under the command of the legendary Vice Admiral Count von Spee was destroyed by British superiority at sea.

To support assertions going beyond the technological and entering the realm of history, I returned to the report eight years ago—when Schmidt was forced out of office and Kohl began the great transformation—appending the reproduction of an oil painting to my otherwise sober analysis. It was a seascape from the brush of Hans Bordt, a well-known practitioner of the genre, showing an armored cruiser sinking during the battle in question. While in the background the ship is going under stern first, in the foreground a German sailor, clinging to a board with his left hand, is holding up a flag, clearly the flag of the sinking cruiser, in his right. It is an unforgettable gesture.

And as you can see, dear friend, the flag is not just any flag. That is why I am writing to you in such detail and reaching back so far into the past. You will recognize in that dramatic painting the military flag of the Reich, the very same flag which made its way back into history recently in the Leipzig Monday demonstrations. They were unfortunately accompanied by scenes of brutal beatings, which I regret. As I have suggested in a report on the unification process, I am of the opinion that the replacement of the empty slogan "We are the people!" with the—as you will recall—politically effective cry of "We are one people!" should have taken place under peaceful, indeed civilized, conditions. On the other hand, we must be glad that the somewhat rough-and-ready skinheads, as those totally shorn youths are called, succeeded in a surprise move to dominate the Leipzig Monday "scene" with their imperial military flags and reinforce—if a bit vociferously—the call for German unity.

It is clear, then, that history may take circuitous routes; indeed, at times she needs a helping hand. How good it was that I remembered my Falkland report and the Bordt seascape when the time was ripe. Back then the people at General Power and Electricity proved utterly lacking in historical perspective and therefore unsympathetic to my bold leap in time. Let us hope that the deeper meaning of the imperial military flag has become clear to them by now. We see the flag more and more. Young people have something to be enthusiastic about again; they enjoy being associated with it, holding it high. And now that reunification is a reality, let me confess, dear friend, how proud I am to have hearkened to history's call and put my report to good use when the time finally came to recall our national values and wave our flag for all to see.

1983

HE WAS ONE OF A KIND, that Strauss! Ever since his heart gave out before the last "Tallyho!" of the fateful hunt—and now that his sidekick, the meat-cheese-and-beer man, is out of the picture and only the third in the troika, who made it over the border just in time, is around to enjoy the fruits of their deals—what's a poor cabaret artist to do? Not even the reigning heavyweight can outweigh those three. It's a drag, let me tell you. "Hey, hold on a second," you say. "What about his parliamentarian sidekicks? The Süssmuths and Blüms and Waigels? They must be good for some laughs." "Tears is more like it," we say.

So the nation's jokesters gathered for a serious meeting in a godforsaken Bavarian town where some established literati once awarded a budding literatus a prize. But we were at a loss. The best we could muster was a paper entitled "On the Plight of the German Cabaret Following the Demise of Franz Josef the Great with Particular Emphasis on the Ensuing Unification." Nobody laughed. The only funny bit was the comics' glum faces.

Oh, how we miss you, dear Franz Josef Strauss. Patron saint of political satirists, your dirty tricks our daily bread. Every tank you bought had a powerful kickback, every business partner was an *amigo* for life. You were on footsie terms with every dictator, yet only the *Spiegel* affair laid you low. German cabaret has always been in the opposition, on the side of the underdog, and the Man-with-No-Neck had a way of turning even thoroughbreds into underdogs. Material galore for our skits, in other words. And on the rare occasions when you let us down, your sourpuss nemesis, Wehner, was always there as a backup. Now he and his pipe are gone too.

Only once did you catch us napping. It was in '83, and there were billions at stake: charity for our poor relations in the East. What we wouldn't have given to be a fly on the wall when an unprecedented triumvirate met in Rosenheim: stocky Strauss, the East-bloc-head Schalk, and Mr. Meat-Cheese-and-Beer März the pickle in the middle. Professing the best of intentions, the Profiteer Trio performed a Musical Joke of epic proportions, the ten-figure finale serving not only to beef up the

East's anemic Western currency reserves but also to provide the host, a major Bavarian importer, with vast quantities of the People's Own Beef for a steal.

It was all in the family, after all. Terms like "red-baiter" and "archenemy of capitalism" fall by the wayside when the meat-cheese-and-beer bill goes sky-high and the East-bloc-head can take the latest Kohl jokes back home to the Lord High Roofer, a.k.a. the General Secretary. I don't imagine they embraced when it was over; let's say—it would be more in keeping with the meeting's great-event-cum-secret-setting framework— they gave one another pan-German winks. Each offered his all: preferential market treatment, rustic charm, Bonn innards, cheap pork, well-aired state secrets, and other such specialties of the eighties acidic enough to warm the cockles of both se- cret services.

An eye-, ear-, and nose-treat it must have been, a pan- German feast: mountains of meat, cheese, and beer. We weren't invited: it must have been saucy enough without us. Our own Strauss soundalike has Strauss-babble down pat, but he could only make a stab at the bloc-head's falsetto, and März the Meat Man must have merely mumbled as he figured on his fingers. So millions changed hands without our input. A pity, really, because we could have used it as a curtain-raiser for the Ger- man unity passion play under the title "In Unity Is Profit." Unfortunately, Strauss and März made their final exit before the Wall fell, and our friend the bloc-head, who is enjoying ever-growing fruits at his Bavarian lakeside villa in the shade of his deals, knows the literal truth of the saying "Silence is golden."

Our comic summit remained a downer, by the way. Maybe German cabaret isn't so hot after all. As for Strauss, Munich's airport was named after him—he had a pilot's license as well as a hunting license—so we're forced to think of him every time we fly in or out of the place. But in 1980, when he bade fair to become Chancellor, prudent voters joined ranks with us comics to forestall the risk of making our "heaviest" comic figure head of state.

1984

YES, I KNOW. Memento mori is easy enough to say, but it entails a huge amount of organizational spadework. For example, we are marking more trails on the former Verdun battlefield at least partly as a result of the symbolic handshake of the President and the Chancellor on that memorable day, 22 September 1984, outside the ossuary, my task being to supply bilingual signs—Mort-Homme Toter Mann (Dead Man's Hill)—especially as there and near the bloodsoaked Bois des Corbeaux Rabenwald (Ravenswood) one can presumably still find mines and duds in the crater landscape that is now completely green and the French keep-off sign *Ne pas piétiner* (No walking on the grass) must be supplemented by our *Betreten verboten* (Walking on the grass forbidden). Nor would it be amiss to point out discreetly that a number of points of interest on the battlefield merit pauses for meditation, for instance, the remains of the village Fleury, where a chapel now invites one to pray for reconciliation, or Côte 304 (Hill 304), which was continually stormed between May and August 1916 and changed hands many times over.

Furthermore, there is a certain urgency to all this, because ever since the Chancellor's visit to our military cemetery at Consenvoye, which followed his visit to the French cemetery on the grounds of Fort Douaumont, where the historic handshake with the President of the Republic took place, the number of tourists has increased considerably. They arrive by the busload and exhibit certain troubling tourist behavior patterns. The ossuary, for instance, with its grenadelike tower rising up over the vault, is often perceived as a house of horrors, and the people peering in through the windows, which by the way give access to only a small part of the bones and skulls of the hundred and thirty thousand Frenchmen who fell here, are often heard to laugh and, worse, make obscene remarks. Other all too grandiloquent comments make it amply clear that the peacemaking process between our two nations, so vigorously promoted by their leaders' symbolic gesture, is far from complete. For example, the not entirely unfounded umbrage our side takes at the discrepancy, hardly to be missed, between the fifteen thousand white crosses inscribed "Mort pour la France" and fifteen thousand rosebushes decorating the graves of the French victims on the one hand and our much less numerous black crosses with neither inscriptions nor flowers on the other.

I should also point out that we have not had an easy time eliciting a response to our complaints. We are likewise at a loss when it comes to fixing the number of war dead. It was long thought that each side had lost three hundred and fifty thousand men. To speak of so many victims in an area of thirty-five thousand square meters, however, is an exaggeration. Most likely a total of only half a million men—approximately seven or eight per square meter—lost their lives in the bitter struggle over Fort Douaumont and Fort Vaux, at Fleury, on

Hill 304, and at Cold Earth (Froideterre, which speaks volumes about the barren, clayey soil of the battlefield as a whole). The term used in military circles is "war of attrition."

Yet no matter how great the losses, our Chancellor and France's President set an eloquent example, one worth far more than figures, when they shook hands outside the ossuary. Because we belonged to the accompanying delegation—the one that included Ernst Jünger, the venerable writer and eyewitness of the senseless slaughter—we saw the statesmen only from behind.

Later they planted a sycamore tree (it having been ascertained in advance that the land was mine-free). Everyone appreciated this symbolic part of the program. The same could not be said of the German-French maneuvers taking place in the immediate vicinity. German tanks on French roads and German Tornados flying low over Verdun were not looked upon here with favor. Our Chancellor would have done better to spend some time at the remains of the dugout known as the Four Chimneys (Abri des Quatre Cheminées), where Bavarian and French troops engaged in a combat both fierce and high in casualties. Quite apart from its symbolic significance, this is a place eminently worthy of a pause for meditation. The Chancellor would best have visited it outside the framework of the official program.

1985

DARLING,

When you first asked me to tell you how I spent the eighties because you needed personal data for your M.A. thesis,

tentatively called "Everyday Life and the Senior Citizen," I
said I'd be glad to. But now you write you're also interested in
"problems related to senior-citizen consumer behavior," and
there I can't be of much help. Your grandmother had no particular problems in that regard. I had everything I needed—
except for your wonderful Grandpa, of course, and he's irre-
placeable. At first, when I could still get around, I worked
half-time at the express cleaner's next door and was active in
the church community. But if you want to know what I did
with my leisure time, then to be honest I have to say I spent a
good part of the eighties in front of the TV set, sometimes just
whiling away the hours, but sometimes quite enjoying it.
Then my legs started giving out, so I was pretty much con-
fined to quarters and, as your dear parents can tell you, had
little use for social gatherings.

Not that there was a whole lot going on. Not in politics, at
any rate, and you keep asking about that. The same old promises, that's all. My neighbor Frau Scholz agrees; we always see
eye to eye. By the way, she did a wonderful job of looking after
me all those years, better than my children, much as I hate to
admit it, your dear father included. She was the only one I
could count on. When she was on the early shift at the post office, she'd come over in the afternoon and bring some home-
baked cake and we'd make ourselves comfortable and watch
whatever happened to be on, right into the evening sometimes.
Dallas, Black Forest Clinic. Ilse liked Dr. Brinkmann, I less so.
But when *Lindenstrasse* came on in the mid-eighties—it's still
on, by the way—I said to her, This is different. This is true to
life. The way things are. The constant commotion, the funny
things, the sad things, the quarreling and getting back together, with all the pain and heartache. It's the same here in

Bielefeld, even though Bielefeld isn't Munich and the corner bar has been turned into a restaurant and is run by Italians, not by a Greek, and they've been doing a decent job of it for years. But our janitor's wife is as much of a shrew as Else Kling in number three Lindenstrasse: she's constantly picking on her husband and she can be pretty nasty to us too. Frau Beimer, on the other hand, is a model of humankindness—always ready to lend an ear, talk over your problems. Just like my neighbor Frau Scholz, who's got plenty of problems of her own with those children of hers, especially Jasmin, who has what I can only call a problematic relationship with a foreigner, the same as Frau Beimer's Marion.

Anyway, we've been following the serial since it began, which must have been some time in December, because on the first Christmas show Henry and Franz got into an argument over a paltry Christmas tree, and even though they got over it, Christmas Eve started out really sad, because Marion had wanted to go to Greece with her Vasily. But then Hans Beimer brought home two orphans, and because the poor lonely Vietnamese boy Gung was invited too, it turned out to be a merry Christmas after all.

Watching *Lindenstrasse* with Frau Scholz made me think back to the early years of my marriage, when your grandfather and I would watch a serial called *The Schölermann Family* in a restaurant that had a TV set. A black-and-white one, of course. It must have been in the mid-fifties....

But you want to know what caught my interest in the eighties. Well, in the year that Frau Beimer's daughter Marion came home late with a bleeding knife wound in her head the "Boris and Steffi" spectacle began. I can't say I'm wild about tennis—all that back and forth, back and forth—but for some reason we'd watch for hours. The players more than the game. Frau Scholz caught on to the terminology pretty well, and there were so many English words—"return," "tiebreak," and the like—that I often had to ask her what was going on. But by the time Wimbledon rolled around and our Boris was up against a South African and then the next year when he played Lendl, the Czech no one could beat, well, I was on pins and needles. After all, he was only seventeen, my little Bobbele. You should have heard me cheer him on. And in '89, even though politics was finally making a comeback, I was glued to the set when he beat that Swede Edberg after three sets. I literally wept for joy. Dear Frau Scholz did too.

On the other hand, I've never been able to warm up to Steffi—Miss Forehand, Frau Scholz calls her—and as for her tax-dodger father with his dirty dealings, well, the less said the better. It didn't bother me that my Bobbele could be unbending, even flip, but neither of us was happy about the way he moved to Monaco to get out of paying taxes. "Now why did he go and do that?" I asked Frau Scholz. And then the two of them, him and Steffi, started having problems, and he took to doing those Nutella commercials. And although he looked perfectly darling licking the goo off the knife and smiling his little-rascal smile afterward, he didn't really need the money: I'm sure he's earned more than he can spend.

But now I've slipped into the nineties, and you want me to stick to the eighties. Well, Nutella and me go back to the sixties, when the children kept wanting to smear the icky mess—I think of shoe polish when I see it—all over their bread. Ask your father if he remembers the daily rows we had over it, him and his little brothers and me. The real thing—door-slamming and all. A lot like *Lindenstrasse,* which, I think I told you, is still on...

1986

PEOPLE LIKE ME FROM THE UPPER RHINELAND area we're known for letting water run off our backs, but this time things went too far. First Wackersdorf, where they wanted to reprocess that infernal stuff; then Chernobyl and the cloud that lay for weeks over Bavaria. Over Franconia too and other places, though less in the north and not at all in the west: the French assure us it stopped short at the border.

Ha! It reminds me of the people who pray to Saint Florian saying, "Protect my house from fire—but not my neighbor's." The local judge here in Amberg has always been against the reprocessing plant, so when the kids camped out there and made a racket by running iron poles along the fence—the papers called it "the trumpets of Jericho"—he fed them a nice Sunday breakfast. Which means that Beckstein of the District Court, who's always been a tough customer and so later became Minister of the Interior, was real tough on him. "People like Judge Wilhelm," he was known to say, "should be professionally destroyed."

And all because of Wackersdorf. I went there too. But only after the Chernobyl cloud came and spread over the Upper Rhineland and the beautiful Bavarian Forest. I took the whole family with me. People told me I shouldn't get all hot and bothered about it at my age, but we've gone mushrooming every autumn for as long as I can remember and I had to do something, I had to sound the alarm. And because that infernal stuff, which is called cesium, has rained down from the trees and saturated the forest soil—and the moss and the leaves and the fir and pine needles—with radioactivity, I decided to take a saw to that fence, even though my grandchildren kept telling me, "Forget it, Grandpa! You're too old."

Maybe they were right. Once, when I was out there with all those young people shouting, "Plutonium kitchen! Plutonium kitchen!" I was knocked off my feet by a water cannon they'd sent specially from Regensburg. They'd put some irritant in the water too, some awful poison, though nothing like the cesium that dripped down on our mushrooms from the Chernobyl cloud and is here to stay.

They had to test all mushrooms in the Bavarian Forest and in the woods surrounding Wackersdorf, all of them, not only the delicious parasol and puffball, because wild animals eat all kinds of russules that we don't and could be contaminated by them too. To those of us who were determined to go mushrooming no matter what, they showed a table indicating that the chestnut boletus, an October mushroom that is particularly tasty, had absorbed the most concentrated doses of cesium. The one with the least cesium was the honey agaric, because it's a parasite that grows on tree trunks rather than in the soil. The ink cap, which has a pleasant taste when young, was also spared. But the yellow cracked boletus, the red cracked boletus, the milk cap, which likes to be near young conifers, and even the brown birch boletus, together with the red riding hood (to a lesser extent) and (unfortunately to a very great extent) the cantharellus or chanterelle were tainted. The edible boletus—which is also called the cep and which, when you can find one, is divine—fared poorly as well.

In the end Wackersdorf fizzled out, because the moguls of the atomic industry found they could brew their infernal stuff in France for less and the French made less trouble than us Rhinelanders. Things are quiet again. You don't even hear anything about Chernobyl and the cloud that covered us. But nobody in my family goes mushrooming anymore. You can't blame them, but it hurts to see a family tradition bite the dust.

Oh, *I* still go. The old people's home the children have put me in is surrounded by woods. I pick up anything I find: hedgehog mushrooms and browncaps, ceps in summer, and the chestnut boletus when October rolls around. I fry them in my tiny kitchenette for myself and some of the people who aren't as mobile as I am. We're all over seventy. Why worry about cesium? Our days are numbered as it is.

1987

WHAT WAS THERE FOR US IN CALCUTTA? What drew me to it? *The Rat* behind me, weary of battles with the German press, I drew rubbish heaps, people sleeping in the streets, the goddess Kali sticking her tongue out in shame, I watched crows perching on piles of coconut shells, observed the remains of the empire in luxuriantly overgrown ruins, and it all so stank to heaven that at first I could find no words. And then I had a dream....

But before the momentous dream, I must admit, came a nagging jealousy: Ute, who is forever reading and reading broadly, Ute, who was forced to put up with Calcutta and growing thinner by the day, read one Fontane after the other. We had packed a number of books to counterbalance everyday Indian reality, but why was she reading only him, the Prussian Huguenot? Why read the effusive chronicler of Mark Brandenburg under the revolving fan? Why under the skies of Bengal? But most of all why read Fontane in the first place? And then one day at noon I had a dream....

But before I unreel it, I must say I have nothing, absolutely nothing against Fontane the writer and his novels. Some of his works made a great impression on me when I first came to them late in life: Effi on the swing, regattas on the Havel, strolls along the Halensee with Frau Jenny Treibel, summers in the Harz... But Ute knew it all—the biblical quotations of every pastor, the cause of every conflagration, whether it be Tangermünde in flames or the fateful smolder in *Beyond Recall*. Even when the electricity went off for long intervals and the fan fell silent and Calcutta sank into darkness, even then she would read *Childhood Days,* read it by candlelight, fleeing West Bengal for Swinemünde's bulwark or Pomerania's Baltic Sea beaches.

And then one day at noon, lying under the mosquito net, I had a dream. I was looking down from the window of my attic studio into our Wewelsfleth garden. It was shaded by the fruit trees. I have told this dream to various audiences and in various forms, but I sometimes forget to mention that the village of Wewelsfleth is located in Schleswig-Holstein on the Stör, a tributary of the Elbe. And what should I see in our Schleswig-Holstein garden, in the shade of a pear tree laden with fruit, but Ute sitting at a round table opposite a man.

I know that to tell a dream is to tell it badly, especially if it is dreamed under a mosquito net and the dreamer is dripping with sweat: everything comes out too reasonable. But this dream had no subplots, no second or third film flickering dreamlike; it was perfectly linear, yet momentous, because the man Ute sat chatting with under the pear tree struck me as familiar: a white-haired gentleman he was, and the more they chatted the more handsome he became. Now during monsoon season Calcutta has a humidity of ninety-eight percent. No wonder that under the mosquito net, which the fan's breezes could penetrate with great difficulty if at all, I dreamed of the north. But how could the elderly gentleman sitting there smiling and chatting with Ute under the pear tree, the sun highlighting his hair, how could he be so like Theodor Fontane?

He *was* Theodor Fontane. And Ute was flirting with him. There was something between her and a famous colleague of mine, a man who first started turning out novels at a ripe old age, novels known for treating adultery. Until then I myself had figured in the dream not at all or only as a distant observer. But as I could tell that the two were quite taken with each other, I dreamed myself jealous and, wit or wiles bidding me keep my jealousy under cover and act wisely or guilefully, grabbed a chair standing near me in the dream and went down the stairs to take a seat in the cool shade of the pear tree with the dream couple, Ute and her Fontane.

From then on, as I always say when telling this dream, my marriage was a *ménage à trois*. The two of them could not get rid of me. Ute actually found this solution agreeable, and I found myself on more and more intimate terms with Fontane; indeed, I began then and there, in Calcutta, to read everything of his I could lay my hands on—his letters to an Englishman by the name of Morris, for instance, which showed him to be quite up on world politics. During a rickshaw trip into the center of town, to the Writers Building, I asked him what he thought of the consequences of British colonial rule and the separation of Bengal into Bangladesh and West Bengal. We were of the same opinion, namely, that the separation had little in common with the current German separation and that Bengali reunification was basically out of the question. I was perfectly willing to have him stay on after our peregrinations back to Wewelsfleth an der Stör, that is, I grew accustomed to his presence as an entertaining if occasionally moody lodger and let it be known I was a Fontane fan. I was not rid of him until history proved herself a ruminant in Berlin and elsewhere and I took him at his voluble word and, with Ute's kind permission, extended his failed life at our century's end by putting it in writing. Now that he has been immortalized in the novel *Too Far Afield,* he has lost his power to disturb my dreams, especially as, in the person of Fonty, he is seduced by a young thing toward the end of the story and disappears in the Cévennes among the last surviving Huguenots.

1988

... BUT BEFORE ALL THAT, BEFORE THE WALL SUCCUMBED to falling sickness, before people took to alienating one another and a great joy still reigned, I began to draw the fallen pines, the uprooted beeches, the dead wood that struck the eye no matter where it looked. "The death of the forest" had been a peripheral topic for some years, report soliciting counter-report. Given that automobile exhaust was harmful to trees, there were renewed if futile calls for reducing the speed limit to a hundred kilometers per hour. I learned terms like acid rain, tree stress, fine-root rot.... And the government published an annual "Report on Damage to Forests" that was later, less disturbingly, called "Report on the State of Forests."

Since I believe only what can be drawn, I drove from Göttingen to the Upper Harz Mountains, holed up in a nearly empty hotel for summer hikers or winter skiers and drew— with Siberian charcoal, a wood product—what had come to grief on the slopes and crests. In some areas foresters had removed the damage, carted off the fallen trees, leaving behind closely packed stumps over large surfaces like graves in a cemetery. I hiked as far as the warning signs and saw that the devastation had made it over the border, crossed it silently, without gunfire, ignoring the wire fence running up hill and down dale and the heavily mined death strip that divided more than the Harz, that divided all Germany, all Europe. Bare hills gave me a unobstructed view of the other side.

I met no one—no witches, not a single wood gatherer. Nothing happened. Everything *had* happened. None of Goethe's or Heine's evocations of the place had prepared me for this Harz journey. My only material was some rough drawing paper, a box of charcoals, and two bottles of fixative, whose instructions claimed they had been made without evil propellants and were definitely not harmful to the environment.

Similarly equipped I went with Ute to Dresden—it was only slightly later, a time when border guards still had orders to shoot—where a written invitation for an entry visa proved helpful. Our hosts, a serious painter and a lively dancer, gave us the key to a comfortable cottage in the Ore Mountains. Immediately—as if I had not seen enough by then—I set about drawing the dying woods near the Czech border. Along the slopes trees lay crosswise on one another, as they had fallen; on the crests winds had battered dead, man-sized trunks. Nothing happened here either except that the mice in the house of the Dresden painter, Göschel, were becoming fruitful and multiplying. In other words, here too everything *had* happened. Exhaust fumes and the residues of two state-run industrial complexes had done their job on this side of the border. While I drew, page after page, Ute read—though not Fontane this time.

A year later the signs and banners of demonstrators in Leipzig and elsewhere were emblazoned with the motto "Ax the bosses! Save the trees!" But things hadn't gone that far when we were there: the state still managed to hold sway over its citizens; the damage still looked permanent.

We actually quite liked the area. The houses in the villages were shingled. Poverty had long been a way of life. The villages had colorful names like Fürstenau (Prince's Pasture), Gottgetreu (True to God), Hemmschuh (Brake Shoe). The road leading to Prague ran through the nearby border town of Zinnwald (Tin Wood). It had been traveled by more than tourists: on an October day fifty years before, motorized units of the German Wehrmacht had headed down it with Prague in view; on an August day twenty years before, motorized units of the National People's Army had followed similar orders. The Czechs couldn't have forgotten the replay. The double-whammy power play. History loves repetition, even if conditions are different. For example, the trees were still standing then....

1989

DRIVING BACK TO LAUENBURG FROM BERLIN, we tuned in as usual to the Third Program, so we got the news late, but when it finally came I cried out in joy and in panic—like thousands of others, I'm sure—"Madness! Sheer madness!" and then—like Ute, who was at the wheel—sank into thoughts running both forward and back. Meanwhile, an acquaintance who lived on the other side of the Wall and worked in the archives of the Academy of Arts, keeping watch then as now over literary estates, was likewise late in receiving the glad tidings, which reached him like a time bomb.

The way he tells it, he was jogging home from the Friedrichshain—nothing out of the ordinary, because even East Berliners had taken up that American-inspired form of self-castigation by then—when at the intersection of Käthe-Niederkirchner-Strasse and Bötzowstrasse he came upon an acquaintance who was likewise panting and sweating from his jog. Bobbing up and down, they agreed to meet for a beer that evening, and that evening he repaired to the acquaintance's spacious flat, where, since his acquaintance was employed in what the East called "material production," my acquaintance was not particularly surprised to find a newly laid parquet living-room floor, an achievement utterly beyond the means of an archival paper-pusher in charge of nothing more than footnotes.

They had a Pilsner, then another, and before long a bottle of Nordhäuser schnapps appeared on the table. They talked about the old days and their children and the ideological constraints at parent-teacher meetings. My acquaintance—who comes from the Ore Mountains, on whose slopes I had sketched dead trees the year before—told his acquaintance he was planning a ski trip there that winter with his wife but was having trouble with his Wartburg—the tires, both front and back, had hardly any tread left—and hoped his acquaintance could put him on the track of some snow tires: anyone who could have a parquet floor laid by a private person under the conditions of "actually existing socialism," as the regime was called at the time, would have an idea of how to get hold of so precious a commodity.

As we arrived home in Behlendorf with the good news from the radio now in our hearts, the volume on the television set in the living room of my acquaintance's acquaintance was turned down low so the two of them could go on undisturbed about the tire problem, and the man with the parquet floor said the only way to get snow tires was to come up with some "real money" but he could find him some carburetor jets. Glancing over at the silent screen, my acquaintance thought the program must be a feature film of some kind because it showed young people climbing the wall and sitting astride it while the border police stood idly by. When my acquaintance's acquaintance was made aware of the flagrant disregard for the wall's protective function, he muttered, "Typical," and the two men quickly dismissed the tastelessness of "yet another cold war product" so as to get back to the subject at hand—the bald regular and unavailable snow tires. The subject of the archives and the papers of the more or less important writers housed there never came up.

As we switched on the TV set, deep in thought by then over the coming post-wall period, my acquaintance's acquaintance had not yet decided to take the few steps over the newly laid parquet floor to turn up the volume, but when he finally did there was not another word about tires: it was a problem the new period and its "real money" could solve instantly. Stopping only to down the rest of the schnapps, they made their way to Invalidenstrasse, which was jammed with cars, more Trabants than the relatively expensive Wartburgs, trying to cross the—wonder of wonders—open border. And if you listened carefully, you could hear everyone, well, nearly everyone who wanted to cross over to the West on foot or in a Trabi, you could hear them all either shouting or whispering "Madness!"

just as I had shouted "Madness!" outside Behlendorf before sinking into my reverie.

I forgot to ask my acquaintance how, when, and for which currency he finally managed to come by his snow tires. I never found out whether he and his wife, who'd been an ice-skating champion during the days of the German Democratic Republic, got to celebrate the New Year in their Ore Mountain retreat. Life just kept moving on.

1990

IT WASN'T ONLY TO BE PRESENT FOR THE BALLOT count that we met in Leipzig. Jakob and Leonore Suhl had come all the way from Portugal and were staying at the Hotel Merkur near the station. Ute and I drove in from Stralsund and had put up at nearby Wiederitzsch in the home of a pharmacist I knew from the Leipzig Round Table.

The first afternoon we set off in search of Jakob's roots. He had grown up in a working-class district that had once been called Oetzsch and was now called Markkleeberg. First his father, Abraham Suhl, who had taught German and Yiddish at the Jewish Gymnasium, emigrated to America with his younger brothers; then, in 1938, fifteen-year-old Jakob followed suit. Only his mother stayed behind in Oetzsch—the marriage had broken up—but then she too was forced to flee, to Poland, Lithuania, and finally Latvia, where the Wehrmacht caught up with her and—as the family later learned— a guard shot her dead as she tried to escape. Her husband and sons had been unable to raise the money necessary for a U.S.

visa, her last hope as wife and mother. Jakob's voice would falter whenever he spoke of their failed attempts.

Though not so mobile as he might have been, he was eager to show us the apartment house where he had lived, the courtyard where the wash had been hung out to dry, his school, and, in a side street, his gymnasium. In the courtyard he had a joyous reunion with the carpet stand, pointing to it, a relic of his youth, with head cocked and eyes closed, as if lending an ear to the regular whacks still resounding from its former life. He wanted Leonore to take his picture under a blue enamel sign that said "Model House Collective of the Municipality of Markkleeberg, 1 May 1982." He also posed for her in front of the blue—unfortunately locked—door to the gymnasium, this time beneath the bust of Friedrich Ludwig Jahn, father of the Young German gymnastics movement, staring severely into the distance out of his niche. "No," said Jakob, "we had nothing to do with the rich 'fur Jews' in the city proper. Everybody here—Jews or non-Jews, Nazis too—they were all low-paid white- and blue-collar workers." Then he asked to leave: he'd had enough.

A young construction engineer took us to the House of Democracy, Bernhard-Göring-Strasse, where the human rights movement had recently set up shop and where we experienced the election disaster. First we spent time with the Greens, then with Alliance 90—young people standing, sitting, and squatting in front of television screens. Here too Leonore took pictures; they capture the mute horror prompted by the first projection: a young woman is covering her face. It was obvious to all that the Christian Democratic Union was in for a devastating victory. "But that's how democracy works," said Jakob.

The next day we found a sign on a corrugated iron fence in front of the side entrance to the Nikolai Church, the center of the Monday demonstrations in the autumn of the previous year. The blue lettering, to make it look like a street sign, said, "Suckers Square," and then, underneath, in small print, "Regards from October's children. Yes, we're still here."

Before we said good-bye to our pharmacist, who had voted for the Christian Democratic Union ("It was the hard-cash argument—I regret it already"), he gave us a tour of his house and garden with the good-natured pride of the wheeler-dealer Saxon not even socialism could keep down. Next to a tiny pond we saw a one-and-a-half-meter bronze head of Goethe he had saved from being melted down by acquiring it for a large lot of copper wire. We marveled at a candelabra that had been part of a lot being sold to Holland for hard currency until he contrived to pinch—in his words, "rescue"—it. He had likewise "borrowed" two stone pillars and a porphyry basin from a cemetery threatened by central planning. And the garden was also strewn with little-used stone and cast-iron benches: he was a man who never sat.

Then our pharmacist, who had managed to remain independent all through socialism, took us to his roofed swimming pool, which he heated with solar panels from April on. But what surprised us more than all the Western goods he'd secured through barter was a group of larger-than-life sandstone figures representing Christ and six of the apostles (including the Evangelists). He assured us he'd managed to save the sculpture at the last minute, namely, just before the Markus Church, like so many other Leipzig churches, was destroyed by the "Communist barbarians." And now Christ (as the late nineteenth century perceived Him) and a few representative apostles stood in a semicircle around the shimmering turquoise pool, blessing the two robots (of Japanese origin) diligently cleaning the tile walls, blessing us, who had come to Leipzig on 18 March to sober up after the first free elections to the People's Chamber, and possibly blessing the coming unity; He stood there under a roof supported by slender "Doric columns," as the pharmacist informed us. "What you see here is a cross between Hellenistic and Christian elements on the one hand and Saxon practicality on the other."

Jakob Suhl, exhausted by his return to Leipzig-Oetzsch, slept through most of the trip past the vineyards along the Unstrut via Mühlhausen to the border. He had seen enough.

1991

"YOU DON'T SEE ANY DEAD PEOPLE. All you see are wobbly gun sights and then hits. Bull's-eyes supposedly. It's like a game...."

"Right. Because CNN's got the TV rights for this war—and the next and the one after that..."

"But you do see oil fields burning...."

"Because that's what the whole thing's about. Oil and only oil! Any kid knows that. That's why they're out in the streets. Leaving their teachers, leaving whole schools empty. In Hamburg, Berlin, Hannover. Even in the East—Schwerin, Rostock. They're carrying candles again, like two years ago...."

"But when we marched against the war in Vietnam and napalm..."

"Don't give me any of your '68 crap. While you're sitting here on your ass, those kids..."

"It's not the same. We had our own perspective, a revolutionary concept, you might say, whereas these kids with their candles..."

"But comparing Saddam to Hitler, that makes sense, doesn't it? Isn't it clear what's good and what's evil?"

"It's more of a metaphor. We should have gone on talking, negotiating, used an economic boycott the way we did in South Africa. Pressure, not war..."

"But this is no war! It's a show put on by CNN. A co-production with the Pentagon. The consumer can turn it on and off at will. Fireworks in the comfort of your own home. Nice and clean. No deaths. A science-fiction extravaganza. Just add pretzels..."

"But you do see the oil fields burning and missiles falling on Israel. There are people down in basements with gas masks on...."

"And who's been arming Saddam against Iran all these years? Right. The Yanks, the French..."

"And German business. Here. Look. A long list of choice goods: missile accessories, poison kitchens with recipes..."

"I guess that's why that Biermann guy, who I always thought was a pacifist, I guess that's why he's for the war. He even says..."

"He doesn't say shit; he just blasts the people who don't agree with him...."

"Know what he calls the kids marching with the candles for peace? Crybabies..."

"Because they have no goal in mind. No broader social perspective, whereas we..."

"What about 'No blood for oil!' Doesn't that say something?"

"Not enough. When we marched against the war in Vietnam..."

"Look, 'Ho! Ho! Ho Chi Minh!' is not what you'd call a brilliant argument. And now it's a bunch of kids out in the streets. Munich, Stuttgart. Over five thousand of them. Play-group kids even. They march a while in silence, then burst out with 'I'm scared! I'm scared!' That's a first for Germany—public confession.... If you want my opinion..."

"Who needs fucking opinions! Look at those kids, will you? What isn't Adidas is Armani. Spoiled brats, scared their designer clothes are in jeopardy, whereas in '68 and later—when we marched against the Frankfurt airport expansion and the Pershing II in Mutlangen—that was the real thing. These toddlers and their candles..."

"Look, isn't that how it began in Leipzig? Every Monday we met at the Nikolai Church for a peaceful march. Every Monday till the bosses got the jitters..."

"It's not the same...."

"But Hitler and Saddam. They go together, don't they?"

"The oil fields are burning...."

"And in Baghdad a shelter packed with civilians was..."

"You won't see that on CNN...."

"Of course not. This is the future. TV rights will be auctioned off before every war. And the time to start preproduction is now. Because there'll be another one soon. Somewhere else if not in the Gulf..."

"In the Balkans? The Serbs and the Croats..."

"No, only where there's oil..."

"And where you don't see any dead people..."

"And only the children are scared..."

1992

I LEFT WITTENBERG A BIT SURPRISED at the invitation from men once in the service of the now defunct state. As a clergyman I had had quite some practice in the pastoral probing of the depths laid bare of late throughout the country. Shortly after the Wall came down, I was one of those who called for a disclosure of the State Security system's activities. Now I was to be personally involved in the process.

The case in question—"Husband Spies on Wife for Years"—was known to me from the extensive coverage given it in the press. The request for advice did not, however, come from the victims of the misfortune, or, should I say, of the legacy of Stasi rule; it came from their parents, who, when they asked for my assistance over the phone, made it clear they had no religious affiliation. As for me, I assured them repeatedly that there was no missionary zeal behind my decision to see them in Berlin.

The couple that had invited me sat on the couch, the other couple, like me, in armchairs. "We simply refuse to believe what the papers say," they told me, "but neither he nor she will talk to us."

"Unfortunately, the children are suffering the most," said the mother of the spied-upon wife. "They're so attached to their father."

They all agreed that their son and son-in-law had always been a good, patient father. They also assured me that while their daughter and daughter-in-law had always been the stronger, domineering member of the couple, both had equally criticized first the Party, then the state. They had refused to see, no matter how often they were told, how much they owed the workers-and-peasants state. Without the socialist system they would never have had the opportunity to become such highly qualified scientists or hold such important posts....

In the beginning I merely listened. I am said to be good at that. What I learned was that one father had been a leader in pharmacological research, the other—the father of the spied-upon daughter—an officer in State Security to the end, and in Personnel Training to boot. The former Stasi officer (now unemployed) regretted his son-in-law's involvement: he knew how things worked from the inside. "If only he'd told me in time, I'd have talked him out of it. It was too risky, his double game. On the one hand, he wanted to offer his services as an informer out of loyalty to the state; on the other, he wanted to protect his all too critical wife—you never knew when she would come out with something—from possible repressive measures on the part of the state. That's what got him into trouble. And he was too weak to stand the pressure. I know what I'm talking about, because I was reprimanded many times by my superiors for having refused to give up contact with my daughter—in other words, renounce her—after her first provocation in a Pankow church. I went on giving her financial support even though she never stopped calling my place of employment 'the octopus.'"

The scientist father had similar complaints: his son had never asked his advice. As a recognized anti-Fascist and long-standing Party member (he had spent the war in Moscow) entrusted with every variety of political deviation and correspondingly drastic responses, he would have urged his son to choose one side or the other. "But no, he dreamed of a 'third way.'"

The mother and mother-in-law said little except to express their concern for the grandchildren and stress the spy spouse's paternal qualities. The mother of the spied-upon dissident daughter said, "Just a few months ago the two of them sat here on this couch with the children. And now everything's a shambles."

The practiced listener in me refrained from commenting. We had coffee and cookies—Bahlsen cookies, a West German brand. I learned that they were sorry, though not particularly surprised to see the German Democratic Republic come to an end. The only thing they found surprising was that the son and son-in-law, whether in spite of or because of his double role, had thought "our state" to be mendable, reformable, and that to the very end. The daughter and daughter-in-law as well. At a time when the "leading comrades" had resigned themselves to the inevitable, she was still ready to go to the barricades for a "one way or other democratic socialism." Which only showed how naive they both were. "No," said the now unemployed Stasi officer, "it wasn't our children who did us in; it was ourselves." After a pause for our cups to be refilled he continued: "In '83, when my daughter and son-in-law began working together—or so we thought—to create a grass-roots 'church from below' in Gotha, the Party and state should have given it, critical as it was, a positive interpretation and reshaped it as a 'Party from below.'"

A series of self-accusations followed, and I, who despite the misgivings of our church hierarchy had also been part of the "church from below" movement, did my best to suppress any sense of triumph in the face of their belated—all too belated—insights. Then the pharmacologist accused the Stasi personnel officer of having delivered the already vulnerable East German population into the hands of the West by having assembled files with excessive ardor, and the Stasi spy's father-in-law admitted that State Security had erred: it had failed to

protect the loyal, trusting informers—some of whom were
family members—by destroying the reports and personal data
in time. Precautionary measures had certainly been called for.
"Don't you agree, Vicar?"

"Certainly, certainly," I said, at a loss for words. "But the
West should also have realized what a time bomb was ticking
away over there in Stasi headquarters. I think the files and
everything in them should have been sealed for twenty years,
say. At least. But the West wasn't satisfied with its material victory.... From a Christian standpoint it would have been...
And to protect the grandchildren, as in your case..."

At that point they showed me a photograph album. I saw
several snapshots of the longtime prominent dissident and her
recently prominent husband. They were sitting with their children on the couch on which the parents of the daughter were
now sitting in their capacity as grandparents of much to be
pitied grandchildren. It was only then that I learned of the
couple's imminent divorce. All the parents-in-law accepted the
idea. "It's all right," said one set. "There's nothing you can do
about it," said the other. Then they thanked me for being such
a good listener.

1993

WHEN YOU'RE JUST A COP, your hands are tied. Oh, not
in principle. A couple of years ago, when there was a well-
guarded border between us and the West and our government
agencies did their job, namely, maintained law and order, you
didn't have these five-six hundred skinheads on the extreme
right going around with baseball bats and swinging—swinging

hard—the minute they got within range of a dark skin. Sure you'd hear people grumbling about the Poles, who'd come in and buy up everything in sight, but real Nazis, tightly organized, with Reich military flags and all—they didn't show up till the end, when there was no order left to speak of and all the big-shot comrades were scared shitless. Skinheads had been around for a long time over in the West; it was normal over there. But when it caught on here too—first in Hoyerswerda and then in our very own Rostock-Lichtenhagen, because the residents were all upset over the Refugee Center and the hostel for Vietnamese workers next door—we pretty much had our hands tied: there weren't enough of us and the men on top couldn't make up their minds. The next thing you know people are saying, "Typical" and "Only in the East" and "The cops just look the other way." Really. That's what people said. They suspected us of secret and even open sympathy with the hooligans. Finally, after they had that fire over in Mölln where three people were killed and then that one in Solingen with five victims, and now that skinhead terror tactics are making headway all over, becoming pan-German, you might say, normal, par for the course, finally people have stopped saying, "You only see that in the East," though it's true that here in Rostock—where we used to have full employment and people had nothing against foreigners—thousands of people have been "temporarily removed from the workforce" or, to call a spade a spade, laid off, and they're perfectly glad that now, since the riots, the refugee hostels are empty and the blacks and Vietnamese gone—well, not gone, but somewhere else, so you don't see them.

Anyway, it wasn't nice—and it didn't make things any easier for us cops—that the people here in Lichtenhagen, like the people in Hoyerswerda, just stood at their windows and watched or even clapped while all hell broke loose, the skin-heads chasing down the poor bastards—Balkan types too—and beating them with their baseball bats, knocking them silly. It was all we could do to save a few Vietnamese from the worst. But we had no deaths the way they had, like I say, in Mölln and Solingen—in the West, that is. They had Turks there. We've got almost none. Though that may change if the West thinks it can load them off on us—Turks and those Bosnians and Albanians, fanatic Muslims the lot of them—because we've supposedly got room for them. And when that kind of thing happens and you're just a cop, you've pretty much got your hands tied, because then these skinhead hooli-gans come in and do what in a normal society you'd expect politicians to do, namely, see to it the borders are secure and clean things up before it's too late. But all the politicians do is talk. They leave the dirty work to us.

Where do *I* stand? The candlelight processions? Hun-dreds of thousands protesting against the way foreigners are treated? What do I think? ... Well, let *me* ask *you*: What's the point? We had them too. Candles galore. A few years ago. In Leipzig, in Rostock even. So what. What did they get us? Fine, the Wall is gone. But what else? Suddenly we've got all these right-wing radicals. And more by the day. Candlelight processions! You think that'll help? Don't make me laugh! Ask people who used to work in the shipyards or anywhere—ask them what they think of candles and what they think of hard, cold reality, namely, what it means to be laid off from one day to the next. Ask my fellow cops. Not the ones they brought in from Hamburg and then recalled the minute things started getting hairy. No, ask the men I work with, the men who were with the force back in the days of the People's

Police. Ask them what they think of candle magic and the rest of your peace crap.

What's that? ... You say it gives our European neighbors a clear sign of our shame at the rise of a new "brown mob" here in Germany. I know I'm just a cop, but let me ask you, Are things so different in France? Or in London, say. Do they handle their Algerians or Pakistanis with kid gloves? Or the Americans their blacks? Well, there you are. So let me be brutally frank. The kind of thing we saw here in Lichtenhagen and the extreme cases later in Mölln and Solingen, regrettable as they were, can in principle be seen as perfectly normal. And Germans—all of us, I mean Germany as a whole—are a perfectly normal people. Like the French, the English, the Yanks...

What's that? ... Well, that's your opinion. I say run-of-the-mill.

1994

HARD AS NAILS, THEY SAY. Well, what the hell! Should I be weak because I'm a woman? May I ask the man who is putting me down on paper here and thinks he can give me a grade (social behavior: unsatisfactory) to acknowledge—before converting all my bottom-line achievements to catastrophes—that I have come through all the fact-finding commissions with a clean bill of health and will be ready to face all fusspots and nitpickers in the year 2000 when the Expo is up and running. And if I do fall—because your social romantics suddenly have the word—I'll land on my feet: I'll retire to the family estate on the Elbe, which Papa, one of the last of the big private bankers, retained after being pushed into bankruptcy. I'll say "What the hell!" and turn my attention to ships, container ships, to be specific, watch them sailing upstream to Hamburg or back down, heavy laden, low in the water, to the mouth of the Elbe, on to the sea and the many seas. And when the sun goes down and the mood comes upon me, I'll watch the play of the colors on the water, yield to the fleetly dissolving images, and turn into pure feeling, all soft and nice....

What do you mean? Of course I love poetry, but I also love monetary risk and the incalculable. Witness my work with, no, my leadership of, the Treuhand, the agency which, because charged with privatizing the East's economy, has moved billions of marks, doing away with many thousands of potentially disastrous businesses and creating the necessary space for development, which has made the man I refer to above—who clearly wishes to offset the top salary I received for services rendered by forcing me to pay damages for supposedly lining my own pocket—think of writing one of his usual overblown novels to compare me to a character from the work of Fontane because a certain Frau Jenny Treibel was as good as I am at combining business and poetry....

Why not? Then I'll be not only hard-as-nails Frau Treuhand and the Iron Lady; I'll be a part of German literary history. I can't understand the envy, the hatred society feels for people like us with high-paying positions. You'd think I'd gone out job hunting. No, each time it was duty calling; each time I was summoned: to Hannover as finance minister and later to Wilhelmstrasse, when my predecessor at the Treuhand was simply bumped off, assassinated—who by, I wonder— and new manpower was called for. It was the same with Expo 2000: I was pressured into it. Why? Because I don't shy at risk, because I'm beholden to no one but the market, because I can put my losses behind me and make debts that pay off, and because I can stick through anything till the end, because I'm hard as nails....

Granted, there was unemployment; there still is. The man putting me down on paper here holds me accountable for hundreds of thousands of jobless Germans. Well, what the hell, I say to myself. They've still got their safety net, and I had other fish to fry. No sooner did the Treuhand complete its monumental task of dismantling the remains of the Communist planned economy than I had to prepare for my next adventure, the world's fair. What does "prepare" mean? Leaping on a galloping horse called Expo, breathing life into the vaguest of ideas. I'd just as soon have lolled in the safety net at government expense—I was myself what you might call unemployed—preferably, of course, in the form of a hammock and on the terrace of our estate on the Elbe, which I seldom have a chance to enjoy and as good as never before sunset, because the Treuhand won't let me be and I'm being threatened with yet another fact-finding commission and the man writing me off under the year 1994 is trying to pin everything on me: I, not the West German potash industry, am responsible for sacking a couple of thousand miners in Bischofferode; I, not Krupp, shut down the steelworks in Oranienburg; I, not Fischer Ball Bearing in Schweinfurt, bought up all the East German ball-bearing factories and put them out of business; I'm the one who invented the trick of using government funds earmarked for the East to buck up ailing Western businesses like Bremen's Vulkan Shipyard; in other words, I, as Frau Treuhand, a.k.a. Jenny Treibel, conned billions of marks at the expense of helpless, floundering little people....

No. Nobody has ever given me anything; I've always had to

take things. I'm not interested in petty social concerns; I care only for large-scale challenges. I love risks and risks love me. When talk about "exorbitant" unemployment rates and monies disappearing "without a trace"—let me repeat: without a trace—when talk like that finally dies down, when after the year 2000 people finally stop going on about subsidized Expo tickets and suchlike nonsense, then it will be clear that the boost the Treuhand gave free enterprise was due to its hard-as-nails cleanup policy and that the boon the Expo proved to be—a boon for the future, our common future—more than made up for any possible shortfall. I'm looking forward to enjoying the poetry of an industrious river and cost-free sunsets from the terrace of my family estate unless, that is, I'm offered another high-risk challenge. I'd be tempted, for example, by the possibility of directing the changeover from the hard German mark to the Euro in paper and coin....

What the hell, I'll say to myself then, and go for it, hard as nails if need be. And no one—not even you, kind sir, who wish to put me down on paper—will save me from the bust that may be in store for me, because without the chance of all-out failure I have no chance for all-out success....

1995

... AND NOW, ALL OF YOU OUT THERE IN RADIOLAND, listen to this, listen to all hell breaking loose, or, as we say in Berlin, the bear on the rampage. Can you hear it? Two or three hundred thousand people crowding the Kurfürstendamm, scene of so many fateful events in our history, yes, all

the way along the Ku'damm, from the Memorial Church on
up to the Halensee, bubbling—no, seething with action. Only
in Berlin could this be happening, only here, where just recently another such one-of-a-kind happening—the magical,
the totally unique "covering" of the Reichstag by world-
renowned artist Christo—caused a sensation that attracted
hundreds of thousands of spectators, yes, here, only here,
where just a few years ago young people boogied on the wall,
threw a bang-up party for freedom, turned the shout "Madness!" into the word of the year, only here, I repeat, could there
be something so brimming with life and flipped-out energy as
the Love Parade, and this year with larger crowds than ever,
even if at first the City Senate was none too eager to give its
blessing and went so far as to ban it, citing the potential refuse
problem, and while we respect its reservations—and I'm sure
all of you out there listening in do too—we were glad when
the senator for Internal Affairs finally okayed a "demonstration," and so now the streets are jumping with "ravers"—a
new English word meaning something like "dreamers, totally
flipped-out visionaries"—and technodancers, making all
Berlin, this wonderful town open to anything and everything
new, "the biggest party in the world," in the words of some,
while shocking others, though what has been going on here
for several hours now—loud as it is in decibels (just listen to
it!)—is also as peaceful as can be, perhaps because this Berlin
version of Rio's carnival has made its motto for the year "Peace
on Earth." That's right, my friends, what these so inventively
dressed young men and women coming to Berlin from the
four corners of the earth, from as far as Australia, what these
young men and women want more than anything else is
peace, peace on earth. But at the same time they want to show

the world, "Hey, look, world! We *are*. And we are *many*. And
we are *different*. We want to have fun. Fun, fun, and only fun."
And when it comes to fun, they have no inhibitions. Because,
as they themselves put it, they're different: they're no thugs, either skinhead or terrorist; they're no born-again sixty-eighters,
always against one thing or the other but never quite clear
about what they're for; they're no goody-goodies with candlelight processions and false alarms about the threat of war. No,
the young people of the nineties—they're horses of many
different colors, so to speak. Just listen to their music, which
some of you out there may think of as nothing but ear-
splitting noise—yes, truth to tell, the constant bass throb up
and down the Ku'damm, the merciless boom-boom chaka-
chaka boom known as techno, is not to everybody's liking—
just listen to their music and you'll know these young people
are in love with themselves and with chaos and all they really
care about is boom-booming their way to ecstasy. I watch
them dance up a storm, dripping with sweat, ready to drop,
yet hanging in there, till finally they depart the Ku'damm in
barely moving vans decorated with the most imaginative de-
signs or in (or on) chartered buses. Just listen. All Berlin is
seething with action. And now that words are beginning to
fail me, I'm making my way, mike in hand, into the rollicking,
frolicking crowd to ask some of these "ravers," these totally
possessed dancers, "What attracted you to Berlin? Why did
you come?" "Because it's really great just to experience all the
people..." "And you, my damsel in pink?" "Because, like,
here at the Love Parade I can, like, finally be me..." "And you,
young man?" "Because I'm for peace, that's why. And the way
things are going down here is the way I picture peace...."
"And you, my beauty in the see-through plastic top? What

brings you here?" "Me and my belly button, we want to be seen...." "And you two in the shiny varnished miniskirts?" "It's awesome...." "Super awesome..." "I really dig the atmosphere...." "And where else could I get away with an outfit like this?" So now you know, ladies and gentlemen, young and old. The key word is "outfit." Because these wild youngsters, these "ravers" have something more on the brain than their Vitus-like contortions: they want to come on strong, make an impression, be seen, "be themselves." So what they cover their bodies with may not go beyond underwear and doesn't cover much in any case. You won't be surprised to hear that name fashion designers are taking their lead, coming out with Love Parade lines, and the tobacco industry, Camel in particular, is featuring technodancers in its ads. By the way, nobody here bats an eyelid at all the advertising hoopla: this generation accepts capitalism hook, line, and sinker. The kids of the nineties are the kids of big business. It's written all over them. They're the product of its markets. They want to be the newest of the new and have the newest of the new. Which accounts in part for the popularity of the latest "high," the latest "dope"—ecstasy. A very mellow young man I talked to a few minutes ago had this to say: "The world's beyond saving, but it can still party." And that's what's happening here today, my friends: the world is "partying." No revolutionary slogans required. Just peace—even if down there in the Balkans, in Tuzla and Srebrenica, they're shooting up a storm—peace today and peace tomorrow. So let me wrap up my report from the Berlin Love Parade with a look at that tomorrow. Because here in Berlin tomorrow has arrived, in the Berlin where the legendary Mayor Reuter once cried out to the world, "Keep your eyes on this town!" and America's President John

F. Kennedy told cheering crowds, "Ich bin ein Berliner," in the once divided, now reunited metropolis and mammoth construction site well on its way to the year 2000 and the post-Weimar, post-Bonn Berlin Republic, here in Berlin the tomorrow generation will resume its ecstatic dancing next year and in the years thereafter, leaving us oldsters, if I may be allowed a little quip by way of conclusion, to clean up the mess, the mountains of refuse that the great technoparty known as the Love Parade leaves in its wake.

1996

PROFESSOR VONDERBRÜGGE, WHOM I'D BEEN PLAGUING with lay questions for some time, actually wished to write something on the subject of genetics for this year—an analysis of the data on Megan and Morag, the cloned sheep twins (the Scottish sheep Dolly, born of a surrogate mother, dates from the following year)—but he had to back out because of an urgent commitment in Heidelberg: a much-sought-after authority, he had been asked to take part in the World Congress of the Human Genome Organization, where, besides cloned sheep, the agenda included the bioethical issue of the increasingly clear prospect of a future without fathers.

As a result, I will fill in with an account of myself, or, rather, my three daughters and myself, their bona-fide father, and of the trip we took together just before Easter, a trip that, while not without its surprises, came off just as we'd hoped.

Laura, Helene, and Nele were sent to me by three mothers who, seen from within and—with a loving eye—from without, could not have been more different and—if they'd ever had a conversation—contradictory. Their daughters, however, soon agreed on the destination of the trip their father had proposed: Italy! I then put in for Florence and Umbria on the basis of admittedly sentimental reasons: years before, in the summer of 1951, to be exact, I had hitchhiked through the region. Back then my rucksack was light—all I had was a sleeping bag, a change of shirt, a sketch pad, and a box of watercolors—and I marveled at every olive grove, every lemon ripening on the tree. Now I was traveling with my daughters, and they, sans mother, with me. (Ute, who had borne no daughters, only sons, said good-bye with a skeptical look on her face.) Laura, the eldest, who vouchsafed her rare smiles on a trial basis only and was herself the mother of three children, took care of booking the hotels and arranging for us to pick up a car in Florence. Helene, well on her way through drama school, struck appropriate poses, mostly comic, in front of fountains, on marble steps, and against classical columns. Nele may have sensed that the trip was her last chance to hold Papa's hand and be his little girl, so she could forget about the coming trials of adolescence and indulge Laura's sisterly attempts at persuading her to finish school if only to spite the silly place. All three were concerned for their father on Perugia's steep steps and during the climbs in Assisi and Orvieto, his legs reminding him at every step of the smoke clouds he regularly emitted. I kept pausing and pointing out sights to show there were in fact things to see— here a portal, there a crumbling façade with a particularly intense color scheme, though occasionally nothing more than a display of shoes in a shop window.

I was less sparing with tobacco than with commentary on art that seemed to cry out for it, first at the Uffizi, then outside

Orvieto's cathedral or in Assisi's Upper and Lower Churches, which were still whole in 1996, but my daughters made up for me in their lively responses. For instance, each time we stopped in front of a Botticelli, a Fra Angelico, or any fresco or painting by the Italian masters depicting women, often three women, gracefully grouped, staggered, aligned, seen from the front or the back or in profile, I would watch Laura, Helene, and Nele's mirror-image reactions to the maidens, angels, and allegorical figures, observe them turning into the Graces or praying in silent devotion, then becoming animated again, prancing in place or striding solemnly back and forth, but still seeming to come from the brush of a Botticelli, Ghirlandaio, Fra Angelico, or (in Assisi) Giotto. Everywhere we went I was treated to a ballet.

And so the removed observer was celebrated as Father. But no sooner did we return to our base in Perugia than, following the Etruscan city wall up- and downhill with my daughters, I had the feeling that, self-confident father that I had just considered myself, I was being observed through the cracks of an otherwise solid stonework. It was as if the three so different mothers had come together in their concern over how I was handling the situation, whether I was playing favorites, whether I was trying to make up for former shortcomings, and whether I was in general living up to my obligations as a father.

During the next few days I avoided the porous Etruscan masonry. Then Easter came with its bells. We paraded up and down the Corso as if we'd come from church and the Mass, arm in arm with Laura, hand in hand with Nele, and Helene making a spectacle of herself out in front. After that we drove into the countryside, and thanks to my fatherly foresight I had a number of not quite Easter eggs but choice surprises like

macaroons, bags of dried ceps, basil paste, jars of olives, ca-
pers, anchovies, and other such Italian delicacies to hide in the
cracked, hollow- and nest-infested trunks of the olive grove
that had invited us for a picnic. While I scampered from tree
to tree, Laura, Helene, and Nele had to stare out at the landscape motionless. Things continued in this childlike vein until
all three had managed to ferret out Daddy's hiding places.
They seemed to enjoy doing so, though Helene claimed to
have uncovered a family of snakes—definitely poisonous—in
a nest among the roots of a tree where she had found a little
pouch of lavender. Thank God they'd slithered off.

At that point I was reminded of the mothers concealed in
the Etruscan wall, a kind of concentrated matriarchy, but
then, driving back past campaign posters for a media shark
or his Fascist allies on the one hand and a left-center coalition
with an olive tree for a symbol on the other, we saw a herd of
sheep—far off, then up close—in which mother sheep and
their Easter lambs drifted past behind the bellwether, so
placidly sheeplike that it was unthinkable that sheep by the
names of Megan and Morag had been cloned, unlikely that
there would soon be a fatherless sheep by the name of Dolly,
and thus possible that fathers would maintain a place for
themselves in the foreseeable future....

1997

Dear Herr Grass,

Between my return from the Edinburgh conference, where
I had ample opportunity to talk shop with that much famed
and much feared embryologist, Ian Wilmut, and my imminent

departure (the day after tomorrow) for Boston to consult with other illustrious colleagues, I have carved out a few moments to respond to your not precisely groundless but wildly overstated fears. Your tendency is to let your imagination range free and unfettered, whereas here the utmost sobriety is called for. For the good of all concerned.

Let us begin with what even the layman should have no trouble understanding, though the quite straightforward modular construction method may strike him as hocus-pocus. Dolly owes her modest existence to three mothers: her "gene" mother, whose udder provided the cells with the genetic information enabling us to engineer the construction of a brand-new sheep; her "egg" mother, whose ovaries provided the ova or reproductive cells, one of which had the genetic information sucked out of it and, thus emptied, was combined by means of electrical charges with the genetic material of the gene mother's udder cells (because only the genotype of the gene mother can give the command to split); and her "surrogate" mother, in whose womb the growing embryo was ready to be transplanted and from whose womb, after the usual period of gestation, our Dolly came into the world, an identical copy of her gene mother—and now for the sensational part—without any input from a male.

That is basically that. And if I understand you correctly, doing away with male participation is the reason for your on-going concern. You fear that the productive and completely fatherless sort of gene manipulation that has now been done with a sheep—and will soon be done with a pig and then with a monkey—will eventually make it possible for humans, or, to be more precise, women, to give birth on their own. And indeed, it is not out of the question. People everywhere are hoping for and dreading the more than likely extension of the modular construction method, and Dr. Wilmut, whom one might call Dolly's "spiritual father," told me stories of highly motivated women offering him their services as gene mothers, egg mothers, and surrogate mothers.

But no, Herr Grass, for the time being it all remains in the realm of speculation, though James Watson, the Nobel Prize winner known for his research on the carrier of genetic information, has not only predicted but also explicitly encouraged human cloning for the purpose of producing copies of exceptional individuals, geniuses like Einstein, Callas, or Picasso. And didn't you yourself use cloned rat-people in a novel (of which I have unfortunately read only excerpts but which must have caused quite a controversy when it appeared), calling your fiendishly clever productions of unchecked gene manipulation, with a touch of irony, "Watstoncricks"?

Joking aside, however, what we need is a scientifically based bioethic that will on the one hand be more effective than repetitive moral precepts at keeping widespread scaremongering tactics within limits and on the other hand have the authority to establish a new social order for the coming clone generations, which one day in the not too distant future will grow up side by side with the standard, primordial human generations, because the juxtaposition of the two is bound to give rise to at least some conflict. It will also be the task of bioethics to regulate the growth of the world population, which in practice means to reduce it. We are currently at a crossroads. We must therefore ask ourselves which part of our human genetic information should be promoted by bioethics and which part should or must be eliminated. We must begin to seek solutions now, because long-term planning is imperative. In other words, no emergency measures, please—though, as we are well aware, science stops for no man.

I don't want to go too far afield, but we've got a lot of land to till and no proper implements for the tilling. They need to be developed—and soon. Time is of the essence!

As for your fears of a "fatherless society," your last letter gave me the impression that they are—please excuse my bluntness—either childish or the result of a still virulent machismo mania. Should we not rejoice in the fact that the habitually conflict-ridden act of procreation is steadily losing significance? Is it not grounds for celebration that the male of the species, unburdened of the responsibility to perform, to be potent, will finally be liberated? Yes, jubilation is in order, because the man of the future, the "emancipated man," as I call him, will be free. Free for fun. Free for games. Free for anything he pleases. A luxury item for the coming generations, one might say. And you are just the person to find ways to use this soon to be available space and ensure that it accommodates not only Dolly & Co. but also your headbirths from the eponymous novel.

By the way, what do you think of the flooding on the Oder? I'm very pleased with the way the army has pitched in. But if the data are correct and we are in for a worldwide shift in climate, we can expect even greater inundations. This is an area in which even I, though basically optimistic by nature, harbor certain fears.

In the hope of having to some extent assuaged your anxieties and with best wishes to your charming wife, whom I happened to have the pleasure of seeing at a Lübeck wine dealer's recently, I remain

Yours sincerely,
Hubertus Vonderbrügge

1998

WE'D DECIDED TO VOTE by absentee ballot, but then arrived in Behlendorf from Hiddensee on the eve of the elections, 27 September, trying to mask the uneasy feeling we'd brought with us by keeping busy. Ute made lentil soup for the election party, hoping it would prove soothing no matter what the results. Bruno, one of her sons, was bringing a friend, and the Rühmkorfs said they would come. Early in the afternoon I slipped off to the nearby woods for a bit of mushrooming.

Behlendorf Wood, which stretches over terminal moraines to the sea, forms part of the Lübeck Woods. Containing as it does a mixture of deciduous and coniferous trees, it looks promising in autumn. But there was not a chestnut boletus or cep to be found. Where I had gathered a hearty meal of saffron parasols in the middle of the month, there was nothing. The naked mushrooms along the wood's edge were yellowish, past their prime. The prospects of my expedition were dim. I should have known: the dog had refused to go with me.

Believe it or not, only a remnant faith in superstition that I, like so many who come to education late in life, hang on to as a kind of alternative moved me not merely to persist in the search but even to establish a relationship between the blind hope of taking home a mushroom booty and the blind hope of winning the elections. But my knife remained idle, my basket empty. I was on the point of giving up, resigning myself to fatalism for the rest of my jaunt; I could picture myself, a past master of defeat, on the losers' bench; I was tempted to ease the generally expected burden of a major coalition by pragmatic cuts of here a gram, there a gram; I was ready to disown my faith—when what did I spy glimmering white among rotting twigs and mossy trunks, one by one and in groups, but unmistakable signs of innocence in mushroom form.

Do you know what puffballs are? Have you ever experienced a puffball? It has no distinguishing lamellae or tubes; it has neither a thin, sticklike stalk nor a bulbous one riddled with wormholes; it has no panama or fedora or skullcap to keep away the sun. Standing there baldpated, it can be mistaken for the common earthball, which is said to be edible though less than toothsome and makes less of a visible impression: the puffball looks like a round glabrous head (which often seems sprinkled with white grains) resting on a proud, slim neck. If cut when young, it proves its youth by being firm to the knife and revealing a white flesh, which can be enjoyed for no more than a few days: beyond that point the head and neck go gray, the flesh decays, becomes greenish, bloated, until finally, in old age, it turns brown and its by then paperlike skin turns to dust. Still, you should be aware that the puffball has a fine flavor and does not cause bad dreams.

I found more and more. It loves rotting wood. One heralds many. They like company. You usually end up with a pile. But each one deserves attention: no matter how alike they seem, each has its own shape. I counted them as I decapitated them with my knife, and soon I had twenty lying among the articles, editorials, and election predictions on the old *Frankfurter Rundschau* I'd brought along for the purpose—twenty small, medium-sized, and mature specimens, the latter still nice and firm. Suddenly the remnant faith in superstition came bubbling up, demanding figures. It began to link the number of puffballs with the probability of promising or disastrous election results and speculated on a favorable projection. But after thirty-five puffballs I ran out of places to look. I began to worry about the Red-Green coalition. Nothing anywhere, or russules at best. But then I had a stroke of luck in a hollow near the brook, which is actually a kind of overflow ditch connecting Behlendorf Lake to the Elbe–Trave Canal.

Now that you know how beautiful the puffball is and have some idea of how it will taste to the mushroomer and his guests, I don't wish to keep you in suspense any longer: even after I'd set aside the specimens that were past their prime and therefore green on the inside, the number of puffballs I spread out on the outdated newspaper and took home to the kitchen table came to forty-seven.

The guests—Bruno and his friend Martin, Eva and Peter Rühmkorf—arrived soon after me. Following the favorable poll reports and just before the first projection, I served the mushrooms as an hors d'oeuvre, and all those present—even P.R., who is known to be a picky eater—trusted me and partook. Since I had increased their number by slicing them, my magic numbers game remained secret, but was nonetheless effective. The guests were amazed. Even Ute, who always knows everything before it happens and has her own, entirely different configuration of superstitions, laid her skepticism to rest. When the votes necessary to ensure Red-Green representation were officially in—with a few extra seats to boot—I saw my faith in superstition vindicated: not a puffball fewer would have been in order, and not a puffball more.

Then Ute's marjoram-scented lentil soup, designed to quell any show of arrogance, made its way to the table. We watched the outgoing Chancellor shed genuine tears on a screen that seemed too small for the event. The victors' surprise at being handed so much unwieldy power made them look younger than they were. Soon they would be so close they'd be at one another's throats. Even that was something to look forward to. The numbers had done their job, but well into October I had no luck with puffballs.

1999

HE DIDN'T FORCE ME INTO IT, he talked me into it, the rascal. He was always good at that. I always said yes in the end. So now he's brought me back to life supposedly: I'm over a hundred and in decent health because he wills it. He was good too, even when he was knee-high to a grasshopper. He would lie like nobody's business and make the most marvelous promises: "When I grow up and have a lot of money, we'll go wherever you like, Mama. To Naples even." Then the war came, and we were shoved out, to the Soviet Zone first, but then we fled to the West, where some Rhineland peasants put us up in the ice-cold room they used for storing fodder, and tortured us with their "Why don't you go back to where you came from!" And they were as Catholic as me....

Then in 1952, long after my husband and I got our own place, they told me I had cancer. I hung on for two years while the boy studied his art in Düsseldorf without a penny to his name and our daughter started working as a secretary but left all her dreams behind, poor thing. I didn't quite make it to fifty-eight. And now he wants me to catch up: he wants his poor old mama to celebrate her hundredth-and-whatever birthday....

I must say I like what he's come up with. Even his cock-and-bull stories, as my husband called them, showed consideration for others, and the home he's put me in—because that's the way he wants it—well, I can't complain: it's called the Augustinum and it's got a view of the water and it's your better-class place. I've got one and a half rooms with bath, kitchenette, and balcony. He had a color TV set installed and a gizmo that plays those newfangled silver discs, and he's bought me all the opera arias and operettas I used to listen to, including "On the Banks of the Volga a Soldier Stands" from *The Tsarevich*. He even takes me on trips. Last time we went to Copenhagen, and next year, if I'm still up to it, we'll finally go south, all the way to Naples....

But now let me tell you what my life was like the first time round. What I remember most is war, war with breaks in between. My father, who was a metalworker in the gun factory, fell right at the start, at Tannenberg. Then two brothers in France. One painted, the other had some poems published in the newspaper. They're the ones my son takes after, I'm sure, because my other brother was only a waiter. Oh, he got around, but it caught up with him in the end. He got infected. One of those sex diseases. Can't say as I know which one. My mother died out of grief for her sons even before the war was over. That left me and my sister, Betty, alone in the world. She was a spoiled brat, so it's a good thing I picked up a little selling and bookkeeping experience at Kaiser's Café. It meant that when I married Willy, which was right after the big inflation, when our currency in Danzig became the gulden, we could open a grocery shop. We did pretty well at first. And then the boy came along—it was 1927, I was over thirty by then—and three years later the little girl....

We had only two rooms besides the shop, which meant the only space the boy had for his books and his paintbox and his modeling clay was under the windowsill, but he made do with that. You should have seen the things he came up with. And now he's brought me back to life, spoiling me silly with "Mama this and Mama that" and bringing his grandchildren—my great-grandchildren that makes them—to the home to see me. They're nice enough, though a little hard to take at times, and I always breathe easy when they go downstairs—the twins, for instance, bright kids, but with a real lip on them— sailing through the grounds on those thingummies that look like ice skates without blades or roller skates without wheels. I can see from the balcony that one is always faster than the other....

The word they use for the thingummies, *Skäter,* reminds me of the card game skat, which I played all my life. Mostly with my husband and my Kashubian cousin Franz at first, but he worked in the post office for the Poles so they shot him as soon as the war came back. It was tough. Not only for me. But it came with the times. Like Willy joining the Party and me going in with the women because the gymnastics was free of charge and the boy getting that classy uniform to wear at youth group meetings. Jungvolk, they called it....

Later my stepfather the cabinetmaker took over as the third in skat, but he'd get too excited and forget to discard, so I'd keep doubling him. I still get a kick out of playing, even now, in my new life, and this time I play with my son when he brings along his daughter Helene, who has the same name as me. She's a pretty cagey player, the girl, better than her father, whom I taught the game when he was ten or eleven but who still bids like a novice. He'll bid his favorite, hearts, when the only heart he's got is a ten....

And while we sit here playing away and my son keeps overbidding, my great-grandchildren are tearing around the grounds of the Augustinum on their *Skäter* at such speed that I'd worry about them if they didn't have those pads all over them. On their knees and elbows and their hands too. They even wear real helmets so nothing can happen. Must have cost a fortune! When I think of my brothers who were killed in the First War or just died, when I think what they would do back in the days of the Kaiser... They'd find themselves an old beer barrel at the brewery in Langfuhr and take it apart, rub the staves with soft soap, and tie them under their shoes, and then go up and down the Erbsberg in the Jaschkental Woods like real skiers. Didn't cost a thing and worked just fine....

When I think what it would have cost me, a small business-woman, to buy real skates, the kind you can tighten with a key, and for two children... The grocery business didn't do so well in the thirties.... Too much "put it on my account, will you," too much competition... And then there was the deval-uation of the gulden. I remember a ditty people sang—"May is here, Makes things grow, Turns one gulden into two"—but things were pretty tight. The reason our currency was the gulden was that Danzig was a free city, free until war started up again and the Führer with his Gauleiter—Forster his name was—brought us "back home to the Reich." From then on we sold everything for Reichsmarks. But there was less and less to sell. And after closing time we had to sort out the ration stamps and paste them on old newspapers. The boy would help sometimes—till they stuck him in a uniform too. And it wasn't till the Russians descended on us and then the Poles and took everything they could and then the big move and all the misery that went with it—it wasn't till then that I got him back. He was nineteen and thought he was all grown up. And then there was the currency reform. Forty marks was all they gave us of the new money. It was especially hard on us refugees from the East.... We had nothing to fall back on.... The picture album ... And his stamp album. I managed to save that too.... But when I died ...

Anyway, now, because that's the way my son wants it, I'm going to see the Euro, if they ever get around to it. But first he wants to celebrate my birthday, my hundred and third, to be exact. He can do as he pleases. He's over seventy, the boy, and he's made quite a name for himself. Still can't stop telling his stories, though. Some of them I like, I must say, but others— well, I'd like to cross out certain parts. Anyway, I've always enjoyed family get-togethers, the kind where you yell a lot and then make peace, because whenever us Kashubians got together there was always a lot of laughing and crying. At first my daughter didn't want to come. She's pushing seventy herself, and she said she found the idea of her brother bringing me to life again for his stories too gruesome. But I said, "Let him have his way, Sis," I said, "or he'll come up with something worse." That's how he is. He gets the craziest ideas. Always exaggerating. You can't believe a word he writes....

The upshot of it all is my daughter's coming for the party at the end of February, and I'm looking forward to standing on the balcony and watching all my great-grandchildren tearing around the grounds on their *Skäter*. I'm also looking forward to the year 2000. We'll see what comes of it....

Contents